T0374864

"Natapoff has written a compelling and searing book about snitching. It not only comprehensively describes the problem, but offers sharp, clear, and unambiguous solutions. If we really want to address the legal and moral implications of snitching, every judge, defense lawyer, prosecutor, and police officer should read this book."

—Charles J. Ogletree, Jr., Jesse
Climenko Professor of Law,
Emeritus, Harvard Law School

"Vital for understanding the legal process and the moral standard of law enforcement. An excellent read and a harsh glimpse at what the future might hold for the fabric of our justice system. A must have for the urban reader."

—Immortal Technique, hip hop artist
and President of Viper Records

"[O]utstanding. . . . [A] concise, powerful summary of the law and social science on informant use, highlighting with more clarity and force than any other source the risk that informant abuses pose in individual cases. [This] book is the only one to make a convincing case that the cumulation of even the best-intentioned judgments about how to use informants in individual cases can, in the aggregate, do serious social harm."

—*Michigan Law Review*

"One of the truly impressive contributions of the book comes in [Natapoff's] explanation of the effects of widespread use of informants for the criminal justice system, our social structures, and our democracy. . . . Snitching should find a place in every law school course looking at legal issues in the criminal justice arena, and on the syllabi of every university course in criminal justice that aims to give students a realistic and nuanced view of how the system really works."

—*Criminal Justice*

"[T]hought-provoking. Natapoff offers the most up-to-date and trenchant analysis of snitching in the criminal justice system [and] insightful proposals for reform. Th[is] impressive text make[s] important substantive and theoretical contributions to the scholarship on race, class, crime, and the legal system."

—*Du Bois Review*

SNITCHING

Snitching

Criminal Informants and the
Erosion of American Justice

SECOND EDITION

Foreword by Barry Scheck

Alexandra Natapoff

NEW YORK UNIVERSITY PRESS
New York

NEW YORK UNIVERSITY PRESS
New York
www.nyupress.org

References to Internet websites (URLs) were accurate at the time of writing. Neither the author nor New York University Press is responsible for URLs that may have expired or changed since the manuscript was prepared.

Library of Congress Cataloging-in-Publication Data
Natapoff, Alexandra.
Snitching : criminal informants and the erosion of American justice, second edition / Alexandra Natapoff.
p. cm. Includes bibliographical references and index.
ISBN–13: 9781479807697 (cl : alk. paper); ISBN–13: 9781479807703 (pb : alk. paper); ISBN–13: 9781479807710 (consumer ebook); ISBN–13: 9781479807741 (library ebook)
1. Informers —Legal status, laws, etc. —United States. 2. Criminal justice, Administration of —United States. 3. Informers —United States. 4. Law enforcement —United States.
I. Title.
KF9665.N38 2009 363.25'2—dc22 2009017397

New York University Press books are printed on acid-free paper, and their binding materials are chosen for strength and durability. We strive to use environmentally responsible suppliers and materials to the greatest extent possible in publishing our books.

Manufactured in the United States of America

10 9 8 7 6 5 4 3 2 1

Also available as an ebook

For Raphael again

CONTENTS

FOREWORD

In the early 1990s, DNA created a revolution in the criminal legal system. The science of DNA permitted us to use new forensic evidence not only to convict but also to identify the wrongfully convicted and to set them free. That revolution opened our eyes to the fact that our system harbors deep flaws. For too long it has tolerated, in even the most serious cases, reliance on faulty evidence, unscientific forensic assays, and unreliable witnesses.

In 1992, we started the Innocence Project to change this unacceptable state of affairs. A national innocence network emerged around the country that has produced hundreds of exonerations and vast amounts of new data. As the innocence community grew larger and more sophisticated, we learned more and more about the destructive influence of criminal informants. Nearly 20 percent of all DNA exoneration cases involve a lying jailhouse snitch.[1] Over 45 percent of all wrongful convictions in capital cases are the result of an unreliable criminal informant, making snitches the leading cause of wrongful capital convictions in the United States.[2] The innocence movement demonstrated that compensated criminal witnesses drive much of the wrongful conviction problem, but we did not initially know how to address it. With this groundbreaking book, Professor Alexandra Natapoff showed us how.

When *Snitching* was first published in 2009, there was little to no discussion about criminal informants and their risks. Today, in large part because of Natapoff's book, there is reform around the country. The Innocence Project's Policy staff refer to *Snitching* as their "informant bible," and its publication spurred the Innocence Project—in collaboration with the Innocence Network—to launch a nationwide campaign to track and regulate the use of jailhouse informants. Since then, at least seven states have substantially reformed their informant systems, from Texas to Nebraska to New Jersey. The foundational research and thoughtful policy recommendations offered in *Snitching* provided a road map for our national campaign, which continues to flourish across the nation.

This book also unearthed crucial connections between wrongful convictions and plea bargaining. Informant deals are a secretive, high-risk type of plea deal in which the government gambles on information obtained from unreliable sources in exchange for giving those sources leniency, money, or other benefits. These deals, and the hope of getting one, have infected our jails and prisons and made jailhouse snitches one of the great threats to innocent defendants. Indeed, Professor Natapoff brilliantly elucidated the problem in a report she authored for an independent panel in Minnesota that analyzed the Myon Burrell conviction. As she explained, the existence of multiple informants, especially in gang-related prosecutions, exponentially increases the likelihood of generating copycat false testimony that a jury could easily believe to be persuasive independent recollections.[3] Mr. Burrell received clemency and release from a life sentence in 2020, in no small measure due to Professor Natapoff's work.

But the problem runs even deeper: we now know that innocent people routinely plead guilty to get out of jail, to avoid crushingly long mandatory minimum sentences after trial (the "trial penalty" dilemma), or to avoid execution. The perverse incentive for the innocent to plead guilty was most eloquently described by New Jersey exoneree Rodney Roberts when he said, "Pleading guilty to a crime I didn't do felt like I was sabotaging and saving myself at the same time." Professor Natapoff's scholarship has helped reveal the terrible dynamics of this cynical plea bargaining market.

I am thrilled to see this updated and expanded edition of *Snitching*. An enormous amount of new thinking and reform has occurred since it was first published, generated in large part by this important book. The second edition, like the first, offers powerful analyses, unique insights, and vital guidance as we continue the campaign for a stronger, better criminal legal system.

Barry Scheck
Professor of Law
Co-Founder of The Innocence Project
Cardozo Law School

Introduction

A Tale of Three Snitches

Ninety-two-year-old Kathryn Johnston was dead, which meant big trouble for police officers Jason Smith and Gregg Junnier.

Three hours earlier, everything had looked so promising. Atlanta police had busted Fabian Sheats for the third time in four months. In exchange for his release, the local drug dealer-turned-informant had tipped them off to a major stash at 933 Neal Street—an entire kilo of cocaine. Sheats wasn't one of their registered informants so they couldn't legally use him to get a warrant, but Smith and Junnier applied for a warrant anyway by inventing an imaginary snitch. They called him a "reliable confidential informant" and told the magistrate judge that this nonexistent snitch had bought crack cocaine at the Neal Street address. The fabrication wouldn't matter in the end, after they got the warrant, busted in, and grabbed the kilo. It would be a major victory.

But nothing went the way it was supposed to. Sheats's tip was bad. There was no kilo at 933 Neal Street. Once inside the house, the police opened fire and killed the innocent grandmother who lived there. With no cocaine anywhere to be found, Smith and Junnier turned to one of their regular informants, yet another snitch named Alex White. They offered him $130 to say that he'd bought drugs at Johnston's Neal Street home and to corroborate their false warrant application. It wouldn't bring Kathryn Johnston back, but at least no one would learn that they'd gambled everything on a weak lead from a bad snitch and that the informant in the warrant didn't exist.[1]

Although it rarely comes to light, criminal informant use is everywhere in the American legal system. Police rely on criminal suspects to get warrants, to perform surveillance, and to justify arrests. Prosecutors negotiate with defendants for information and cooperation, offering to drop charges or lighten sentences in exchange. Especially in the expansive arena of drug enforcement, turning suspects into so-called snitches is a central feature of the way America manages crime, while the secretive practice of trading lenience for information quietly shapes major aspects of our penal process.

In the movies, informants usually show up in high-octane stories about mafia gangsters and drug dealers. But in real life, the practice affects ordinary families and their children. Rachel Hoffman was twenty-three years old and recently graduated from Florida State University. In 2008 she was caught with a small amount of marijuana and a few pills, and Tallahassee police convinced her to become an informant to avoid going to jail. Unbeknownst to her lawyer or family, she agreed to engage in an undercover sting to buy a gun and a large amount of drugs from two criminal targets. During the sting, the targets discovered the wire in her purse. They killed her with the gun she had been sent to buy.

Three years after Rachel Hoffman's murder, Detroit police caught nineteen-year-old Shelly Hilliard smoking marijuana. Police threatened her with prison, a potentially lethal threat for Hilliard, who was a transgender woman. Hilliard immediately agreed to cooperate and engage in a sting. Within hours of the sting, the dealer-target was released. He tracked Hilliard down and strangled, burned, and dismembered her. "I lost my baby for an ounce of weed," mourned Hilliard's mother. "It's like they just threw her away."[2]

As stories like these reveal, the use of criminal informants is risky in many ways and for many different stakeholders. It can harm vulnerable informants like Hoffman and Hilliard. It can harm people like Kathryn Johnston who live in neighborhoods where informants are deployed. It invites mistakes, sometimes lethal ones, when the government relies on unreliable sources like Fabian Sheats. It invites official deceit and even corruption when law enforcement officials like Smith and Junnier can operate in secret and without accountability.

At the same time, informants are also a potent crime-fighting tool. They can permit the infiltration of drug cartels, powerful corporations, terrorist conspiracies, and other organizations often impervious to law enforcement. Offering lenience to low-level offenders is sometimes the only way to get information about well-insulated, high-level criminals. From the challenges of organized crime to political corruption, criminal informants can be uniquely productive helpmates for the government.

Informant deals span all kinds of information and cooperation. An especially dangerous yet common version is when law enforcement deploys active criminal informants to generate new arrests and new cases. In Hearne, Texas, for example, a federally funded drug task force swept through town in 2000 and arrested twenty-eight people, mostly Black residents of the Columbus Village public housing project. The task force was relying on the word of informant Derrick Megress, a suicidal former drug dealer on probation facing new burglary charges. Megress had cut a deal with the local prosecutor. If he produced at least twenty arrests, Megress's new charges would be dropped. He'd also earn one hundred dollars for every person he helped to arrest. One of his innocent victims was waitress Regina Kelly, mother of four, who sat in jail for weeks. Another target, Detra Tindle, was in the hospital giving birth at the time when Megress alleged that she had sold him drugs. A lie detector test finally revealed that Megress had been mixing flour and baking soda with small amounts of cocaine to fabricate evidence of drug deals. Charges against the remaining Hearne suspects were dropped, although several had already pleaded guilty.[3]

The Hearne case was unusual in that it triggered national attention, an ACLU lawsuit, and a film. But it was not an unusual scenario. In 2017, Tina Prater cut a similar deal with local Tennessee police to produce arrests in exchange for cash for her own drug dependency while she was on probation for smuggling drugs into the local jail. Prater fabricated recordings and used fake drugs to allege the sale of illegal pills. Without checking either the recordings or the drugs, police made dozens of arrests before an innocent couple sued the city to stop the practice. When asked by a journalist about the scandal, the local prosecutor shrugged it off: "I'm not saying things aren't sometimes messy," he conceded, "but that's how it happened here."[4]

The Big Picture

The idea behind "snitching" is simple: a suspect provides incriminating information about someone else in exchange for a deal, maybe the chance to avoid arrest and walk away, or the promise of a lesser charge or sentence. The reality of snitching is complicated: anyone can become an informant, and the government has unfettered discretion over the benefits that it can offer, including money, leniency for past crimes, and the freedom to commit new ones. In exchange, the government can seek nearly anything from its informants, including the demand that they risk their lives. In effect, snitching represents an enormous unregulated market in which the government is authorized to pressure and reward anyone it chooses, in almost any way it pleases, in exchange for almost anything it wants.

As a result of this market flexibility, informant deals are wildly varied. Some are quick and informal. In the "buy, bust, flip" technique, a police officer might release a drug user or dealer like Fabian Sheats in exchange for a tip. Some deals are unconstitutional. In Orange County, California, sheriff deputies strategically placed Mexican Mafia gang members in jail cells next to other defendants and paid the gang members to extract information.[5] Other informant deals are complex, high-profile, and relatively formal. In 2006, corrupt lobbyist Jack Abramoff avoided decades in prison by agreeing to snitch on the politicians he bribed. Fifteen years before that, hit man Salvatore "Sammy the Bull" Gravano testified against mafia boss John Gotti in exchange for drastically reduced punishment and years of witness protection. The unfettered reach and negotiating flexibility of the informant deal has made it a key weapon in the law enforcement arsenal.

Snitching is, in turn, the ubiquitous legal loophole available to even the most serious criminal as a way of escaping liability. The Orange County gang members, Jack Abramoff, and Sammy the Bull all avoided punishment for crimes that the government knew they committed, including drug dealing, racketeering, bribery, and murder.

For these kinds of reasons, using criminal informants exacerbates some of the worst failings of the U.S. criminal system. The practice invites inaccuracy, crime, violence, and sometimes corruption. It inflicts special harms on vulnerable individuals such as poor people of color, individuals with substance use or mental health challenges, and low-income defendants who lack robust legal representation. Because it is secretive and largely unregulated, it evades the traditional checks and balances of judicial and public scrutiny, even as it determines the outcomes of millions of investigations and cases. And finally, like the criminal system itself, the phenomenon is enormous.

Philosophically, the informant deal represents a tense compromise with two core goals of the justice system: crime prevention and proportionate punishment. Informants escape liability for their own crimes when they give information to the government and can even earn the ability to continue offending. Informants may work both ends of the deal, maintaining relationships with the police and turning in other people even as they continue to break the law. In this sense, unlike civilian witnesses, using criminal informants by definition requires the toleration of crime. Indeed, the ability of cooperating drug dealers to remain in business has made snitching a subject of heated debate in communities from Atlanta to East Harlem.[6] The same problem haunts Wall Street where corporate wrongdoers routinely work out cooperation deals to escape prosecution for their multimillion-dollar crimes.[7]

At the same time, the informant deal skews who we punish and how much we punish them. The informant market tends to reward those with the most information to offer, who in turn tend to be more serious or experienced criminals. Minor players, by contrast, have less to trade and therefore, counterintuitively, get punished more harshly. The more culpable are punished less. This is not how criminal justice is supposed to work.

Turning suspects into informants has implications that extend well beyond the criminal process. The practice has political, cultural, even intimate dimensions. For example, when police threatened first-time offender Amy Gepfert with a forty-year sentence for drug distribution, they offered to drop all charges if she had paid sex with another target so that police could charge him with prostitution. She did; no charges were filed against her.[8]

Sometimes the creation of an informant disturbs an entire community. The orthodox Jewish community in Los Angeles was shaken when a prominent member of a well-known congregation turned state's evidence against a Hasidic rabbi in exchange for lenience in his own fraud case. The betrayal was all the more traumatic because traditional Jewish law prohibits informing against another Jew.[9] Fifty miles south of Los Angeles, the FBI paid fitness instructor Craig Monteilh $11,200 per month to pretend to be Muslim and to infiltrate Southern California mosques and other Muslim organizations. Monteilh—who had a previous conviction for fraud—lost his cover when the Islamic Center of Irvine reported his extremism, ironically, to the FBI and filed a restraining order against him due to his violent jihadist rhetoric.[10]

Informant use disrupts vulnerable communities more than others. Because police make disproportionately more drug arrests in Black neighborhoods,[11] the practice of "flipping" drug arrestees, i.e., turning suspects into snitches, naturally creates more informants in those communities. This means that such neighborhoods must routinely bear the costs of snitching—including informant crime and unreliability. One study, for example, found that innocent Black and Latinx households in San Diego were disproportionately the target of bad search warrants, 80 percent of which relied on confidential informants.[12] Such communities must also contend with friends and neighbors who may be actively seeking information in order to "work off" their own charges.

Because the criminal system occupies such a central place in our social fabric, law enforcement tactics like informant use are not merely penal policies: they are influential features of the way we govern. It is through the penal system that we collectively debate and respond to right and wrong, punish serious wrongdoers, and vindicate victims while simultaneously announcing how we will permit the state to treat its own citizenry. For better or for worse, the criminal system educates the public about the law, about democratic values, and about power.[13] It can instill public confidence or send fear and distrust coursing through a neighborhood.

The penal system, moreover, is a multibillion-dollar industry controlling the lives of the millions of people who are in jail, in prison, and under court supervision. It employs millions of law enforcement workers and influences the local economies of thousands of cities. Over the decades, it has altered the shape of American government itself, investing it with increasingly vast powers to surveil, investigate, coerce, and punish.[14] Using criminal informants is an integral part of this matrix, with many of these same weighty educational, equitable, and governance dimensions.

Our penal system is also famously flawed—harsh, expensive, inaccurate, and unfair. It is the most punitive system on the planet, incarcerating more people than any other nation. It pulls billions of dollars into policing and prisons and away from social services and schools. It is secretive and sloppy, routinely convicting the innocent for the most serious as well as the most minor of crimes. Money matters too much: rich people fare better than poor people. And the system is racially skewed, punishing Black and Latinx people more often and more heavily than whites and deforming the life trajectories of individuals and communities of color.[15] Snitching practices are intimately tied to many of these failings as well.

Understanding the U.S. criminal system in its complex entirety is one of the great challenges of modern legal and social studies; understanding criminal informant use is central to that challenge. This is because snitching is paradigmatic of the American criminal system, an extreme expression of three of its key characteristics: discretion, secrecy, and plea bargaining. Like all arrests and prosecutions, informant deals are crafted at the broad discretion of police and prosecutors. Informants are powerful tools of investigation and surveillance, but because their arrangements with the government are mostly confidential, these law enforcement investigative methods are cloaked in secrecy. At the same time, informant deals permit the clandestine resolution of informant liability. In effect, snitch deals are informal, secretive plea bargains: they let the government negotiate and resolve informant criminal guilt and punishment off the books and under the table.

Put differently, the vibrant market for informant deals is possible only because the United States relies so heavily on plea bargaining to resolve the vast majority of criminal cases and U.S. law gives prosecutors such unfettered discretion to do so. Ninety-five percent of all criminal convictions in this country are the result of a plea, not of a trial: this is the dominant legal and market reality within which informant deals take place. Conversely, informant deals strongly shape plea bargaining culture by injecting the theoretical possibility of cooperation into every case, from traffic stops to murder. The pervasive use of such deals, in turn, has transformed key aspects of the adversarial process, including public transparency, the role of defense counsel, trials, and sentencing. Unearthing the full story of informant use is thus revelatory precisely because it uncovers significant, paradigmatic features of the criminal process that usually remain hidden. By understanding snitching, we can learn deep and often disturbing truths about how our entire penal system really functions.

Snitching also offers a powerful opportunity to improve the criminal system. When I wrote the first edition of this book in 2009, there was only a smattering of informant reform at the local, state, and federal levels. I predicted that would change—and it did. Today, more than half of all states have considered or passed significant informant reforms, some of which I have helped to draft. Those reforms span new rules regarding disclosure, tracking, reliability hearings, notice to victims, and protections for vulnerable informants. Chapter 8 describes the trajectory of this reform and documents its many new features.

Informant reform has been fueled by several related developments, most of which involve disruptions to the informant culture of secrecy and impunity. First, the innocence movement has uncovered hundreds of wrongful convictions and revealed the raw unreliability of compensated witnesses who are promised lenience.[16] In 2004, the Northwestern University Center on Wrongful Convictions traced over 45 percent of documented wrongful capital convictions to false informant testimony. This made "snitches the leading cause of wrongful convictions in U.S. capital cases."[17] In 2015, the National Registry of Exonerations concluded that 23 percent of wrongful capital convictions are due to jailhouse snitches alone.[18] As a result of such revelations, numerous states have passed legislation demanding more accountability from prosecutors who reward their criminal witnesses.

Interest in change has also been prompted by the growing volume of media coverage publicizing the violence, corruption, and injustice that often accompany the use of criminal informants. The *New York Times Magazine* and ProPublica, for example, jointly published an eye-popping series on jailhouse informants in 2020. It zeroed in on the government's sordid reliance on a con man named Paul Skalnik to convict dozens of people, including four men who were sent to death row. Skalnik had multiple convictions for fraud; in 1983 he was charged with sexually molesting a seventh-grade girl, but the charges were soon dropped and he was permitted to keep working as an informant.[19]

The popular podcast series *In the Dark* devoted several episodes to uncovering the government's heavy reliance on jailhouse informants in the Curtis Flowers murder case. Flowers, a Black man from Mississippi, was vindictively prosecuted six times over the course of twenty years for the same crime despite the lack of any physical evidence against him.

The prosecution relied on multiple jailhouse informants, all of whom claimed that Flowers confessed to them and all of whom later changed their stories. The government's main informant was Odell Hallmon, who was repeatedly given leniency and released despite facing a broad array of serious criminal charges himself, including an attempt to run over a police officer. In 2016, after testifying four times against Flowers, he went on a shooting rampage and killed three people. In 2018, Hallmon recanted and said his own testimony had been "all make-believe." The next year, the U.S. Supreme Court overturned Curtis Flowers's conviction, the government dropped the case, and Flowers was exonerated after spending twenty-three years in prison.[20]

The public has also learned that informants themselves can be victims of the informant market. Spurred in part by the death of Rachel Hoffman, the *New Yorker* published a groundbreaking exposé of the widespread use and abuse of young informants; *60 Minutes* followed up with its own investigation of murdered young informants.[21] In 2014, the University of Massachusetts Amherst was rocked by the fatal heroin overdose of a student named Logan. Logan became an informant for campus police to avoid getting suspended from school. Campus police, in violation of university policy, did not tell Logan's parents or the university about his substance use disorder and thus prevented him from getting help before he died.[22]

Stories like these over the past decade have opened the door to a deeper public awareness of this clandestine law enforcement practice, its pervasive influence, and its deep flaws. As the debate progresses, it cries out for more and better data. But the criminal system has not been forthcoming. Even with stark evidence of the risks and costs of informant use, law enforcement and prosecutorial practices remain largely undocumented and nonpublic. With a few exceptions described in chapter 8, prosecutors' offices are not required to document the informant deals they make, the crimes they use informants to solve, or the informant crimes that are forgiven. Likewise, most police departments are not required to keep or report data on their informant use. As a result, public data on informant practices still come largely from sources external to the conventional criminal process: journalism, innocence projects, nonprofit investigations, and advocacy. Much of this disclosure, moreover, is triggered by scandal and tragedy.

The lack of public data flows from the larger culture of secrecy that has long characterized informant use and is explored in chapter 5—"Secret Justice." The informant deal itself is secretive and informal, typically taking place in unrecorded conversations between suspects and law enforcement. Law enforcement jealously guards its informant practices against disclosure to courts and defendants and sometimes even to other law enforcement agencies. The single most powerful transparency mechanism in the U.S. criminal system is the trial: it is at trial where a defendant becomes legally entitled to information about the informants used against them and the public accordingly gets to learn about those informants too. But this mechanism is inherently limited because most criminal cases in the United States never go to trial, and so the best informant disclosure requirements are rarely triggered.

From a policy perspective, the lack of transparency and the paucity of data mean that there can be no meaningful cost-benefit analysis of informant use, only assumptions. The benefits of informant use are well-recognized and mostly taken for granted. It is commonly said, for example, and I have said it myself, that the FBI could not have dismantled the mafia without using serious criminals as informants—many of them murderers themselves. But the downsides and dangers of those deals remain invisible. We do not know how many other crimes those mafia informants committed, or how many other violent informants were deployed and rewarded without producing any law enforcement benefits at all. The same is true for drug informants, street snitches, terrorism informants, and all the other secretive classes of informant whose deals and criminality rarely come to light. As we will see in chapter 7, this invisibility abates somewhat for white collar and public corruption informants whose deals and cooperation tend to be formal, lawyered, and publicly documented. But such cases represent a relatively small fraction of the criminal process and thus provide a limited window. In order to move forward, we need to know more.

This Book

The culture of secrecy surrounding informant practices means that the public has little information, and many misunderstandings, about this important arena of public policy. This book is an effort to remedy that deficit. When I wrote the first edition, I included the data publicly available at the time. We now know more than we did then—mostly because of scandals, exonerations, and journalism, not because the state has become more transparent—and the second edition is updated throughout to include that new information. More broadly, the book analyzes the key features and consequences of the widespread use of criminal informants throughout the American penal system. While it acknowledges the well-known strengths of the practice as a crime-fighting tool, the bulk of the book is spent in the shadows, uncovering the hidden realities and troubling implications of informant use. The aim is not to present an unbalanced view but to even out what has historically been a largely one-sided debate.

Importantly, this is *not* a book about everyone who gives information to the government. It does not address civilian witnesses, whistleblowers, undercover police officers, or even noncriminal paid informants, although these groups are obviously important in their own right and can be indirectly affected by criminal informant policies. It is also not a book about "snitching" or loyalty in noncriminal arenas of society, such as schools, workplaces, or families. Rather, it is about the enormous criminal market for guilt and information that rests on the specific, widespread governmental practice of rewarding informants who themselves have broken the law. Chapter 1—"The Real Deal"—explains in detail how that market works. It provides an overview of the players and practices, and it identifies the most important implications for individuals, communities, and the criminal system as a whole.

This book is for written for anyone curious about how our legal system authorizes and regulates snitching. It is also designed to be useful to lawyers, judges, and legislators who professionally engage this body of law. Chapter 2 lays out the contours of "informant law," namely, all the legal rules that govern criminal informants: from investigations to sentencing rewards to discovery rules to civil rights. Because there are so many facets of informant use, the chapter brings together a broad range of laws not usually associated with one another. It analyzes police and prosecutorial authority to create and reward informants as well as Fourth Amendment search and seizure law, defendants' rights when informants are used against them, and informants' civil rights against the government. Taken together, this collection of rules and practices comprises a body of law characterized almost uniformly by unfettered law enforcement discretion, pervasive informality, secrecy, and toleration of lawbreaking—characteristics of the American legal process that distinguish it from many other democratic nations.

One especially rich development since the first edition has been new psychological research into how juries evaluate informant witnesses. Our adversarial system relies heavily on juries to decide whether witnesses are lying, and it turns out that, when it comes to compensated criminal witnesses, ordinary people are not very good at it. Jurors routinely believe lying informants and convict innocent people based on informant testimony. In response, defense attorneys sometimes call academic expert witnesses like me, or former law enforcement officials with informant experience, to educate jurors who may not be familiar with informant culture and the workings of the informant market. Chapter 3—"Juries and Experts"—shares the new research on juries and evolving developments in the law regarding informant experts.

Chapters 4, 5, and 6 represent the normative heart of the book: they explore the profound risks and costs of informant use. Chapter 4—"Beyond Unreliable"—covers one of its best-known dangers. The chapter analyzes the various mechanics through which unreliable informants exacerbate the risk of wrongful conviction and the ways that police and prosecutorial incentives impede the system's ability to check informant misinformation.

Another, less recognized consequence of informant use is its tendency to render the entire criminal process more secretive and less publicly accountable. Because informant practices tend to remain informal and undocumented, investigations and cases involving informants recede from public view. On the theory that confidentiality is necessary to protect investigations and witnesses, courts and legislatures tolerate high levels of executive secrecy. As a result, numerous disclosure rules involving discovery and public record keeping have been rolled back to accommodate informant confidentiality, with widespread impact on governmental transparency and accountability. Chapter 5 explores this strain of "secret justice." It also discusses some burgeoning issues surrounding informants and the internet, social media, and new surveillance technologies.

Of all the problematic aspects of informant use, the consequences of the practice for poor communities of color have been the least recognized, even though they represent some of the most costly, violent, and unfair aspects of the practice. Chapter 6—"The Community Cost"— examines the impact of pervasive informant use on heavily policed low-income communities, in particular on the Black men who tend to live there. The chapter roughly estimates the localized extent of the snitching phenomenon and discusses its harmful effects on crime, violence, families, youth, and community stability. It argues that informant practices contribute to the long-standing phenomenon of community distrust of police and that snitching is intimately related to the destructive culture of mass incarceration and the racial inequalities that plague the U.S. criminal system.

Drugs, street theft, and violent crime make up the bulk of the criminal system, and much of the book addresses informant use in those contexts.[23] Particularly at the federal level, however, informants are deployed in the investigation and prosecution of all sorts of offenses, including securities fraud, antitrust, political corruption, and organized crime offenses such as racketeering and money laundering. Chapter 7— "How the Other Half Lives"—examines informant use in the prominent arenas of organized crime, white collar crime, political corruption, and terrorism, each of which has its own set of histories, practices, and challenges. The chapter also reveals the existence of a rich man's version of snitching. White collar and political corruption suspects tend to be wealthier, whiter, better educated, and often socially and politically powerful. The state deploys the informant deal more carefully and lawfully with them, as compared to its treatment of poorer, unrepresented, and otherwise more vulnerable individuals. While all forms of snitching retain core problematic features, informant use generally works more reliably, transparently, and fairly in the more regulated law enforcement environments characterized by wealthier, better-represented defendants.

Because this book exposes the many harmful, sometime shocking consequences of snitching, it poses serious questions about the basic validity of the practice. Nevertheless, the book does not advocate banning all informant use. Rather, it diagnoses the practice as a downstream consequence of two larger structural features of the U.S. criminal system: plea bargaining and a high tolerance for law enforcement discretion. These structural features not only make snitching possible; to some extent they make it inevitable. As long as police and prosecutors have complete discretion over whom to target, useful suspects will evade arrest and prosecution. And as long as law enforcement can freely negotiate with suspects over what crimes to charge, some suspects will be able to trade cooperation for better treatment. In other words, we cannot eliminate snitching without dismantling much of the United States' dominant policing and plea bargaining apparatus, a project that exceeds the scope of this book.

To recognize the practical limits to change, however, is not to abandon it. While some horse-trading over guilt and information may be inevitable in a system like ours, the complete lack of regulation and oversight is not. The process can be rendered less opaque and more accountable. Egregious aspects of informant use can be reined in. Some—for example the use of child informants—can be eliminated. Chapter 8—"Regulation and Reform"—thus proposes a new global approach to the meaningful regulation of the informant market aimed at its most problematic features: its secretive lack of accountability, the harms it inflicts on the vulnerable, and its unprincipled tolerance of crime, victimization, inaccuracy, and inequality. The chapter then connects that rethinking to the exciting array of new reforms currently occurring at the federal, state, and local levels.

A perennial challenge of penal reform is that the criminal system withholds key information about its own operations and consequences: informant reform suffers from an especially strong version of this problem. This book itself represents the most comprehensive collection of publicly available information regarding informant use and the most far-ranging analysis of its implications to date, and yet throughout it acknowledges that many of its conclusions are provisional due to the lack of systemic data. Because the criminal process is primarily designed to conceal, not to evaluate, informant use, it prevents rigorous conclusions about when snitching practices are too destructive to tolerate or, alternatively, when their crime-fighting benefits are worth important compromises. We do not know with any certainty how many neighborhoods have been devastated by the police use of informants or how many innocent people have been convicted by false snitch testimony, although we know that both things happen. Conversely, we do not know how many criminal organizations have been disabled or how many crimes have been prevented or solved by the practice, although we know that these things happen too. It is precisely this kind of information that is needed for an informed democratic debate over the phenomenon, one that can address the fundamental principles of justice at stake as well as the crime-fighting cost-benefit analysis.

Of all the changes proposed in chapter 8, therefore, the most important is the most difficult: disrupting the culture of secrecy and deregulation that permits informants and officials alike to break rules, harm others, and evade accountability. It is this culture that fosters snitching's worst dangers: unchecked criminal behavior, harm to the vulnerable, wrongful convictions, official corruption, public deception, and the weakened integrity of the criminal process. It is also the feature that prevents us from addressing the ultimate public policy questions with clarity. The system currently handles the problem by asking us to accept on faith that unregulated snitching is worth the risks, without demonstrating its full benefits or revealing its true costs. For a public policy of this far-reaching importance, such faith is not enough.

I end the book by sharing some of my own experiences with the informant market and explaining my ultimate conclusion that informant use is a high-order governance problem. Because the practice touches nearly every aspect of the criminal process—from policing to prison—it provides a unique window into the routine workings of mass incarceration. Indeed, snitching perpetuates one of the most destructive legacies of mass incarceration culture, which is its reductive, dehumanizing approach to the millions of people affected by our criminal system. In all these ways, snitching implicates some of the hardest issues raised by modern-day policing and punishment. It is time to bring this important practice into better conformity with basic principles of equal justice and democratic accountability.

A Note About Terminology

The scholarly and public conversations around how we refer to people— people in the criminal system, people in different racial groups, people struggling with substance use—have changed enormously since I wrote the first edition. I have done my best to update the language in light of these evolving conventions, including using the medically preferred term "people with a substance use disorder (SUD)."[24] I often use male pronouns to refer to informants and defendants, in large part because the majority of people who directly encounter the criminal apparatus are male, but I also use female and gender-neutral pronouns. Finally, as I did in the first edition, I use the terms "informant," "cooperator," and "snitch" interchangeably throughout, even though each term carries its own distinctive cultural baggage.

1

The Real Deal

I want these new shoes, I want this or I want drugs to sell,
or something like that . . . and the police asked me for information. I'm just gonna give it to them to get what I want,
even if they gonna give me some drugs or give me some
money, or whatever, whatever they gonna give me I'm still
gaining. . . . I'm gaining to get something in my pocket. . . .
And in another way, I could fucking well get caught with a
gang of cocaine and I know the man they want, they'll tell
me, "I'm gonna let you stay on the street a little bit longer if
you tell me where he is." Sure I'm gonna tell him, he's right
over there.
—Interview with a street snitch[1]

The central, defining characteristic of snitching is the deal between
the government and a suspect. In that deal, the government ignores or
reduces the suspect's potential criminal liability in exchange for information. From street corners to jailhouses and courtrooms around the
country, thousands of suspects work off their guilt by cooperating with
police or prosecutors. Their crimes may go lightly punished or not punished at all. Indeed, if the deal takes place early enough, these crimes
may never be officially recorded.

This method of resolving criminal liability contradicts the conventional story about how we handle questions of guilt. In theory, if the government suspects a person of wrongdoing, it will arrest and then charge
them with a specific crime.[2] Such charges are a matter of public record
and trigger numerous consequences, including the onset of the defendant's right to counsel. Likewise, a person charged with a crime must
either go to trial to contest their guilt or publicly admit liability by pleading guilty. These processes of filing charges, going to trial, and pleading guilty are heavily regulated by procedural rules, many of which are

grounded in the U.S. Constitution. The process is monitored by lawyers and judges and leaves a paper trail. While conventional plea bargaining involves significant negotiations over facts and guilt, and much of that bargaining process takes place in private, an interested member of the public can usually discern after the fact the basis on which a person was found guilty and what their punishment was.[3]

Snitching is the clandestine, black-market version of this process. It resolves guilt mainly off the record, without rules, at the discretion of individual law enforcement officials. For example, instead of serving a sentence for running an identity-theft ring in San Francisco, Marvin Jeffery became an informant. While providing information to the police on the street, Jeffery continued to expand his illegal ring. Although he committed new offenses, violated his probation, and incurred several arrest warrants, police permitted him to remain at large because of his cooperation. These numerous deals remained largely secret: even investigators on related cases were unaware of Jeffery's special status. Finally, after he sold an illegal AK-47 machine gun that was used to kill a police officer, Jeffery disappeared. Jeffery's long history of ongoing cooperation and wrongdoing came to light only because of the happenstance of his link to that lethal weapon.[4]

In Omaha, Nebraska, informant Jorge Palacios was an MS-13 gang member working for the FBI. His FBI handler, Greg Beninato, admitted that he knew that Palacios was a suspect in two Los Angeles cases—one involving a drive-by murder, the other involving the sexual assault and murder of a thirteen-year-old girl—but he never inquired about them or questioned Palacios. "It's a fine line between getting involved in someone else's investigation," Beninato said. "I wasn't going to question him without the [other agencies'] permission or their request to do so." The Omaha FBI paid Palacios more than $300,000 over the course of his cooperation before he was convicted in California of rape and murder.[5]

Informant practices such as these represent a fundamental alteration of the criminal system's response to wrongdoing. Not simply the basis for arrest, prosecution, or punishment, criminal conduct becomes instead the starting point for negotiations that may never be publicly revealed and in which police and prosecutors may tolerate ongoing crime. Such negotiations are highly instrumental and often short on principle.

In deciding that an informant's usefulness outweighs his or her culpability, for example, police often implicitly downplay the seriousness of the informant's crimes and the significance of holding such offenders accountable while elevating the importance of future cases that the informant might help them make. Likewise, when prosecutors tailor charges not just to the magnitude of the crime but to the cooperativeness of the criminal, they are making similar judgments.

Such practices represent a retreat from some core purposes of the criminal law, such as evaluating individual moral culpability or publicly condemning crime. Instead, they elevate instrumental values such as an offender's immediate investigative usefulness, law enforcement efficiency, or even mere convenience. This swap erodes key legitimating features of the criminal process. As one federal appeals court complained, "[t]he judicial process is tainted and justice cheapened when factual testimony is purchased, whether with leniency or money."[6]

Informant practices also alter some basic features of criminal procedure, from the ways in which investigations are conducted to the terms of plea bargains to the respective roles of defense counsel, judges, and juries. As law professor Graham Hughes once wrote, cooperation agreements are "sharply different from the general phenomenon of plea bargaining. They are exotic plants that can survive only in an environment from which some of the familiar features of the criminal procedure landscape have been expunged."[7]

Although all snitching requires a deal, informant arrangements vary widely, from Marvin Jeffery's informal understanding with his police handlers to elaborately written cooperation agreements worked out by counsel for both sides. The nature of the deal will be affected by the type of underlying crime and the extent of involvement by police, prosecutors, or defense counsel. The resulting obligations imposed on informants—and their potential rewards—vary enormously as well. What follows is a description of the general contours and variables of the informant bargain—in practice, each individual deal may look very different.

I. Anatomy of an Informant Deal

Police and prosecutors are the primary state officials who create and control informant deals, and they engage informants in distinct ways.

Police are generally authorized to conduct investigations, make arrests, and sometimes determine the nature of initial criminal charges. Prosecutors typically appear later in the process to file formal charges and handle plea bargaining, trials, sentencing, and other public aspects of the legal case. Police and prosecutors may also work together throughout a particular investigation or case, making decisions about informants' conduct and rewards.

A. Police

Sometimes referred to as "handlers," police officers and investigative agents are on the front lines of the informant phenomenon, with the most information about and influence over informants and their ongoing relationships with the government. Because police handle arrests, they typically make the first contact. Dennis Fitzgerald, retired DEA special agent and former Miami police sergeant, explains the process as follows:

> Offering an arrested individual the opportunity to cooperate and mitigate his situation is the technique most frequently used to recruit an informant. . . . [T]he incident should have taken place discretely [sic] and without fanfare. If not, word of his arrest will have spread quickly "on the street." Once booked into jail, his value to the agents as an informant may rapidly diminish.[8]

Police may also approach or arrest people expressly for the purpose of turning them into informants, even if there is insufficient evidence to prosecute them. According to Dr. Stephen Mallory, a twenty-five-year narcotics agent, former police trainer, narcotics bureau director, and member of DEA and FBI task forces, "[another] method that can be effective for recruiting informants is an 'informed bluff.' If the investigator . . . has failed to produce an indictable case, a bluff may be his only alternative. . . . When a potential informant believes that a case is pending on his activities, he/she may agree to cooperate."[9]

As Fitzgerald acknowledges, the tactics used to recruit informants may themselves be illegal. Police, for example, may target a prospective informant and wait until he commits a crime or is suspected to be in possession of a controlled substance or other contraband. He is then "arrested" following what is usually an illegal search and seizure. The subject, fearful of going to jail, may immediately agree to cooperate (flip) and be "unarrested." He will work as an informant laboring under the impression that charges will be filed unless he cooperates.[10]

There are no legal constraints at all on the kinds of underlying offenses that police can leverage to develop an informant. FBI agent John Connolly helped mafia snitches James "Whitey" Bulger and Stephen Flemmi avoid prosecution for murder in exchange for their cooperation. At the other end of the spectrum, police can use mere traffic stops to pressure drivers into cooperating. Police stopped Bianca Hervey for driving on a suspended license, for example, and although she had no drug ties, they threatened her with jail unless she became a drug informant.[11]

Once the suspect agrees to cooperate, the officer will strike a deal. The deal may be verbal, with details to be worked out later, or it may involve a written agreement. As the street snitch quoted at the beginning of this chapter explains, sometimes the deal can be as simple as the police's agreement not to arrest the suspect and to let him "stay on the street a little bit longer" in exchange for a tip. By contrast, the FBI requires its agents to write down all informant agreements.

Even if an informant is arrested and charged with a crime by a prosecutor, an active informant's most frequent contact will be with the police or investigative agent. The handler will control the informant's activities, tell him what to do, receive his information, and potentially act on it. The handler in turn will report to the prosecutor about the information obtained from the informant, about the informant's other activities—for example, if he has committed additional crimes—and about whether or not he has been cooperative. The police handler is thus the government official closest to the informant, with the most knowledge, control, and day-to-day contact with him.

The relationship between an active informant and their handler is complex, personal, and a two-way street. The more heavily police rely on snitches, the more important it becomes for them to work with, retain, and protect their informants. Mallory describes the importance of maintaining an officer's personal reputation among criminals.

The reputation of an investigator is paramount to informant recruitment. The criminal elements of a community know who the fair, productive, and professional investigators are in a police organization. They know who to trust, whose word is good, and who will demonstrate persistence toward solving crimes. They also know who has influence with prosecutors, judges, and other law enforcement agencies. In other words, they know who to "weigh in" with. . . . After a successful prosecution, my telephone would begin to ring. . . . These informants may be seeking help with their charges, calling out of fear of being charged, or just in need of money.[12]

Mallory further describes handling informants as a form of employee management, dependent on "motivation, leadership style, and job satisfaction."

Informants, like other productive people, must be motivated to reach their potential. . . . Once the investigator's positive reputation has become known in the community, informants will be more easily recruited and controlled by the investigator. He will be known as a police officer who understands and works with people.[13]

Views differ within the law enforcement community about how best to handle informants. For example, according to Mallory, keeping informants motivated may involve delegating power to the informant to design investigations or select targets to enhance his job satisfaction. "The investigator may use empowerment to motivate a potential informant. Although care must be used when allowing informants to exercise too much control or to have too much input into case planning, participat[ion] by the informant does seem to produce more cooperation."[14] By contrast, John Madinger, senior special agent with the Criminal Investigative Division of the IRS and a former narcotics agent, believes that authority should never be delegated to informants, even though it may well produce good results.[15]

Police may work with an informant on more than one case and in different ways. While a particular informant may be a key witness for one crime, he or she may merely provide corroboration or other information regarding another. Police may maintain their relationships with informants as a way of keeping feelers out in the community or tabs on a situation unconnected to any particular investigation. Madinger describes one investigator in a small county who developed dozens of criminal informants, maintaining a set of cross-referenced three-ring binders in which he recorded all the information and crimes about which he learned. In the course of a single evening, this one agent might meet with six or seven individuals for debriefing.[16]

Investigative agents thus have immense power to decide the course of the criminal informant's relationship with the government. They are the most directly involved with the day-to-day instructions and management of investigations, including keeping tabs on the informant's ongoing criminal activities. They also heavily influence the eventual criminal charges that will be lodged against the informant, if any, because they have the discretion to decide whether to arrest him in the first place, what to charge him with initially, and what to tell the prosecutor.

B. Prosecutors

Prosecutors typically do not start working on a case until a police officer or investigative agent has made an arrest or produced some evidence of a crime. Once police have initiated a case, the prosecutor must evaluate the evidence and decide whether to file charges or to continue the investigation or both. Prosecutors may thus meet an informant for the first time after an investigative officer has already established a working relationship. Or a suspect may be brought in for questioning and the prosecutor can decide to flip the suspect by offering a deal.

In the federal system, once a suspect has been formally charged, an informant deal will often come about as a result of a "proffer session." The defendant, their lawyer, the prosecutor, and, typically, the agent will all sit down in a room together. The parties will sign an agreement that nothing the defendant says in that room during that proffer session will be used as evidence against them. And then the defendant will talk.

In an effort to better understand the cooperation and proffer process, law professor Ellen Yaroshefsky interviewed numerous prosecutors and other attorneys in the Southern District of New York. Those prosecutors explained that they spend a great deal of time and effort trying to discern the value and veracity of information obtained from informants, including extensive debriefings, investigation, and corroboration. They also described the dangers of the proffer process. "[C]ooperators are eager to please you," one prosecutor explained. "Telling them that you just want the truth is meaningless." According to another prosecutor, "Many of them come in believing that This is What They Want to Hear Time rather than This is What Happened Time." All the former U.S. attorneys reported that cooperators do not tell the truth in the first few sessions.[17]

Depending on what the defendant says, the prosecutor may decide that his information was not helpful and the defendant will get no benefit. Or he may get a sentencing break for being cooperative. Or he may embark upon a longer relationship with the government in which he agrees to testify before a grand jury, wear a wire, set up a meeting, arrange a deal, or engage in some further activity for which the government may, but is not required to, confer some benefit. If the defendant is released, the agent will typically take more control, acting as the handler for the informant and periodically reporting back to the prosecutor.

Prosecutors have a wide range of negotiating tools. They can delay an indictment or an existing case to give an informant a chance to testify before a grand jury or to go back into the community or organization and gather information, sometimes known as "working off a charge." They can drop charges, alter charges, or promise to make favorable recommendations to the judge at sentencing.

Prosecutors can also negotiate with respect to third parties, for example by bringing charges against an informant's family. After the multibillion-dollar collapse of the company Enron due to financial fraud, the government charged Enron's chief financial officer, Andrew Fastow, with numerous crimes. Fastow resisted cooperating against Enron CEO Kenneth Lay, and so the government prosecuted Fastow's wife, Lea, for tax fraud, a move that threatened to incarcerate the couple at the same time and leave their young children without parents. Fastow's cooperation permitted Lea Fastow to negotiate a plea and serve time in a way that would protect their children.[18] Alternatively, a defendant who has nothing to offer the government or who cannot cooperate themselves may recruit a "brokered informant," a family member, friend, or associate whose cooperation will be credited to that defendant.[19]

Prosecutors and law enforcement agents do not always share the same attitude toward informants. A prosecutor may want to flip and reward a defendant who the police believe should be prosecuted to the fullest. Conversely, agents may not want to expose a valuable source and therefore may not share all their information with the prosecutor. For example, police in Chicago and New York used to maintain "double file" systems in which police created two sets of investigative reports but gave only the public versions to prosecutors.[20] Furthermore, agents may not trust prosecutors with various aspects of informant management. Agent Fitzgerald voiced this concern when he asserted that "[m]any prosecutors are poorly prepared to deal with experienced criminals as they negotiate their fate as an informant."[21] And finally, police may want to reward their sources in ways that prosecutors do not approve. In Detroit in the 1990s, for example, police officers working the infamous ninth floor of the jail went behind prosecutors' backs to get benefits for their numerous jailhouse snitches.[22]

A law professor and former prosecutor, Daniel Richman explains that federal agents and prosecutors have different relationships to the cultivation of informants and that "cultural difference can drive a powerful wedge between agents and prosecutors" in ways that lead to nondisclosure:

> Agents or even agencies seeking to justify their refusal to share information about sources and methods with prosecutors will assert a fear that such data will be misused when the prosecutor enters private practice. This tendency towards non-disclosure is bolstered by concerns that prosecutors have less "on the line" when it comes to investigative security. An agent's promise to an informant is bonded by his and his agency's professional reputation. The prosecutor who will soon move into another world is not so bound.[23]

The relationship between agent and prosecutor is thus an important wild card in the informant scenario.

C. Defense Counsel

Whether an informant has an attorney makes an immense difference to the nature and course of a cooperation deal. For a range of reasons, most informants do not have lawyers. As a matter of law, when a suspect is first stopped by police they do not yet have the right to counsel. If they are given Miranda warnings and decide to ask for a lawyer, they will be given counsel for the purposes of an interrogation, but the vast majority of suspects do not invoke their rights and therefore end up talking directly to police on their own.[24]

As a practical matter, police will often purposely approach suspects before they are represented precisely in order avoid involving defense counsel. As Fitzgerald explains,

> The first attempt to recruit the individual occurs during the postarrest interview, commonly referred to as interrogation. The interview occurs shortly after the arrest. The defendant is unnerved, confused, frightened, angry, or experiencing a combination of these emotions. Of greatest importance to the agent, however, is that the individual is probably not yet represented by counsel. This is the period when most defendant informants are recruited.[25]

A smaller percentage of informants negotiate cooperation deals with the help of a lawyer. Once a defendant is charged with a crime, they acquire the constitutional right to counsel, and prosecutors are ethically prohibited from contacting a represented defendant.[26] Whether suspects get lawyers in the first place, however, is a function of many factors, including their economic status, educational level, the kind of crime they are suspected of, and their independent access to counsel. In white collar and political corruption cases, for example, defendants are more likely to have or retain counsel. In such cases, the government may even put a suspect on notice that they are a potential target of investigation and give them the opportunity to get a lawyer. For example, in 2008, federal prosecutors sent a "target letter" to Nicole Gestas, wife of personal trainer Greg Anderson. Anderson had refused to testify against his client, baseball star Barry Bonds, in connection with allegations that he provided Bonds with illegal performance-enhancing drugs. The letter informed Gestas that she might be charged with conspiracy and that she should contact the public defender's office if she could not afford counsel.[27]

As the use of cooperation has ballooned in the white collar context, so have the issues surrounding the role of counsel. For example, the U.S. Department of Justice formerly made a practice of pressuring corporate entities and employees to waive their rights to counsel and confidentiality as part of entering into cooperation deals. These developments are discussed in more detail in chapter 7.

There are big differences between a counseled and uncounseled informant deal. To mention a few, counseled deals are typically written, determinate, and witnessed. There is a modicum of formality and scrutiny that is lacking in the informal street negotiation. At the most basic level, there is another witness to the deal. A defense attorney will know if the government is being unduly coercive, if improper pressure is being brought to bear, and what sort of cooperation the informant has provided.

An informant is also likely to get a better deal if they are represented. Professor Richman explains the "critical role of defense lawyers" as follows:

> Her legal knowledge and experience will help the defendant assess the likely outcome of a trial, the value of his information, the nature of both parties' obligations under a cooperation agreement, the likelihood and extent of a sentencing discount, and other such factors. Even more importantly, as a repeat player in the market where the government buys information, the defense lawyer helps guarantee that the government will meet its obligations in good faith.[28]

Unlike white collar and other wealthier defendants, street and drug informants tend not to have counsel, a significant difference that permits many of the irregularities and dangers of the practice.[29]

D. The Crimes

What kinds of crimes does law enforcement investigate using informants? The short answer is "all of them," but different types of criminal investigations create and deploy informants in distinctive ways. The two dominant models come, respectively, from the worlds of organized crime and drug enforcement.

Many of the best-known instances of snitching involve long-term, high-level investigations of organized crime. This type of informant use tends to be internally regulated and documented. The Department of

Justice has formal published guidelines governing the use of confidential informants by the FBI, DEA, and other federal agencies that require relatively extensive documentation and monitoring. High-level organized crime investigations also tend to demand communication, coordination, and access to high levels of decision-making within governmental organizations. For example, the use of hit man "Sammy the Bull" Gravano as an informant required coordination over several years among the FBI, federal prosecutors, local police, the court, and eventually the federal witness protection program, and left an extensive public paper trail.

By contrast, the practices surrounding drug informants are extremely varied and largely unregulated. This is in part because drug investigations are more common and diverse than high-profile mafia cases and take place at the state and local as well as the federal level. In contrast to the Department of Justice's extensive guidelines, state and local police departments and prosecutor's offices may not have any written policies governing the use of informants at all. Where guidelines are lax or nonexistent, informant practices are left up to individual police and prosecutor discretion to craft on a case-by-case basis. As a result, some snitches are street-corner drug users, while others are active dealers with control over large amounts of drugs. Some are family members or intimate partners; some may have already been charged with a crime, or are incarcerated or on probation, while others remain uncharged and at large at the discretion of their handlers. Recall Derrick Megress, the snitch in Hearne, Texas, who ran wild through the public housing project fabricating evidence against dozens of innocent residents.[30] If the high-level mafia informant is supervised, aimed at specific targets, and documented, drug informants are loosely controlled, widely targeted, and often leave no paper trail at all.

Between these two polar extremes, snitching is sprinkled throughout the system like salt, flavoring every kind of case from burglary to corporate fraud and political corruption, hacking, murder, and terrorism. The Department of Justice indicates that federal defendants have been rewarded for cooperation in connection with every single type of federal crime, including murder, sexual abuse, and child pornography. In sum, while law enforcement in different jurisdictions uses informants to varying degrees, and some kinds of investigations are more dependent on the practice than others, informing permeates every kind of criminal case.

E. The Rewards

This book focuses on the most common and potent informant reward: lenience for crimes. Informants can obtain lenience in various forms, from avoiding arrest or the filing of charges in the first place, to reduced or dropped charges on a particular case or in other jurisdictions, to sentence reductions if the informant is eventually convicted. As noted above, informants can also earn lenience for friends and family.

Police and prosecutors often intervene personally in their informants' criminal matters. For example, as reported by the *Boston Globe*,

> Massachusetts State Trooper Mark Lemieux has spent most of the morning sitting on a hard wooden bench in Newton District Court, waiting for his confidential informant Patrick's case to be heard. . . . Lemieux must persuade the district attorney and judge to let Patrick back on the street quickly, despite today's charge of driving without a license, so the informant can act as a liaison with Fidel, a heroin trafficker. . . . Just as the case comes up, Lemieux whispers to the court officer, passes behind the dock, and confers with the assistant district attorney for less than a minute. Patrick's case is resolved: a fine of $450 and the continued suspension of his license. Lemieux walks out of the courtroom. "Everything is fluid," he says. "You gotta go with the flow." Outside, Patrick gets in his own car— already violating the new agreement with the court.[31]

Informants can also receive other sorts of benefits above and beyond lenience. Most famously, they get paid. In one year alone, the federal government paid nearly $100 million to its confidential informants. Over five years, the DEA and ATF together paid nearly $240 million to their informants.[32] Forfeiture statutes authorize paying informants a percentage of the value of assets seized on the basis of their information. DEA "super snitch" Andrew Chambers earned as much as $4 million over the course of his work for various federal agencies, notwithstanding a lengthy rap sheet of his own.[33]

Local police departments maintain informant funds that can range from hundreds to thousands of dollars.[34] Alex White, the snitch to whom Atlanta police turned after they killed Kathryn Johnston, typically received thirty dollars for each buy. Indeed, White subsequently sued the City of Atlanta for wrongful termination, arguing that, by involving him in the scandal surrounding Kathryn Johnston's death, the police ruined his $30,000-a-year employment as a drug informant.[35] In Durham, North Carolina, the police department ran a secret bonus program for years—issuing payments of hundreds of dollars to informants willing to testify—without telling prosecutors or defendants about the money.[36]

Some informant reward arrangements are dangerous and illegal. Police from New York to Los Angeles have been known to reward their informants with drugs. In 2006, Baltimore detectives William King and Antonio Murray were convicted of, among other things, "robb[ing] drug addicts in West Baltimore to reward their sources on the street."[37] The Los Angeles Rampart scandal revealed that officers not only gave drugs to informants but also stole drugs and money from them. Officers also used informants to frame suspects, fabricate cases, and cover up for police shootings. The ensuing federal consent decree required Los Angeles to restrict the LAPD's ability to operate and pay informants; for several years Los Angeles banned the use of street-level informants by most police officers.[38]

Illicit reward arrangements can take place at the highest levels of governmental decision-making. During the federal prosecution of the El Rukn gang in Chicago, the government was so heavily dependent on six cooperating gang leaders that federal prosecutors permitted those incarcerated defendants to buy and use drugs and steal legal documents. As described by the court, "'benefits' included money, gifts, clothing, radios, beer, cigarettes, services and privileges, including the government providing means by which the witnesses' acquisition, possession and use of illegal drugs was facilitated." Informants were "observed snorting cocaine and/or heroin while in MCC [the Metropolitan Correctional Center] on a number of occasions." The government gave the informants telephone privileges, which one informant used to call his drug supplier to "complain[] about the poor quality of the cocaine he had recently received." Because the informants were allowed to move about freely within the U.S. Attorney's Office, they were able to steal a confidential "preindictment prosecution memorandum and other materials related to the case."[39]

As the Chicago story reveals, incarcerated informants can also receive a myriad of incidental benefits including better jail conditions, food, cigarettes, phone and visitation access, and other basic amenities typically denied to the incarcerated.

The best-documented type of informant reward is the lower sentences afforded to cooperating defendants under the U.S. Sentencing Guidelines. As described in detail in chapter 2, federal law authorizes reduced sentences for defendants who provide "substantial assistance" to the government. Such reductions are particularly valuable in the context of federal mandatory minimum drug sentences, which can be reduced only if the defendant cooperates. In state courts that lack comparable guidelines, judges typically reward cooperating defendants with lower sentences as well.

For non–U.S. citizens, informing can carry immigration benefits. The S-visa, sometimes referred to as the "snitch visa," can be available to deportable noncitizens who provide the government with information about a criminal or terrorist organization.[40]

Finally, a small number of cooperating defendants may be given witness protection benefits, which can involve relocation, payments, or even new jobs and identities. Such benefits are available mostly to federal defendants; state witness protection programs are relatively small or sometimes nonexistent.[41]

II. Implications of Informant Practices

The use of criminal informants has wide-ranging implications for the legal system. The following discussion charts the breadth of these implications: the rest of the book explores them in depth.

A. Crime-Fighting Benefits

Informant deals are a powerful law enforcement tool. As one court put it, "our criminal justice system could not adequately function without information provided by informants. . . . Without informants, law enforcement authorities would be unable to penetrate and destroy organized crime syndicates, drug trafficking cartels, bank frauds, telephone solicitation scams, public corruption, terrorist gangs, money launderers, espionage rings, and the likes."[42] Or as an old law enforcement saying goes, "good informant, good case. Bad informant, bad case. No informant, no case."

Informants make it uniquely possible to penetrate group or organizational crimes. Henry Hill was a mafia drug dealer with a twenty-five-year career in organized crime whose life story was depicted in the popular movie *Goodfellas*. Arrested in 1980, Hill testified against many of his mafia colleagues in exchange for witness protection.[43] Pedro and Margarito Flores were twin brothers from Chicago who smuggled at least 1,500 kilograms of Sinaloa cartel cocaine into the United States every month between 2005 and 2008 while sending nearly $1 billion in cash back to the cartel in Mexico. Their cooperation helped make possible the 2019 prosecution and conviction of Joaquín "El Chapo" Guzmán, the drug kingpin who headed the Sinaloa cartel.[44] Not only does the informant deal make possible such prosecutions of high-level operatives, but informant use can also destabilize organized crime and group criminality because of the ever-present possibility that a member of the conspiracy may someday flip.

The informant deal also enables the government to go after politically powerful or otherwise insulated criminal actors. Lobbyist Jack Abramoff used bribes, favors, and illegal influence to help his clients obtain favorable legislation. In 2006, in exchange for a heavily reduced sentence, he agreed to cooperate with the government. His assistance made possible the prosecution of Congressman Robert Ney and several other high-level administration officials.[45] Likewise, it took the cooperation of Enron CFO Andrew Fastow to bring down Enron CEO Kenneth Lay.[46]

Similarly, the 2008 federal investigation into illegal doping in track and field was based heavily on the testimony of Trevor Graham, a cooperating witness who provided prosecutors with names and documentation regarding numerous elite athletes. Graham agreed to cooperate in order to avoid being charged with drug trafficking and money laundering.[47] The prosecutions of wealthy and occasionally famous parents in a wide-ranging college admissions scandal in 2019 also depended on a snitch. The scam involved high-profile Hollywood parents who bribed college officials in order to get their children admitted to elite schools. The ringleader of the scam—William "Rick" Singer—turned FBI informant and secretly recorded his conversations with the parents in exchange for leniency for himself.[48]

Informant deals are powerful in another way: they make law enforcement activities easier and cheaper. By using informants, investigators can often avoid the need for search warrants, wire taps, and other time-consuming procedures that require court authorization.[49] The secrecy that surrounds informant use can enable the government to avoid judicial scrutiny and to move more quickly and quietly against criminal activity.[50]

With respect to individual defendants, converting a defendant into an informant can be a quicker, easier way of resolving a case than going to trial or even negotiating a conventional plea. Unlike a plea bargain, an informant deal is temporary and partial: the government provisionally agrees to reduce or eliminate the suspect's criminal liability, while the suspect temporarily relinquishes his or her right to contest his guilt while promising to provide information about others. Instead of litigating the defendant's guilt or the precise terms of a plea agreement, the informant deal permits the government to come to an agreement while leaving the ultimate question of liability and punishment open-ended. In our overloaded criminal system in which prosecutors lack the resources to pursue every case, the informant deal can be a time-saving, resource-efficient method of case management.

The informant deal thus offers many benefits to the government. At the same time, snitching can be extremely beneficial for criminal offenders as well. It permits them to avoid liability, to escape punishment, and sometimes even to continue offending. These mutual benefits explain in part why the informant deal has become such a popular way of managing criminal cases, for law enforcement and lawbreakers alike.

B. Compromising the Purposes of Law Enforcement

While using informants produces certain kinds of benefits, it also threatens some of the very purposes of the law enforcement endeavor. Most obviously, it inherently involves the toleration of crime. The practice of letting known criminal actors walk away in exchange for information, and even facilitating their criminality to enhance their informational value, flips the law enforcement endeavor on its head. Numerous judicial cases and press accounts reveal handlers who turned a blind eye when their informants committed murder, extortion, fraud, money laundering, bribery, theft, tax evasion, fencing stolen goods, illegal weapons possession, domestic violence, and child abuse.[51] The Department of Justice reports that 10 percent of the FBI's own informant files contain evidence that the informant was committing unauthorized crimes about which the government knew.[52]

Drug enforcement suffers from a particularly strong version of this problem. Police, for example, give thousands of dollars' worth of cash and drugs to informants who suffer from substance use disorders, purportedly in the name of conducting the "war on drugs." In 2008, Brooklyn police officers were caught paying informants with drugs taken from dealers who were arrested after the informants pointed them out. One officer bragged about the practice on tape, explaining that officers would seize drugs but report a lesser amount, keeping the unreported drugs to give to informants later on.[53] A decade later, a police whistleblower recorded fellow police engaging in similar practices—including protecting and supporting drug dealers who served as their informants—in Mount Vernon, New York.[54]

Some informants commit new crimes under cover of their informant status. Tony Warren, for example, started working as a Secret Service informant in 2001 investigating a Nigerian check-fraud scheme, after which he started his own check-fraud scheme involving the theft of hundreds of thousands of dollars.[55] Armando Garcia, already convicted once for cocaine importation, was earning some extra money by helping the FBI intercept 1,200 kilograms of cocaine headed for Florida in a submarine. Garcia used his relationships with the FBI and DEA to cloak his own unauthorized 25-kilogram cocaine deal.[56]

Sometimes the lines blur between authorized and unauthorized informant crimes. In 2004, police told Troy Smith that he needed to produce six arrests in order to escape charges himself. In 2005, Smith sold methamphetamines to another informant. When Smith was charged as a dealer, he claimed that his handler had been pressuring him for a new arrest and that he was therefore authorized to sell the drugs in pursuit of his quota. The court did not permit Smith to call the police handler to the stand or to make the argument to the jury, and Smith was convicted and sentenced to thirteen years.[57] Similarly, when Ralph Abcasis was charged with importing heroin, he asserted that his New York drug enforcement handlers knew about and had implicitly authorized the scheme, while the agents asserted that Abcasis had been terminated as an informant prior to the heroin bust.[58] In such cases, whether new crimes have actually been authorized by the government is often a matter for debate and speculation.

Using informants alters other fundamental aspects of the criminal process, for example, the principle that the worse the crime, the worse the punishment. This foundational rule is routinely flouted in the world of snitching. For example, in the drug prosecution of Cedric Robertson—Crips gang member, drug dealer, and paraplegic—prosecutors also charged his girlfriend, Lakisha Murphy, as well as four active gang members. Although the judge recognized that Murphy was not part of the gang or Robertson's drug business but was only marginally involved because she lived with and cared for her paraplegic partner, Murphy received a mandatory ten-year sentence. Because the four active gang members cooperated against Robertson, they received lower sentences than Murphy did, even though their crimes were far worse. Even the judge complained of the disparity, telling Murphy that "it seems unfortunate in this case that you're doing more time than some of these guys did . . . and there's nothing I can do about it."[59]

Sometimes such disparities have racial dimensions. In 1999, mafia hit man John Martorano agreed to cooperate against his Boston mafia colleagues Whitey Bulger and Stephen Flemmi. In exchange, he received a twelve-year prison sentence for the twenty murders to which he admitted, in addition to extortion, money laundering, and racketeering charges. African American leaders in Boston complained that, even as federal prosecutors cut the deal with cold-blooded killer Martorano, they were considering seeking the death penalty against young Black local gang members accused of committing two murders. "It fosters distrust in our criminal justice system," asserted one Massachusetts state representative. "It mocks the fundamental principle that justice is blind and evenly applied."[60] More generally, studies have shown that federal Black and Latinx defendants who provide substantial assistance receive smaller sentencing reductions than do cooperating white defendants.[61]

Such cases reflect the more general phenomenon that snitching skews the system's evaluation of guilt and innocence. As law professor William Stuntz put it:

[D]efendants who have the most information to sell get the biggest discount.... Trading plea concessions for information means giving the biggest breaks to the worst actors.... [W]orse,... [i]n order to make their threats credible, prosecutors must punish defendants who fail to give them the information they want.... In a system (like ours) that rewards snitches generously, some defendants will be punished very harshly—nominally for their crimes, but actually for not having the kind of information one gets only by working at high levels of criminal organizations.[62]

Or as federal district judge Roger Vinson once mourned, "the problem ... is that the people who can offer the most help to the government are the most culpable."[63]

This shell game of criminal liability weakens the force of the legislative process. When legislatures craft criminal laws, they define the conduct for which liability will attach and specify the range of punishment. The California robbery statute, for example, defines "robbery" as "the felonious taking of personal property in the possession of another, from his person or immediate presence, and against his will, accomplished by means of force or fear," and the statute sets specific sentences ranging between two and nine years, depending on the nature of the underlying conduct.[64] When legislatures define culpable conduct, and set the punishment for a particular crime at a higher level than for other offenses, this is a grave societal statement that we collectively consider such conduct to be worse.[65]

The ability of informants to escape punishment for more serious behavior erodes the force of these highly specific legislative decisions. Instead, punishment turns on the amorphous and sometimes momentary decisions of police and prosecutors regarding the usefulness and convenience of an informant, even when he or she may have committed acts that the legislature has decided deserve substantial punishment.[66] In effect, snitching is the universal loophole to every substantive criminal law. It is as if each code provision read: "Here is the crime. Here is the punishment. Unless you cooperate."

C. Who's in Charge around Here?

"You're only as good as your informant," explained the police officers to the sociologist.[67] "Informers are running today's drug investigations, not the agents," complained a twelve-year veteran of the DEA, "[and] agents have become so dependent on informers that the agents are at their mercy."[68] Even prosecutors worry: "These [drug] cases are not very well investigated. . . . [O]ur cases are developed through cooperators and their recitation of the facts. . . . Often, in DEA, you have little or no follow up so when a cooperator comes and begins to give you information outside of the particular incident, you have no clue if what he says is true." Another prosecutor revealed that "the biggest surprise is the amount of time you spend with criminals. You spend most of your time with cooperators. It's bizarre."[69]

Particularly in drug investigations, police and prosecutors rely heavily on informants to make basic decisions about cases: Who should be investigated? What should be the charges? Which accomplice should be the witness and which one should be the defendant? Because criminal informants are often key sources of information, their choices about what to reveal or conceal become crucial ingredients in the official decision-making process. As a result, government actors are all too often at the mercy of their own informants.

Heavy dependence on informants also displaces more independent decisional processes: according to one former DEA and customs agent, "reliance on informants has replaced good, solid police work like undercover operations and surveillance."[70] Prosecutors in Yaroshefsky's study described violent gang cases as "all based on cooperators . . . [and evidence] for which there is only one rat after another."[71]

Another consequence of this interdependence is to concentrate police attention on poor neighborhoods of color from which drug informants tend to come. Relying on informants naturally focuses attention on the people closest to those informants, since snitches are unlikely to know people outside their own socioeconomic group or community. As discussed in more detail in chapter 6, the use of snitches thus becomes a kind of focusing mechanism on a community, guaranteeing that law enforcement will disproportionately identify new targets there.[72]

Finally, police and prosecutors often inadvertently validate the interests of their criminal informants. Law enforcement agents universally recognize the danger that informants may be cooperating in order to further their own aims: to eliminate competition, for example, or take revenge.[73] When this happens, it means that the state has effectively placed its penal power at the disposal of criminal actors. This is deeply problematic because the integrity of law enforcement discretion turns heavily on how the system selects within a nearly unlimited pool of potential targets.[74] Indeed, because the vast majority of potential cases will never be pursued, it is the quintessential role of police and prosecutors to choose which crimes will be addressed in ways that validate broad public values of fairness and efficiency.[75] The more police and prosecutors rely on informants in selecting targets, the more the integrity of the system is compromised.

D. Mishandling and Corruption

According to the DEA, "Failure in the management of cooperating individuals constitutes, perhaps, the most obvious single cause of serious integrity problems in the DEA and other law enforcement agencies."[76] Former DEA agent Fitzgerald tells of one inexperienced agent who gave his informant free rein to commit new crimes and who was so thoroughly at the informant's mercy that the agent actually served as a lookout during a burglary.[77] The Office of the Inspector General for the U.S. Department of Justice concluded in a 2016 audit that the DEA mishandled hundreds of its informants, including paying unreliable and deactivated sources millions of dollars without tracking, supervision, or documentation.[78]

The FBI's use of mafia informants during the 1970s, 1980s, and 1990s has been called "one of the greatest failures in the history of federal law enforcement" by the U.S. House of Representatives Committee on Government Reform. Over the course of those three decades, the FBI "made a decision to use murderers as informants. . . . Known killers were protected from the consequences of their crimes and purposefully kept on the streets."[79] Perhaps the most infamous incident of the era took place in the FBI's Boston office. For twenty years, Agent John Connolly and a handful of others managed a relationship with Irish mob hit men James

"Whitey" Bulger and Stephen "The Rifleman" Flemmi, who provided the Boston FBI with valuable information about their rivals in the Italian mafia, La Cosa Nostra. As part of that relationship, Connolly protected Bulger and Flemmi from discovery and prosecution for their racketeering activities, extortion, and the murder of at least nineteen people. Connolly lied to prosecutors and other FBI agents in order to protect his sources. In order to protect their informants, FBI agents also permitted four innocent men to be convicted of murder and to serve decades in prison, a violation of law for which, in 2007, the FBI was ordered to pay a judgment of $101 million.[80] Connolly is currently serving a forty-year sentence. Flemmi, now eighty-eight years old, is serving a life sentence for ten murders. Bulger was a fugitive for sixteen years before he was caught in 2011; he was killed in prison in 2018. The saga was sufficiently infamous that Hollywood turned it into the 2015 film *Black Mass*.

More commonly, informant-related misconduct takes place on a smaller scale. Police officers in Columbus, Ohio, were having sex with their informant Michelle Szuhay and wanted to help her get a job as a stripper. So police took Ohio resident Haley Dawson's identity—in the form of her driver's license and Social Security number—and gave it to Szuhay without Dawson's knowledge. An arbitrator ruled that the officers' actions in taking Dawson's identity and giving it to Szuhay were not illegal, although they constituted "a serious error in judgment."[81]

Sometimes police use informants as a cheap and easy way to meet performance goals. Dallas police paid informants to plant fake drugs on immigrant workers, who were then arrested and sometimes deported before the scam was discovered. The busts were used to inflate the department's performance statistics.[82]

From the prosecutorial end, sometimes misconduct takes the form of misleading courts and defendants in order to obtain convictions. In prosecuting Blufford Hayes for murder, for example, a California prosecutor cut a deal to dismiss Andrew James's pending felony charges in exchange for his testimony against Hayes. James also received immunity for his own possible involvement in the murder. The prosecutor then lied to the court, insisting that no deal had been made, and elicited James's perjured testimony in front of the jury.[83]

Similarly, in the effort to obtain a conviction in a gruesome double murder, another California district attorney cut a deal with Norman

Thomas, one of the murder defendants who had admitted to dismembering one of the victims. In exchange for Thomas's testimony against his codefendant, the government dropped his murder charges and arranged that Thomas would avoid a psychiatric exam that might have undermined his reliability as a witness. The prosecution concealed this deal from the defense attorney and the court. Thomas's testimony was the sole evidence that the defendant personally committed the murder.[84]

Disturbing stories exist of law enforcement officials who exploit the secrecy and deregulation of informant use to deploy snitches for their own personal gain, for example, when Boston police detective David Jordan teamed up with an informant to steal $81,000 worth of cocaine from a drug dealer.[85] In another scandal, Baltimore police officer Victor Rivera and two other officers stole three kilograms of cocaine from a drug bust. They gave the cocaine to one of their informants to sell on the street, with whom they then split the tens of thousands of dollars in proceeds.[86] But the far more common scenario is that of the agent or prosecutor who bends or breaks the rules on behalf of his source in pursuit of other criminals and cases. In these ways, otherwise well-meaning public officers end up breaking the law in their efforts to fight crime. Because using informants inherently demands the toleration of some levels of criminality, such official lawlessness is a predictable consequence of the practice.

E. Crime Victims

Although one of the central purposes of the criminal system is to provide relief and vindication to crime victims, using informants requires constant compromises with that purpose. As one frustrated victim of Marvin Jeffery's identity-theft scheme put it, "I do everything legally. I vote. My credit is clean. I try to do all the right stuff, follow all the rules. Then there's this guy, driving around in a gold Escalade, laughing it up, cashing my checks."[87] Karen Parker was the twelve-year-old girl molested by informant Paul Skalnik in Florida. Parker reported the sexual assault to the police, even passing a lie detector test, but Skalnik was too valuable as an informant and was never prosecuted. "No one ever said, 'That's wrong,'" said Parker years later. "The message I got was that what he did was O.K.—that it wasn't serious, it wasn't a crime."[88]

Releasing dangerous informants inherently runs the risk that they will commit new crimes. Darryl Moore, for example, was a known hit man, drug dealer, robber, and rapist with a substance use disorder. His history of perjury was so extensive that his own mother indicated that she would not believe him under oath. Nevertheless, in exchange for his testimony in a murder case, Chicago prosecutors offered him a deal: weapons and drug charges against him would be dropped and he would be paid cash. Moore testified in the case, although he later stated that he fabricated his testimony. After being released and returning to his home neighborhood, he attacked an eleven-year-old girl with a gun and raped her.[89] Odell Hallmon, the snitch who testified falsely four times against Curtis Flowers in Mississippi, avoided punishment in seven felony cases and was released multiple times. He subsequently killed three people.[90]

As trading liability for information has become increasingly common, it desensitizes decision makers to the profound compromises that such law enforcement practices entail. For example, it is a common drug enforcement practice to excuse property crime or violent offenders who provide drug-related information. Because property and violent crimes have victims, the practice conveys the message to those victims that their personal suffering or need for vindication is less significant than drug enforcement goals. As discussed at length in chapter 6, this problem has reached it zenith in poor urban communities in which the pervasive use of criminal informants may actually be exacerbating crime and insecurity.

F. Vulnerable Informants

Bosco Enriquez was fifteen years old when Miami police recruited him into becoming an informant against local drug gangs. The teenager wore a wire and provided information in dozens of cases. As a result of his dangerous work for police, he acquired a substance use disorder. Police carelessly released his name in court documents, which led to brutal attacks against Enriquez and his family by angry gang members. His substance use disorder landed Enriquez in prison, where he was raped. In 2012, the U.S. government deported him to Nicaragua, where he had not been since he was four years old. "They betrayed me," said the young man to a reporter. "I put my life on the line on seven or eight occasions. . . . [W]hat really makes me angry is that [the police] didn't help me when I was thrown out of the country. I asked them, and they said there was nothing they could do."[91]

Six years later and over a thousand miles away, New York law enforcement betrayed Henry, a high-school junior who agreed to inform on other members of his MS-13 gang in exchange for protection and a new life. After he cooperated, police turned Henry over to ICE. ICE used the information that Henry himself provided to police to deport the seventeen-year-old back to El Salvador, where, marked as a snitch, he was likely to be killed.[92]

Our penal system has little sympathy for people in the criminal system. People whose rights are violated or who are physically or psychologically harmed during the criminal process are often perceived to be getting what they deserve for having broken the law in the first place. This hostility is part of what legal scholar Sharon Dolovich calls "the dehumanized, essentialized, and unforgiving conception of the penal subject."[93] It is what Bryan Stevenson mourns as our institutional tendency to "reduce people to their worst acts and permanently label them 'criminal,' 'murderer,' 'rapist,' 'thief,' 'drug dealer,' 'sex offender,' 'felon'— identities they cannot change regardless of the circumstances of their crimes or any improvements they might make in their lives."[94]

In the informant context, this unsympathetic posture has translated into a high tolerance for the risks and harms that often accompany cooperation with the government, to the point of explicitly devaluing informant lives. As Judge Richard Posner of the federal Seventh Circuit Court of Appeals bluntly reasoned,

> confidential informants often agree to engage in risky undercover work in exchange for leniency, and we cannot think of any reason, especially any reason rooted in constitutional text or doctrine, for creating a categorical prohibition against the informant's incurring [costs such as] the usual risk of being beaten up or for that matter bumped off by a drug dealer with whom one is negotiating a purchase or sale of drugs in the hope of obtaining lenient treatment from the government.[95]

As an ethical matter, tolerating such violence against informants is reductive and dehumanizing, a way of writing off their value as people.

As an intellectual matter, it reflects an uncritical acceptance of the informant deal: specifically, the assumption that informants and the government bargain on an equal footing and that the risks informants incur are thus their own responsibility. This uncritical assumption overlooks the lopsided power dynamics of the way informants are often created in the first place. Informants can be the most defenseless players in the criminal justice drama—those without counsel or education, those with substance use disorders, young, frightened, alone, or otherwise susceptible to official pressure. As one sociologist puts it, the creation of an informant "is not a paradigm of simple bargaining between equals but, rather, a complex interaction between personnel of the criminal justice system and vulnerable people."[96]

Indeed, part of the process of creating informants involves the purposeful manipulation of their vulnerability. As Agent Fitzgerald describes it, "The method selected for exerting the pressure [on the informant] varies and is limited only by the imagination, experience, and skill of the investigator."[97] Former narcotics agent Mallory is even more direct:

> It is a widely accepted fact that individuals are most vulnerable to becoming cooperative immediately following arrest. . . . [I] learned to "strike" while the "iron is hot." Informants will often rethink their exposure and decide not to cooperate if given too much time to contemplate their decision. However, a night or two in jail can work for the investigator to help the informant decide to cooperate.[98]

As noted above, one of a suspect's most important resources is defense counsel, not only to advise them about how valuable cooperation might be but also to dispel the panic that many suspects feel when confronted with the possibility of prosecution or incarceration. Accordingly, well-represented, educated, well-resourced informants are in a better position to make rational judgments about whether and to what extent to cooperate or whether to invoke the adversarial process and fight the charges against them. Vulnerable suspects such as drug users, juveniles, people with mental disabilities, or those for whom prison is especially life-threatening are more likely to agree to cooperate even if the benefits are uncertain or small or the risks very high. They may also be more likely to provide false evidence under pressure to produce information.

Because police and prosecutors have wide leeway in negotiating informant deals, there are few limits to the concessions that can be extracted from informants. Many highly extractive arrangements are perfectly legal. Amy Gepfert, for example, agreed to pose as a prostitute and engage in oral sex with another suspect in order to avoid cocaine charges.[99] Similarly, the FBI used Helen Miller—a sex worker dependent on heroin and a fugitive from Canadian drug charges—as an informant to investigate Darrel Simpson by having sex with him for five months. The court held that neither the FBI's use of deceptive sexual intimacy against Simpson, nor the pressure on Miller to have sex in order to escape criminal charges herself, nor Miller's continued illegal drug and sex work activities while serving as an informant constituted outrageous government conduct.[100]

Some arrangements are illegal but happen anyway. Police all over the country have been fired for pressuring their informants into having sex with them.[101]

Since the first edition of this book was published, the problem of informant vulnerability has received far greater public attention. In 2012, journalist and MacArthur "Genius" Fellow Sarah Stillman published a widely read article in the *New Yorker* titled "The Throwaways," in which she chronicled story after story about the government's use of young informants and the violence inflicted on them. Three years later, *60 Minutes* aired a segment about young people who were killed while working as informants. The story focused on North Dakota college student Andrew Sadek, whom police pressured into becoming a drug informant and who was found dead months later. Numerous colleges have now been exposed and criticized for permitting campus police to pressure students into becoming informants, including the University of Massachusetts Amherst, University of Mississippi, University of Wisconsin, and the U.S. Air Force Academy.[102]

Transgender people can be especially susceptible to the pressure to cooperate. Because they face heightened danger of violence in jails and prisons, they may go to great lengths to avoid even brief periods of incarceration. Shelly Hilliard, the transgender teenager whose murder was described in the introduction, agreed to cooperate to avoid incarceration even though she faced only a minor marijuana charge.[103]

Immigrants are vulnerable too: they can experience unique pressures to cooperate in order to obtain a visa or to avoid deportation. ProPublica, the *Intercept*, and other journalistic outlets have chronicled how ICE and the FBI use the promise of a visa—sometimes called the "immigration relief dangle"—in conjunction with the threat of deportation to pressure immigrants into providing information about others in their communities, often at great risk to those informants. Muslim immigrants in particular have been targeted by the FBI; the agency sometimes interferes in the immigration process in order to obtain cooperation, even though the practice violates FBI regulations.[104]

For people with mental health issues, cooperation can be especially risky. Montana police pressured twenty-one-year-old Colton Peterson into becoming an informant even though they were aware of his suicidal tendencies; he killed himself the next day.[105] Individuals with mental disabilities can also be coerced or swayed into providing information that may not be accurate. For example, Derrick Megress, the informant in Hearne, Texas, who fingered numerous innocent residents, suffered from mental disabilities.[106]

One of the central challenges of informant use is the pervasive risk and harm it inflicts on people with substance use disorders. Police routinely give cash to informants, knowing that they will use the money for drugs, or require people with a substance use disorder to engage in risky drug transactions. When UMass Amherst police pressured Logan into becoming an informant, instead of reporting his heroin addiction to the university and to his parents as required, they pushed him into further drug exposure while preventing him from getting medical help. Logan died of an overdose. Legislatures are starting to respond to these kinds of tragedies by considering new rules governing the use of vulnerable informants. These legislative efforts are discussed in more detail in chapter 8.

To be sure, not all criminal informants are vulnerable in these ways. Mafia hit men, international drug dealers, and high-level political operatives with well-paid defense attorneys have a wealth of resources at their disposal in negotiating with the government. Indeed, some of the worst debacles described in this book are the result of the government's inability to check or control such informants. But for the typical person confronted by police without counsel or other protections, or for the indigent suspect sitting in a jail cell, the government can be a formidable opponent indeed. Such suspects may agree to become informants out of fear, ignorance, and their perception that they have no choice.

G. Witness Intimidation and the Spread of Violence

In 2004, fourteen-year-old Jahkema "Princess" Hansen witnessed a murder in her Washington, D.C., neighborhood. She refused to talk to police and instead asked the killer and his associate Franklin Thompson to compensate her for her silence. "For real, little sis, you better not be snitching," Thompson told her, according to a bystander. Hours later, Thompson shot and killed Princess.[107]

Witness intimidation is connected to informant use in a variety of ways. Criminal informants are routinely subject to threats or harm. To a lesser degree, civilian witnesses may also experience threats, or the fear of retaliation, when they agree to cooperate in a criminal case. While most civilian witnesses and criminal informants inhabit different worlds, the violence associated with criminal snitching has spilled over into the realm of civilian witnessing. A 2009 investigation by the *Philadelphia Inquirer*, for example, blamed "an epidemic" of witness intimidation, and the city's failure to address it, for Philadelphia's high dismissal rates in violent crime cases.[108] Police and prosecutors in numerous cities have stated that it is difficult to get witnesses to serious crimes to come forward. In a 2016 survey, most federal criminal legal officials stated that they were aware of threats or harms to cooperating defendants in one or more cases. The survey identified hundreds of cases in which cooperators or witnesses were threatened or harmed.[109] Various aspects of the criminal system are responses to this form of informant-related violence, from witness protection programs to solitary confinement provisions for cooperating prisoners.

Witness intimidation, however, is just one of the ways in which using informants creates and spreads violence. The widespread culture of snitching promotes violence against informants themselves; it tolerates violence against victims of crimes perpetrated by informants; and it exacerbates violence against innocent bystanders who must live cheek-by-jowl with the violent methods used by gangs to police themselves against betrayal from the inside. For example, sixteen-year-old Martha Puebla was killed by Los Angeles gang members because police misinformed Jose Ledesma, a murder suspect, that Puebla had identified him and was cooperating with the police. In fact, Puebla had told the police that she had not seen Ledesma, but police forged Puebla's signature on a fake photo array and showed it to Ledesma in order to pressure him to confess. Instead of confessing, Ledesma ordered Puebla's murder.[110]

Indeed, nearly every informant story contained in this book constitutes an example of informant-related violence, from Darryl Moore's attack on his eleven-year-old victim to the death of ninety-two-year-old Kathryn Johnston at the hands of Atlanta police operating on a bad informant tip. One sociological study concludes that "snitching is a pervasive element of inner-city street life that poses dangers for street criminals and law-abiding residents alike."[111] Increases in violence are thus a particularly devastating cost of informant policies.

H. Systemic Integrity and Trust

The final set of implications associated with informant use has to do with the perceived legitimacy of the criminal system itself. Law enforcement depends on the trust, acceptance, and cooperation of the people and communities that it polices. Without that trust and acceptance, the entire system breaks down.[112]

Informant use erodes public trust in the criminal system in numerous ways that are explored throughout this book. For example, the fact that more culpable defendants routinely receive lesser sentences undermines the public sense of the system's fairness and evenhandedness. The deterrent effect of the law is eroded by the fact that, as one court put it, "[n]ever has it been more true than it is now that a criminal charged with a serious crime understands that a fast and easy way out of trouble with the law is . . . to cut a deal at someone else's expense."[113] That violent and destructive people may be permitted to remain at large in exchange for information is frightening to the people who must live with the consequences. The secrecy surrounding informant use exacerbates all these problems, obscuring the real costs and benefits of informant use and driving a wedge between the law enforcement officials who use informants and members of the public who are supposed to be the ultimate beneficiaries of the practice.[114]

Finally, the tragedy of Princess Hansen's death reveals another kind of destructiveness: the fourteen-year-old's jaded understanding that justice is for sale and that if she cooperated with criminals she would be paid—in precisely the same way that police pay criminals for their cooperation. A car wash attendant in Los Angeles likewise once explained to me that, in his old neighborhood (which he declined to identify), "three will set you free." The adage referred to the widespread understanding that if you were charged with a felony but gave the government information about three other people, they would let you go.

In all these ways, informant use inflicts significant wounds on the integrity of the criminal process, even as it contributes to the law enforcement project in unique ways. The remainder of this book explores this conundrum.

2

Informant Law

Courts have countenanced the use of informers from time
immemorial.
—Judge Learned Hand[1]

From the outside, informant use often looks like a game without rules, in which everything is negotiable and no law is sacrosanct. This state of affairs is a direct function of "informant law": that body of laws and court doctrines that define the legal parameters of the relationship between informants and the government. "Informant law" is centrally characterized by official discretion and flexibility, the inapplicability of many traditional criminal procedure constraints, and the overt toleration of criminal behavior and secrecy. In other words, the official rules of the informant game are that the usual rules do not apply.

The legal rules governing criminal informants fall roughly into four categories. One set covers police and prosecutorial authority to create and reward informants, to persuade criminal suspects to become informants, and to let them off the hook when they cooperate. Another set governs the way informants may be deployed as investigative tools against other people. A third set of rules defines the procedural protections and information to which defendants are entitled when faced with evidence obtained from an informant. And finally, a narrow group of rules sets limits, telling the government what it cannot do in connection with or to its informants.

Each of these arenas has its own laws regarding record keeping and disclosure. Taken together, the informational rules regarding snitching have such a potent effect on the rest of the criminal system that chapter 5—"Secret Justice"—is separately devoted to them.

I. Creating and Rewarding Criminal Informants

Police and prosecutors have vast discretion to create and reward informants. Central to this discretion is the authority to tolerate or authorize crimes committed by those informants. There are few legal limits on the extent to which government officials can reduce a criminal's potential liability or punishment in exchange for information or, conversely, to increase liability when a defendant refuses to cooperate.

A. Police

As described in chapter 1, police, detectives, and investigative agents are the main officials who typically create and manage informants. It is initially up to them to decide whether to arrest or flip a suspect, to evaluate the potential usefulness of a source, and to convey information about the informant to the prosecutor. An informant and their law enforcement handler may maintain a relationship over many years, with the informant providing ongoing information in exchange for the handler's help in evading criminal liability.[2]

When an officer first confronts a potential informant, prior to an arrest or formal criminal charge, there are very few legal constraints. For example, a suspect's right to receive Miranda warnings is triggered only if they are in custody, so if the suspect has not yet been taken into custody or arrested, their unwarned statements to police can potentially be used against them.[3] Similarly, the Sixth Amendment right to counsel applies only once a suspect has been formally charged with a crime, so police can legally—and often do—negotiate directly with uncharged suspects without a lawyer.[4] As a result, police have wide latitude to confront, threaten, and negotiate with potential informants without the presence of defense counsel or other witnesses.

Police can legally reward informants in a variety of ways. They can refrain from arresting them in the first place, thereby permitting the informant to remain at liberty without creating an arrest or other record of the suspected offense. If they do arrest the informant, police can limit the initial description of the crimes or omit other information. For example, in *United States v. White*, the court described how Officer Mike

Weaver manipulated the report-writing process as part of his negotiations with a suspect:

> Weaver stated that if defendant cooperated with the questioning, Weaver would write the police report to reflect only a charge of possessing drug paraphernalia, a misdemeanor, and that if defendant did not cooperate, he would send the glass pipe [containing methamphetamines] to the crime lab and charge defendant with felony drug possession. These matters were entirely within Weaver's control, and in fact he fulfilled the promise: after defendant made the statements, Weaver wrote the police report to reflect only a misdemeanor charge.[5]

This discretionary police power translates into the practical ability to forgive informant crimes simply by declining to arrest informants or by failing to record their conduct. This authority is rooted in constitutional law: the Supreme Court has held that no one can force police to arrest a criminal suspect.[6]

Police also have the power to permit informants to commit new crimes, and police departments each handle this thorny question differently. Some agencies deny that active informants are permitted to commit crimes at all. For example, the standard policy manual adopted by numerous police and sheriff's departments throughout California has an informant policy section, which states that "criminal activity by informants shall not be condoned."[7] The Las Vegas Police Department informant guidelines state that "[c]riminal law shall not be violated in gathering of information," even though those same guidelines provide procedures for the purchase of "evidence" such as illegal drugs.[8]

By contrast, the U.S. Department of Justice has issued several sets of comprehensive guidelines governing the way the FBI and other federal investigative agencies handle informants. These guidelines designate "Tier 1" and "Tier 2 Otherwise Illegal Activity" that can be authorized by the handler. Tier 1 Otherwise Illegal Activity includes violent crimes committed by someone other than the informant, official corruption, theft, and the manufacture or distribution of drugs, including the provision of drugs with no expectation of recovering them. Tier 2 activity includes all other criminal offenses. The guidelines state that informants may never be authorized to participate in an act of violence except in self-defense, to obstruct justice, to commit illegal acts that would be unlawful if committed by a law enforcement official, such as breaking and entering, or to initiate a plan to commit a criminal offense. The guidelines also provide that illegal activity by confidential informants must be authorized in advance, in writing, and for a specific period of time and that the authorizing agent must make a determination that "the benefits outweigh the risks."[9]

Police and investigative agents do not have the legal authority to bind prosecutors. This means that police cannot confer so-called immunity, i.e., they cannot promise informants that they will not be prosecuted for a crime they did or will commit.[10] But courts occasionally give weight to such promises anyway, on the theory that it is unfair to informants who reasonably believed that they would not be prosecuted for crimes they committed in order to provide the government with information. For example, in *United States v. Abcasis*, the defendants claimed that government agents authorized their heroin importation scheme. The court reasoned that

> [i]f a drug enforcement agent solicits a defendant to engage in otherwise criminal conduct as a confidential informant, or effectively communicates an assurance that the defendant is acting under authorization, and the defendant, relying thereon, commits forbidden acts in the mistaken but reasonable, good faith belief that he has in fact been authorized to do so as an aid to law enforcement, then estoppel bars conviction.[11]

The Federal Rules of Criminal Procedure even have a special provision governing cases where defendants allege that they committed their crimes with "public authority," meaning that the government authorized them to do it.[12]

If police do arrest an informant, file a complaint, or otherwise initiate criminal proceedings, then a prosecutor becomes in charge of that informant's case. At this stage, the defendant acquires the right to counsel, which means that police and prosecutor alike are not supposed to try to elicit further incriminating information without the lawyer's presence.[13] For this reason, charged defendants constitute an important subgroup of criminal informants because they are represented by counsel and therefore tend to cooperate in more formal, better-documented ways.

B. Prosecutors

Prosecutors have near-absolute discretion over charging decisions.[14] This means they can add, drop, or alter criminal charges in exchange for cooperation from a defendant in any way they please.[15] Prosecutors can also confer formal or statutory immunity from prosecution pursuant to various immunity statutes or confer informal immunity by entering into written agreements in which they promise not to pursue certain charges in exchange for a witness's testimony. Statutory immunity agreements are binding on prosecutors in other jurisdictions as well, although informal negotiated immunity grants may not be binding.[16] In practice, prosecutors are often willing to drop or reduce charges against someone who is cooperating with law enforcement in other jurisdictions, although this may depend on the seriousness of the new offense.

Prosecutors can also charge third parties, such as family members, in order to pressure a defendant to cooperate. This is sometimes referred to as a "wired plea" because the outcome of the family member's case is attached or "wired" to the defendant's cooperation.[17]

In deciding whether to turn a defendant into an informant, prosecutors may negotiate with defense counsel over a defendant's cooperation, potential charges, and sentencing concessions. They may also seek more information from the defendant before they decide.[18] Often the prosecutor and the defense will agree to postpone the case while the defendant tries to "work off" charges by obtaining more information or generating new suspects.[19]

If a defendant does not want to cooperate, prosecutors can charge them with more serious offenses in order to induce a plea or cooperation. If the defendant remains uncooperative, the Supreme Court has held that the government can seek and a court can impose harsher punishment.[20]

In an example that became nationally infamous, Kemba Smith was charged with drug conspiracy in order to pressure her to testify against her boyfriend, a suspected drug dealer. Because she did not cooperate, she received a twenty-four-year sentence even though she had no prior record and had never handled or sold any drugs herself. She served six years before her sentence was commuted by President William Clinton in 2000.[21]

Prosecutorial charging decisions are unreviewable by courts. The only exception is where there is clear evidence that a prosecutor has charged someone on an impermissible basis such as race, vindictiveness, or to punish a defendant for exercising their constitutional rights.[22] In the context of negotiating with informants, prosecutors have near-complete latitude.

C. Sentencing and the U.S. Sentencing Guidelines

Once a defendant has been convicted—typically as a result of pleading guilty—he or she can seek a lower sentence from the court for having cooperated with the government. The general theory is that a defendant who has been helpful to the government has mitigated their crime and shown some remorse and therefore should be punished less harshly. Judges routinely impose lower sentences on defendants who have cooperated. In some jurisdictions, judges may do so however they see fit as a matter of sentencing discretion.[23] In other jurisdictions, notably in federal court, sentencing is governed by "guidelines" that tell judges what kinds of sentences they should impose. Such guidelines typically have special provisions authorizing judges to award lower sentences to cooperating defendants.[24] In Virginia, for example, the fact that a defendant "cooperated with authorities" is the reason most often given by courts in justifying the reduction of a sentence.[25]

During the 1980s, Congress created special sentencing statutes and the U.S. Sentencing Guidelines, which have strongly influenced the law and culture of federal cooperation. First, as part of the war on drugs, Congress established high mandatory minimum sentences for drug crimes that can be avoided only through cooperation. It also created sentencing guidelines to guide all federal judges. The guidelines set presumptive sentences in addition to a system of "departures" through which courts can impose higher or lower sentences than those contemplated by the guidelines. Because these provisions make cooperation central to a defendant's ability to get a lower sentence, they turned cooperation into a dominant feature of federal plea bargaining and sentencing, ensuring that a large percentage of federal defendants become informants of one kind or another. Approximately 10 percent of federal defendants receive departures, namely, reduced sentences, on the basis of their cooperation—more than for any other reason—and they do so in every category of federal offense, including child pornography and murder. Drug offenders constitute the largest class of cooperators, with just under one-quarter of all drug offenders receiving lower sentences.[26] Many additional defendants cooperate and never receive public credit at all.[27]

The first way in which the federal system incentivizes cooperation is by permitting courts to impose sentences below the minimum sentence prescribed by statute if the government files a motion stating that a defendant has provided "substantial assistance." The statute reads:

> Upon motion of the Government, the court shall have the authority to impose a sentence below a level established by statute as a minimum sentence so as to reflect a defendant's substantial assistance in the investigation or prosecution of another person who has committed an offense.[28]

This provision is crucial because the statutory minimum sentences contained in the U.S. criminal code—especially for drug sentences—can be extremely high. For example, an offender charged with distributing 28 grams of crack cocaine (approximately two tablespoons) faces a mandatory sentence of at least five years.[29] The only way such an offender can obtain a lower sentence for that offense is by providing the government with "substantial assistance."[30]

Separate and apart from these statutory requirements, the U.S. Sentencing Guidelines have a specific provision governing cooperation rewards. The provision is section 5K1.1, and it reads: "Upon motion of the government stating that the defendant has provided substantial assistance in the investigation or prosecution of another person who has committed an offense, the court may depart from the guidelines."[31] Typically, when the government is satisfied with a defendant's cooperation, the prosecutor will file a motion—often referred to as a "5K" motion—acknowledging the defendant's substantial assistance. The judge will then consider the motion in deciding whether to reduce a defendant's sentence below the range recommended by the guidelines. Cooperating defendants can also bring evidence of their cooperation directly to the judge, even if the government does not file a 5K motion.[32]

The Federal Rules of Criminal Procedure contain an additional provision that makes defendant cooperation even more valuable. Rule 35 is titled "Correcting or Reducing a Sentence," and it permits courts to reduce sentences after they have been set, sometimes years after, as a reward for a defendant's further cooperation. Rule 35 reads in part:

(1) In General. Upon the government's motion made within one year of sentencing, the court may reduce a sentence if the defendant, after sentencing, provided substantial assistance in investigating or prosecuting another person.

(2) Later Motion. Upon the government's motion made more than one year after sentencing, the court may reduce a sentence if the defendant's substantial assistance involved:

(A) information not known to the defendant until one year or more after sentencing;

(B) information provided by the defendant to the government within one year of sentencing, but which did not become useful to the government until more than one year after sentencing; or

(C) information the usefulness of which could not reasonably have been anticipated by the defendant until more than one year after sentencing and which was promptly provided to the government after its usefulness was reasonably apparent to the defendant.

Rule 35 thus permits a sentenced defendant to continue to try to provide information to the government while incarcerated in an effort to reduce their sentence. Over one thousand federal defendants receive such sentencing reductions every year.[33] Some judges have publicly complained of the dangers inherent in this arrangement, pointing out that it encourages jailhouse snitches to fabricate information.[34]

In sum, the use of informants plays a powerful role during sentencing, and at least in the federal system, this is true by legislative design. Defendants, lawyers, and judges alike all recognize that a defendant's eventual sentence may depend heavily on whether he or she provides information to the government. This realization influences investigations, plea negotiations, legal strategies, disclosure rules, and all sorts of other decisions that shape sentencing and beyond.

D. Additional Benefits: Money and Drugs

Informants often work for money. The FBI and DEA have budgets of millions of dollars for paying informants. In 1993, federal agencies paid informants approximately $100 million.[35] Over a five-year audit period from 2010 to 2015, the DEA and ATF together paid nearly $240 million to their informants; the FBI paid out another $42 million each year.[36] Through the rules of forfeiture, informants can also receive up to $500,000 or 25 percent of the take in a drug bust or seizures of other property or cash, whichever is less.[37] For example, Rob Roy was facing up to eighty years' imprisonment for cocaine distribution in Philadelphia. Instead, as a result of his substantial cooperation with the FBI over four years, he eventually received a sentence of five years' probation, a $100,000 lump sum payment, and $84,424.77 to cover expenses.[38] Local police departments typically pay small-time informants through vouchers or in cash.[39]

Police also give drugs directly to informants, legally and illegally. The legal justification for doing so is to give informants the ability to set up deals. But many police admit that informants "skim" drugs from buys or that police give small amounts of cash to informants knowing that they will use the money for drugs for themselves. Sometimes police even give drugs directly to informants with substance use disorders in exchange for information.[40]

In addition to money and drugs, informant benefits can include anything of value that the government is willing to give. As the stories throughout this book reveal, those benefits can include better conditions of confinement for informants who are incarcerated, housing for those who aren't, travel, licenses, and immigration concessions.

II. Using Informants as Investigative Tools

For the government, the central benefit of using informants is to obtain information. The U.S. Constitution places significant limits on the government's ability to obtain and use incriminating information. Under the Fourth Amendment, for example, the government cannot engage in unreasonable searches and seizures; the government must get a warrant for certain kinds of searches; and the government needs a certain amount of evidence—"reasonable suspicion" or "probable cause"—before police can stop or arrest or otherwise deprive individuals of their liberty. The Fifth Amendment privilege against self-incrimination, famously embodied in Miranda warnings, protects suspects against being pressured to provide self-incriminating information. The Sixth Amendment right to counsel means that, once a defendant has been charged with a crime, the government cannot question him or her without the presence of defense counsel.[41] Federal and state law further regulates the government's ability to obtain records or to deploy in private places bugs, wiretaps, video cameras, and other types of surveillance.[42]

These rules, particularly those in the Bill of Rights, famously protect individuals against official coercion and invasions of privacy. But the government's ability to use informants is a powerful and often easy way to circumvent many of these restrictions. Because constitutional restraints generally apply only to official actors, a private individual acting as an informant can obtain information that the government could not easily obtain on its own. Criminal informants are thus potent investigative tools, not only because they can be effective information gatherers but also because they are exempt from many of the rules that otherwise constrain official investigative techniques.

In 1966, the Supreme Court decided that the governmental use of compensated criminal informants is constitutionally permissible. That case—*Hoffa v. United States*—upheld the government decision to use and reward Edward Partin, a corrupt union official, to infiltrate the inner circle of Teamsters president Jimmy Hoffa and to eavesdrop on Hoffa's conversations with his associates and his attorney. The government recruited Partin out of a Louisiana jail, where he was facing multiple serious state and federal charges including manslaughter, kidnapping, embezzlement, and perjury. Because Hoffa let Partin into his private hotel room unaware that Partin was working for the government, the Court held that Hoffa had assumed the risk that the informant would share the information he learned and therefore that Hoffa's right to privacy under the Fourth Amendment was not violated. As the Court put it, "The risk of being overheard by an eavesdropper or betrayed by an informer or deceived as to the identity of one with whom one deals is probably inherent in the conditions of human society. It is the kind of risk we necessarily assume whenever we speak."[43]

The Court also decided that the government's use of Partin to obtain Hoffa's incriminating statements did not trigger Hoffa's Fifth Amendment's protection again self-incrimination, because Hoffa was not officially compelled to speak. In *Illinois v. Perkins*, the Court went further, holding that an incarcerated suspect questioned by a jailhouse informant at the government's instigation did not have the right to be given Miranda warnings or to obtain counsel, even though he would have if the exact same questioning had been conducted openly by police. The Court reasoned that, because the defendant did not know the snitch was acting as a government agent, he was not being coerced to confess in an impermissible way.[44]

After *Hoffa*, the Supreme Court approved the extension of informant use through technology. In *United States v. White*, the Court held that the warrantless use of a "wired" informant—i.e., an informant wearing a transmitter permitting police to hear the conversation—did not violate the defendant's Fourth Amendment privacy rights, even though one of the transmissions took place in his home. In dissent, Justice Douglas worried that the Court had missed the significance of the new technological advances. "Electronic surveillance," he wrote, "is the greatest leveler of human privacy ever known. . . . [M]ust everyone [now] live in fear that every word he speaks may be transmitted or recorded and later repeated to the entire world?" Also in dissent, Justice Harlan opined that "the practice of third-party bugging, must, I think, be considered such as to undermine that confidence and sense of security in dealing with one another that is characteristic of individual relationships between citizens in a free society."[45]

The convergence of informant use and new technologies has opened the door to even more intrusive and powerful forms of surveillance. Federal law imposes significant restrictions on official use of electronic surveillance, requiring police to obtain a court order before intercepting communications. A court may not approve a request for electronic surveillance unless it makes numerous findings, including a finding that that there is probable cause that a crime is being committed and that "normal investigative procedures have been tried and have failed or reasonably appear to be unlikely to succeed if tried or to be too dangerous."[46] But the federal electronic surveillance statute, typically referred to as "Title III," contains an exception for one-party consent: if an informant is party to the communication and consents to the recording, there is no need for court authorization. In other words, while the government must get a court order before it can wiretap a phone or place a camera in a private place such as a home or hotel room, it does not need a warrant to wire an informant to record communications or videotape in those same private spaces.[47] For example, in *United States v. Nerber*, the U.S. Ninth Circuit Court of Appeals held that the government could place a video camera in a hotel room with the consent of the informants who were inside, although once the informants left the room, it was no longer permissible to videotape the occupants absent a warrant.[48]

Thirty-eight states follow Title III by authorizing one-party consent to electronic surveillance. A few states, however, have held that informant electronic surveillance in a person's home or other private places requires more regulation. The West Virginia Supreme Court has held that, in contrast to federal constitutional and statutory law, the West Virginia Constitution prohibits wired informants from videotaping or recording transactions in an individual's home without a warrant.[49] Similarly, the supreme courts of Montana, Vermont, Massachusetts, Alaska, and Pennsylvania have all held, under their respective state constitutions, that wired informant surveillance in a person's home requires a warrant.[50]

III. Defendant Rights against Official Informant Use

For defendants who are charged with a crime based on evidence from a criminal informant, the central protections are informational and procedural. The government must turn over certain kinds of information about its informants, usually referred to as "discovery," and defendants can in turn use this information to challenge the veracity and credibility of informants in front of the jury or sometimes before a judge.

In *Brady v. Maryland*, the Supreme Court held that, as a matter of fundamental due process, the government must provide the defendant with all "evidence favorable to an accused . . . where the evidence is material either to guilt or to punishment."[51] Evidence is considered "material" if it is reasonably likely to affect the outcome.[52] In *Giglio v. United States*, the Court held that evidence impeaching a government witness's credibility—i.e., evidence indicating that the witness might be lying—constitutes a form of Brady material and therefore must be disclosed as well.[53] The specific impeachment material at issue in *Giglio* was the government's undisclosed promise to its criminal informant witness not to prosecute him in return for his testimony.[54] Typical impeachment material also includes the informant's prior inconsistent statements, his or her criminal record, benefits conferred on the informant by the government in exchange for information in the instant case, and the informant's history of testimony and rewards in other cases.

In 2002, the Court restricted these informant disclosure requirements. In *United States v. Ruiz*, the Court held that the government need not produce Giglio material to a defendant before the entry of a guilty plea, but only if the defendant decides to proceed to trial.[55] This means that, if a defendant goes to trial, he is entitled to information about informant witnesses, but if he pleads guilty—as do the majority of defendants[56]—he may never see that information. The broad implications of this increased secrecy are discussed in chapter 5.

State courts, plus roughly a third of federal districts, have specific rules governing Brady disclosures. Many states and districts simply track the constitutional requirements, but others impose greater disclosure requirements, different deadlines, and other additional procedures.[57] Massachusetts, for example, requires among other things that prosecutors provide "a statement whether any promise, reward, or inducement has been given to any witness whom the government anticipates calling in its case-in-chief, identifying by name each such witness and each promise, reward, or inducement, and a copy of any promise, reward, or inducement reduced to writing."[58] In 2014, the Florida Supreme Court amended its state discovery rules to require more extensive disclosures regarding state informant witnesses.[59]

Sometimes the government will want to withhold the identity of an informant for protective or investigative reasons. During the investigative phase of a case, this so-called informers privilege is strong. For example, the police need not reveal the identity of an informer who provides them with information leading to an arrest or a warrant.[60] At trial, the privilege is more limited. The government may "withhold from disclosure the identity of persons who furnish information of violations of law to officers charged with enforcement of that law" only if the court decides that the government's need to withhold outweighs the defendant's right to a fair trial. "Where the disclosure of an informer's identity, or of the contents of his communication, is relevant and helpful to the defense of an accused, or is essential to a fair determination of a cause, the privilege must give way."[61] In deciding whether the government may withhold that information, the court must "balance[e] the public interest in protecting the flow of information against the individual's right to prepare his defense." If the government refuses to disclose information necessary to a fair trial, the court may dismiss the case.[62] In addition, the Confrontation Clause of the Sixth Amendment guarantees defendants the right to cross-examine witnesses and therefore limits the government's ability to use evidence from confidential informants at trial without actually producing the informant in person.[63]

Congress has limited the federal government's obligation to disclose an additional form of informant-related material: prior witness statements. Under the Jencks Act, federal prosecutors need not produce a witness's prior statements until after the witness has testified on direct examination.[64] Such prior statements might include inconsistent statements, admissions of perjury or recantations of prior assertions, admissions of the falsity of other statements, or statements regarding the defendant.

Because of growing concerns regarding informant unreliability, an increasing number of states have imposed additional discovery and disclosure obligations on the government when it wants to use a criminal informant as a witness. For example, Illinois passed a law that requires additional discovery and a "reliability hearing" whenever the government seeks to use an in-custody informant, or jailhouse snitch, as a witness.[65] Connecticut requires informant reliability hearings in all murder and rape cases.[66] Texas and California both require that jailhouse informant testimony be corroborated.[67] The American Bar Association, the American Legislative Exchange Council (ALEC), and numerous public interest organizations and innocence projects have advocated heightened scrutiny of informant testimony, and an increasing number of states have imposed new disclosure rules.[68] These reforms are discussed in chapter 8.

IV. Legal Limits: What the Government Can't Do

As this survey reveals, there are few legal limits on the government's authority to create, reward, and use informants. Police and prosecutors have broad discretion to forgive informant crime, to offer lenience and other rewards, to deploy informants to obtain information against others, and to keep information about the process out of the hands of defendants and off the public record.

One federal appellate court briefly considered limiting prosecutorial authority. In 1998, in *United States v. Singleton*, the government promised Napoleon Douglas reduced charges and other sentencing benefits as a reward for his testimony against Sonya Singleton. A panel of the Tenth Circuit held that this reward essentially constituted a bribe and that prosecutors could not pay witnesses in this way without violating the federal antigratuity act, which prohibits providing "anything of value" to a testifying witness. The full Tenth Circuit court reversed, holding that this provision against bribery did not apply to prosecutors.[69]

There are, however, some things the government may not do. For example, if a police officer lies in a warrant application about an informant's tip, it may invalidate the warrant. If a prosecutor knowingly uses a lying informant to obtain a conviction or permits an informant to lie about their reward for testifying, the conviction may be overturned.[70] Because proving such falsehoods after the fact is extremely difficult, however, such rules provide few practical controls.[71]

As a matter of due process, the government may not use an informant in a way that constitutes "outrageous government conduct."[72] Courts rarely deem the official use of informants to be "outrageous," but it occasionally happens in extreme cases. For example, in *United States v. Twigg*, the court reversed a conviction for drug manufacture because the government, through its informant, had so thoroughly set up the defendant. The informant provided the defendant with key ingredients for the drug, a place to manufacture it, and chemical expertise, all of which was paid for by the government. The court considered this level of government promotion of crime fundamentally unfair to the defendant, who, as the court said, was "lawfully and peacefully minding his own affairs" before the informant came along.[73]

In a related doctrine, law enforcement cannot use an informant to entrap a defendant into committing a crime, as long as that defendant is not predisposed to commit the crime in the first place. The entrapment defense is available, as the Supreme Court wrote in 1958, "when the criminal design originates with the officials of the government, and they implant in the mind of an innocent person the disposition to commit the alleged offense and induce its commission in order that they may prosecute."[74]

Both the entrapment defense and the outrageous government conduct defense are very difficult for defendants to raise. For example, between 2001 and 2010, the majority of the highest-profile federal terrorism prosecutions relied on informants, many of whom provided encouragement, support, supplies, and instructions to defendants. Approximately one-third of those defendants raised the entrapment defense; not a single one was successful.[75] Similarly, in a series of "stash house" cases, the federal Bureau of Alcohol, Tobacco, Firearms and Explosives (ATF) used informants to lure dozens of defendants into attempting to rob imaginary stash houses for nonexistent drugs. Most of the defendants tried to raise either the outrageous government conduct defense or the entrapment defense; no one was successful.[76] Consequently, due to these kinds of restrictive judicial interpretations, the government can effectively use informants to suggest, promote, support, assist, and encourage people to commit all sorts of crimes and then prosecute those people afterward.[77]

When the government uses an informant in a way that violates a defendant's rights, the typical remedy is to overturn the conviction. Whether the government can also be sued civilly—either by defendants or others—is a separate question that depends on the nature of the violation and whether the government actor is immune from suit.

Sometimes an informant will hurt people in the course of cooperating with the government. While courts have been reluctant to characterize informants as government employees,[78] where informants act with the knowledge and acquiescence of their government handlers, they may qualify as government agents subject to the same constitutional restrictions as other official actors, thus rendering the government liable for their actions.[79] Private parties cannot, however, force the government to prosecute its bad informants or sue the government for failing to do so.[80]

Some individuals harmed by informants have sued the federal government under the Federal Tort Claims Act (FTCA), with varying results. The FTCA has a "discretionary function exception" under which the federal government cannot be sued for decisions that are "discretionary . . . a matter of judgment or choice" and that "required the exercise of judgment based on considerations of public policy."[81] Because informant use is highly discretionary and involves numerous public policies, it will often be protected. For example, in 2019 the Tenth Circuit dismissed the Estrada family's lawsuit against the DEA where the DEA's active informant sexually molested their five-year-old son and then murdered the father when the father found out.[82] Similarly, in *Ostera v. United States*, the court found no governmental liability for the FBI's decision to release an informant with known violent tendencies. By contrast, in *Liuzzo v. United States*, the court found that the government was potentially liable for authorizing an informant to participate in a KKK operation that led to the murder of civil rights worker Viola Liuzzo.[83]

What if police harm an informant or otherwise violate their rights? Police have qualified immunity from suit, which means that they are not liable if "their conduct does not violate clearly established statutory or constitutional rights of which a reasonable person would have known."[84] For example, police lied to Amy Gepfert about her potential sentence in order to pressure her to perform oral sex on another suspect. She complied in order to avoid drug charges, but later sued the police. Even though the court found that the police might have violated Gepfert's rights by using threats and fraud to get her to have sex, it concluded that the police were immune from suit because the right was not clearly established at the time in a way that a reasonable police officer would have known.[85] The court was also careful to note that not all threats or frauds will render such arrangements illegal and that there is no general rule against police obtaining sex-related or other dangerous or distasteful cooperation from a suspect who wants to avoid criminal charges.[86] Similarly, in *Shuler v. United States*, the court held that an informant who was shot in the back because the FBI blew his cover, and then failed to protect him as promised, nevertheless could not recover damages from the government under the Federal Tort Claims Act.[87] By contrast, in a rare decision, the U.S. Court of Federal Claims found that the DEA breached its duty to its informant, referred to as "the Princess," by failing to protect her from being kidnapped by the Columbian drug traffickers against whom she was informing. The court awarded the Princess $1.1 million for the lifetime of damages to her health.[88]

In a new and provocative turn, the Second Circuit recently held that people in prison have a First Amendment right to *refuse* to snitch.[89] New York correctional officers threatened to put Mark Burns into restrictive protective custody—twenty-three-hour-a-day lockdown—unless he became their informant. He refused, and they put him in solitary for six months, repeatedly pressuring him to become a snitch. The federal court of appeals concluded that this violated Burns's First Amendment right not to speak, noting that "[s]afety risks as well as legitimate concerns about personal loyalty play a role in the decision to divulge information and incriminate others." The court traced this fundamental right back to the Founding era, where the British use of writs of assistance "ignited the fury of the colonists largely because they forced individuals to serve as 'snitches and snoops' for the Crown."[90] The court also concluded that "forcing an inmate to serve as an informant on an ongoing basis is not reasonably related to a legitimate penological purpose—namely, safety."

The decision is specifically about prison and does not change the rules of plea bargaining. As the Second Circuit emphasized, prosecutors may legally pressure defendants to cooperate by offering benefits or threatening harsher charges without violating defendants' First Amendment rights. But after *Burns*, prison officials cannot threaten harsher conditions of confinement in retaliation for a prisoner's refusal to snitch.[91]

Unlike police and correctional officers, prosecutors are absolutely immune from suit—and therefore cannot be sued civilly at all—for decisions or conduct that is "intimately associated with the judicial phase of the criminal process," such as initiating a case and deciding what charges to file, what evidence and which witnesses to use, and what arguments to make. This includes knowingly using false evidence or lying criminal informants in a particular case, even when such use leads to a wrongful conviction.[92]

However, prosecutors do more than just charge and litigate cases. They may initiate or direct investigations, select potential targets, and otherwise work closely with law enforcement agents. Courts have found that prosecutors, when they act either administratively or like investigative agents, relinquish their absolutely immunity from civil suit and may be sued for things they do while "advising the police during the investigative phase of a criminal case" or performing investigative acts generally considered functions of the police.[93] For example, the Eighth Circuit held that a prosecutor did not possess absolute immunity for pressuring and then using a jailhouse informant they knew to be lying. The court reasoned that "immunity does not extend to the actions of a County Attorney who violates a person's substantive due process rights by obtaining, manufacturing, coercing and fabricating evidence before filing formal charges, because this is not 'a distinctly prosecutorial function.'"[94]

In sum, while governmental liability for informant misconduct is limited, there remain a number of legal theories under which the government might be held responsible for the informants it deploys.

V. Informant Use in Comparative Perspective

The United States permits law enforcement to use criminal informants more freely than do many other countries. These differences highlight some fundamental policy choices adopted by American law enforcement and courts. One is the tolerance of high levels of informant unreliability. Another is the notion—central to the practice of plea bargaining—that it is permissible to trade away criminal liability in exchange for information. Another is reflected in the governmental acceptance of, and even engagement in, ongoing criminal activity. These are controversial precepts that many other nations have resisted or declined to accept altogether.[95] As law professor Jacqueline Ross explains with respect to Europe in particular, "The United States and European nations conceptualize, legitimate, and control undercover policing in substantially dissimilar ways."[96]

For some countries, the unreliability associated with informants has made them a highly disfavored tool. In 1997, for example, the government of Ontario, Canada, appointed a commission to review the wrongful murder conviction of Guy Paul Morin. After hearings that lasted over five months and called 120 witnesses, the Kaufman Commission concluded that Morin's wrongful conviction was due in large part to the testimony of two jailhouse informants who fabricated evidence that Morin had confessed to the murder. The commission also found that "the systemic evidence emanating from Canada, Great Britain, Australia and the United States demonstrated that the dangers associated with jailhouse informants were not unique to the Morin case. Indeed, a number of miscarriages of justice throughout the world are likely explained, at least in part, by the false self-serving evidence given by such informants." The commission issued dozens of recommendations for reform, including limiting the use and reward of informants, increased disclosure, and improved police and prosecutorial training.[97] As a result of the commission's recommendations, the Canadian attorney general established new policies limiting jailhouse informant use.[98]

For other countries, the covert practices associated with informant use are considered legally and morally problematic. Methods such as the "bust-and-buy" sting and informant lenience deals, while standard in the United States and United Kingdom,[99] have been resisted by other European countries, often on the principle that the government should neither engage in criminal conduct nor tolerate it. Well into the 1970s, "[t]hroughout most of continental Europe, . . . virtually all these [undercover] techniques were viewed, even by police officials, as unnecessary, unacceptable, and often illegal." Today, many European countries engage in some form of these tactics, but to a lesser degree than does American law enforcement.[100]

In the Netherlands, for example, the Dutch began adopting American-style undercover tactics in the 1970s. In the 1990s, the government was rocked by scandal when it was revealed that police and highly paid criminal informants were actively running drug operations, importing tons of drugs into the country, some of which were released onto the streets. The resulting Parliamentary Inquiry from 1995 to 1996 led to significant restrictions on law enforcement authority to use criminal informants and to engage in U.S.-style undercover operations.[101]

Central to the Dutch public debate over informant use has been the contrast with American practices. According to Police Commissioner René Karstens, Dutch and American law enforcement take fundamentally different approaches to questions of informant legality and the need for regulation: "[T]he philosophies on infiltration [by informants] were rather divergent. Where we [Dutch] feel that certain limitations are needed on infiltration as a method, the Americans are inclined to let the end justify the means. With them anything goes."[102]

In Italy, criminal informant use is broadly constrained by the "concern that undercover operations might corrode the rule of law by enabling police to engage in 'crime.'" If they have not obtained explicit authorization, Italian law enforcement officials may be prosecuted for crimes they commit or permit in pursuit of criminal targets and investigations. In order to permit some undercover investigations, Italian law thus contains a series of narrow exceptions that relieve police of criminal liability for specific acts such as the simulated drug buy or postponing arrests and seizures for investigative purposes—acts that would otherwise be deemed illegal police conduct.[103] Under U.S. law, by contrast, such decisions are committed to law enforcement discretion without threat of criminal liability or even judicial review.

Similarly, the legal culture in Germany includes a prohibition against the official toleration of lawbreaking. In 1992, under pressure to permit greater use of undercover tactics, Germany passed reforms designed to legitimize a limited form of undercover policing. Those reforms permit the use of undercover informants only in connection with serious crimes and only when it is extremely difficult for police to obtain evidence by other means. The reforms were accompanied by great controversy: as one German official commented, "undercover investigations should always be considered a tactic of last resort."[104]

Such social and legal distaste for informant use stands in stark contrast to the former Soviet Union, where the use of informants was considered not so much a "necessary evil" as a "fundamental means of pursuing both ordinary criminals and individuals who might prove a political threat to the regime." There, a lack of legal safeguards and the official premium placed on the state's interest made informant recruitment and use widespread.[105]

Snitching has been a prominent feature of authoritarianism in other countries. The former East German government was infamous for conducting pervasive surveillance of its own citizens through informants working for the state secret police, known as the "Stasi." Indeed, the use of informants in that context came to be seen as a paradigmatic aspect of authoritarianism precisely because it reflected such offensive disrespect for citizen privacy and autonomy.[106] The use of informants has also been associated with the Israeli occupation of Palestinian territories and the British occupation of Northern Ireland.[107]

The ongoing evolution of informant use around the world reflects broader developments in international law enforcement. Collaborative international drug enforcement efforts, for example, have had a significant impact on the law and practices of European nations. Drug policy expert Ethan Nadelmann describes the "Americanization of European drug enforcement" as the gradual adoption of DEA-style methods of drug investigation by countries such as Germany, the Netherlands, Austria, Belgium, France, Spain, and Italy.[108] Such methods have introduced more reliance on undercover criminal informants, more trading of liability, and more tolerance of ongoing crime than European criminal systems have historically accepted.

In the antiterrorism arena in particular, there have been calls for the harmonization of legal standards to permit more international collaboration. Professor Ross has pointed out the significant challenges that such cooperation entails:

> Nations would need to renegotiate the tense political compromises legitimating undercover operations (which are everywhere controversial, but for different reasons). And they would need to revise the practices and procedures not just of undercover investigations, but of their domestic policing regime, including in areas that at first glance appear unrelated. Champions of closer cooperation who call on countries to overcome insularity in the interest of collective struggles against international crime and terrorism do not appear to appreciate the scale and depth of the requisite transformation of domestic policing regimes or the difficulty of reshaping the political compromises currently legitimating undercover operations.[109]

VI. American Informant Law

The laws of informant use embody a nation's stance toward weighty issues: Are guilt and punishment negotiable? What are the appropriate limits on police and prosecutorial authority? How much protection should be afforded to individual privacy? Each nation's "informant law" reflects the confluence of legislative, judicial, and executive authority, as well as these kinds of important public values. The United States is notable for the ways in which the legislative and judicial branches have ceded authority on this issue to executive law enforcement. As the sociologist Gary Marx pointed out years ago, "Unlike some Western European countries or Japan, legislatures in the United States have indirectly supported undercover practices by their consistent failure to set standards and goals for police performance. Legislatures, like the courts, generally prefer to leave such matters to police, thus enacting a kind of legitimacy by default."[110] The U.S. philosophy of informant law thus stands at the far end of the international spectrum, privileging law enforcement authority, discretion, and secrecy over the dangers and intrusions posed by criminal informant use.

The overall picture of American informant law is one of tremendous official authority and discretion to use, reward, and pressure criminal informants with few legal limits. The constraints that do exist tend to focus on the government's informational obligations rather than substantive limits on the government's choices, and even those informational obligations are tied to litigation and trials that occur infrequently. The end result of this laissez-faire, unregulated approach is that the American informant market is centrally shaped by the individual decisions of police and prosecutors, with few external controls and little judicial oversight or legislative or public scrutiny.[111]

3

Juries and Experts

It was a grim and violent case, with allegations of murder, rape, and a missing body. In 2009, George Leniart was charged in a Connecticut court with multiple crimes involving a teenage girl who had disappeared thirteen years earlier. The body of April Dawn Pennington had never been found. There was no physical evidence tying Leniart to the crime. There were, however, four witnesses; three out of four were informants testifying in exchange for deals.

The government's key witness, Patrick Allain, was the alleged accomplice. He had been the missing girl's boyfriend. He admitted to raping her before she disappeared but claimed that Leniart had killed her. At the time of Leniart's murder trial, Allain himself was incarcerated, serving ten years in prison for a different felony sexual assault. In exchange for agreeing to testify against Leniart, Allain avoided being charged with the murder himself. With regard to his admitted rape, the statute of limitations had passed, so he could not be prosecuted for that crime either. Allain acknowledged on the stand that the prosecutor had promised not to oppose his early release if he cooperated and testified.

Three other central witnesses in the case had been incarcerated with George Leniart and claimed that he confessed to them while in jail. Two of them admitted that they were testifying in order to get reduced punishment. Only the third witness had no discernable incentives: he was no longer incarcerated and was facing no pending charges when he related Leniart's statements to the police.[1]

In sum, the case rested overwhelmingly on the word of incentivized criminal informants. It was also the kind of shocking, high-profile case in which informants tend to be richly rewarded when the government wins. With so much at stake, the defense attorney reached out to me to ask if I would testify as an expert to educate the jury about the culture and common practices of jailhouse snitches, how they sometimes collude, and how often their testimony leads to wrongful convictions. The defense also wanted me to explain the widespread, informal understanding within U.S. jails that entrepreneurs who come forward with incriminating evidence about other prisoners—especially high-profile suspects—can expect to be rewarded.

I flew to Connecticut and appeared before the presiding trial judge, where I described the kinds of data and research that I would provide to the jury. The judge would not let me testify, stating that jailhouse informant behavior and unreliability were within "the common experience, ken, or common knowledge of the jury."[2] So I went home. The jury convicted George Leniart, and he was sentenced to life in prison.

I. Juries

The Leniart case was unusual in that the defendant actually went to trial. Fewer than 5 percent of all convictions in the United States are the result of a jury trial, which means that juries do not decide cases all that often. But the jury remains one of the system's most important structural checks on informant reliability. The threat of a trial in which a snitch might have to testify in open court is an incentive for law enforcement to ensure that its informants are accurate. Once at trial, the informant must convince a jury of ordinary people that he or she is telling the truth. The jury will typically learn that the informant is receiving a benefit for their testimony and may hear about previous instances in which the informant testified in exchange for lenience. In some jurisdictions, the court will also instruct the jury that the informant's testimony should be carefully scrutinized for potential unreliability. Trials also perform an important public transparency function: it is only when a defendant decides to go trial that the public will learn about the informants that the government uses to make its case.

In 1966, in *Hoffa v. United States*, the Supreme Court upheld the constitutionality of using and rewarding criminal informants. The Court approved the practice in large part because it believed that the jury trial provides a good check against the risks of compensated criminal witnesses notwithstanding their strong incentives to lie. The Court relied on what it called "[t]he established safeguards of the Anglo-American legal system [that] leave the veracity of a witness to be tested by cross-examination[] and the credibility of his testimony to be determined by a properly instructed jury."[3]

The Supreme Court was partially right: sometimes jurors can be an effective check against lying informants. One prominent observer, Judge Stephen Trott, himself a former federal prosecutor, concludes that "[o]rdinary decent people are predisposed to dislike, distrust, and frequently despise criminals who 'sell out' and become prosecution witnesses. Jurors suspect their motives from the moment they hear about them in a case, and they frequently disregard their testimony altogether as highly untrustworthy and unreliable, openly expressing disgust with the prosecution for making deals with such 'scum.'"[4]

Juror distrust, for example, cost the government its massive 1981 racketeering case against the Hell's Angels motorcycle gang. In that case, jurors felt that the government's key witnesses—former Hell's Angels members, one of whom was paid $30,000—were "despicable and beneath contempt."[5] That same kind of distrust led to Todd Ruffin's acquittal by a Connecticut jury for the charge of selling drugs to an informant. "They just didn't believe a word [the informant] said," said the prosecutor, who spoke with jurors after the trial. "He has a terrible record, so they felt he was inherently untruthful."[6]

But the Supreme Court was also fundamentally wrong. Jurors—and the adversary system more generally—have proven to be ineffective protection against informant unreliability. The first and biggest reason is structural: because 95 percent of criminal convictions are the result of a plea, informants in those cases will never testify or be subject to cross examination at all, even when their allegations strongly influence the case and its eventual outcome. Most of the time, the defense will never see impeachment material regarding those informants, their criminal histories, or their deals. Most of the time, jurors will never evaluate their credibility. In a system with so few trials, jurors are at best a backstop, not a frontline mechanism for checking informant reliability.

Even when defendants do go to trial, however, it turns out that jurors are not very good at evaluating informant veracity. A 2004 report found that over 45 percent of the innocent people on death row were convicted because jurors believed a lying criminal informant.[7] For example, jurors believed Paula Gray, an accomplice to a double murder in the infamous 1985 "Ford Height Four" case. Her testimony led to the wrongful conviction of three men before the actual killer confessed ten years later. Likewise, jurors at Randy Steidl's 1986 murder trial believed informant Debra Reinboldt, even though later evidence revealed that Reinboldt could not possibly have witnessed the murder about which she testified because she had been at work at the time.[8] Two different Mississippi juries believed Odell Hallmon when he testified against Curtis Flowers, even though in an earlier trial Hallmon had told an entirely different story and later admitted that his testimony had been "all make-believe."[9] Dozens of additional exonerations in noncapital cases reveal just how often juries believe unreliable criminal informants, even when jurors are told that the informant is being compensated and has the incentive to lie.

II. Limits to the Trial Truth-Seeking Process

Such cases indicate that the "established safeguards of the Anglo-American system" such as discovery, cross-examination, and jury instructions do not effectively protect defendants from unreliable informant witnesses. We now know a lot more than we did in 1966 about why. One reason is that discovery is a partial and flawed mechanism for disclosure. As described in chapter 2, "discovery" is the legal term for the process by which the government discloses select information about its case, including government witnesses. As a matter of due process, the government is constitutionally obligated to disclose any exculpatory material, that is, evidence that the defendant might actually be innocent. When a defendant goes to trial, this disclosure obligation includes so-called impeachment evidence that a government witness might be lying, including incentives, deals, and prior criminal records.[10] This is key evidence that defense attorneys use to cross-examine informants and on which jurors ultimately decide credibility.

Unfortunately, discovery is not always forthcoming. Sometimes the state's failure to disclose is illegal. We have seen numerous cases in which prosecutors violate their constitutional obligations and withhold impeachment information about their informants, hiding promises and deals or past criminal conduct.[11] In Roderick Johnson's murder case, for example, the Pennsylvania prosecutor "blatantly lied" about his key informant witness, hiding the informant's serious criminal conduct, his ongoing cooperation with the police department, and the many benefits he received. Johnson, who was facing the death penalty, was exonerated in 2020.[12] Similarly, Stanley Mozee and Dennis Allen were wrongfully convicted of murder because the prosecutor knowingly presented false informant testimony at their trial and hid evidence of the state's agreements with those informants. Mozee and Allen were exonerated in 2019.[13]

Police and prosecutors can also avoid disclosure by taking steps to prevent the creation of an evidentiary record in the first place. Using what one scholar calls "soft words of hope," prosecutors may refrain from making explicit promises to an informant, even though both parties fully expect the informant to be rewarded, to avoid creating a formal deal that would have to be disclosed to the defendant and to the jury.[14] This kind of hide-the-ball gamesmanship can occur on an institutional level, rising to the level of official policy. In the aftermath of the high-profile snitch scandal in Los Angeles, the grand jury concluded that the Los Angeles District Attorney's Office had intentionally refrained from creating an informant tracking system in order to avoid triggering its discovery obligations.[15]

Sometimes prosecutors may not have all the relevant information. Police and investigators often offer under-the-table deals to their informants, or hide information about their informants' criminal conduct, in order to protect their sources. For example, in the infamous case of the mafia informant James "Whitey" Bulger, FBI handler John Connolly hid information about Bulger's ongoing crimes from prosecutors for years.[16] In Orange County, California, the sheriff's department maintained secret informant logs that deputies were trained not to disclose, even when testifying in court under oath.[17] Prosecutors cannot disclose such informant-related material to the defense if police do not share it in the first place.

The *Hoffa* Supreme Court also relied heavily on cross-examination as a way of ensuring informant reliability, noting that the informant in that particular case "was subjected to rigorous cross-examination, and the extent and nature of his dealings with federal and state authorities were insistently explored."[18] The nineteenth-century legal expert John Wigmore once wrote that cross-examination "is beyond any doubt the greatest legal engine ever invented for the discovery of truth."[19] But in real life, cross-examination does not work that well, especially for compensated witnesses who have personal incentives to stick to their stories. The Connecticut Supreme Court has noted that "false confessions are easy to fabricate, but difficult to subject to meaningful cross-examination."[20] Cross-examination cannot uncover unspoken understandings and deals when an informant knows that he is a more valuable witness when such things remain unsaid. As one scholar has pointed out, "the more the witness's fate depends on the success of the prosecution, the more resistant the witness will be to cross-examination. A witness whose future depends on currying the government's favor will formulate a consistent and credible story calculated to procure an agreement with the government[] and will adhere religiously at trial to her prior statements."[21] Moreover, an effective cross-examination depends on full discovery: a defense attorney cannot cross an informant regarding information the prosecutor has not disclosed.[22]

The third classic safeguard in the Anglo-American adversarial toolkit is the jury instruction. The Supreme Court in *Hoffa* wrote that a "properly instructed jury" is a strong defense again lying informants, and some jurisdictions instruct juries to consider informant testimony with special care. For example, California requires judges to instruct juries that "[t]he testimony of an in-custody informant should be viewed with caution and close scrutiny. In evaluating such testimony, you should consider the extent to which it may have been influenced by the receipt of, or expectation of, any benefits from the party calling that witness."[23] In Oklahoma, Utah, and Connecticut, juries are told that the testimony of informants "must be examined and weighed by you with greater care than the testimony of an ordinary witness."[24]

In practice, however, jury instructions can be ineffective. In the most recent study from 2020, researchers tested the efficacy of the Connecticut cautionary informant instruction. That instruction tells jurors: "You must look with particular care at the testimony of an informant and scrutinize it very carefully before you accept it. You should determine the credibility of that witness in the light of any motive for testifying falsely and inculpating the accused." The study found that the instruction had no meaningful effect on juror decision-making.[25] More generally, jury instructions have long been understood to have significant weaknesses. At the end of a case, a judge might read the jury dozens of different instructions, many of which will be in complicated legalistic prose or otherwise difficult to process. As Judge Learned Hand wrote in 1944, "It is exceedingly doubtful whether a succession of abstract propositions of law . . . has any effect but to give [jurors] a dazed sense of being called upon to apply some esoteric mental processes, beyond the scope of their daily experience."[26] More scientifically, studies have shown that many jury instructions are "incomprehensible" to jurors and that jurors often ignore them and rely instead on their common sense.[27] And finally, to the extent that cautionary informant instructions have value, numerous jurisdictions do not use them at all.[28]

III. Human Psychology

Another reason that jurors are not very good at evaluating informant reliability has to do with basic structures of human cognition. Over the past decade, we have learned much more about how people's minds work when they evaluate witness credibility, and it turns out that some basic features of our psychology get in the way. People are reluctant to evaluate witness reliability based on incentives, preferring to attribute reliability to dispositional, personal factors rather than external, situational ones. Human beings are generally programmed to believe that others are telling the truth; it takes strong medicine to get them to think otherwise. And jurors' minds are heavily swayed by the mere allegation of a confession. At the same time, incentives do in fact exert a strong effect on people's willingness to falsely implicate others. All these common psychological features conspire to make jurors prone to believing informants when they shouldn't.[29]

A core assumption behind informant disclosure rules is that, if jurors know about an informant's deal or other incentive to lie, they will discount or disbelieve the informant's testimony. But this assumption is flawed. Psychological studies indicate that jurors often simply ignore the fact that informants are compensated, preferring instead to accept informant testimony at face value. In one study, mock jurors were divided into two groups. The test group was told that the witness was being given a lenience deal in exchange for his testimony, while the control group was not told this fact. The test group convicted at approximately the same rate as the control group. In other words, knowing the informant's incentives to lie did not undermine the jurors' belief in his testimony.[30]

Another study found similarly that jurors did not discount jailhouse informant testimony even when they knew an incentive had been offered.[31] By contrast, a different study found that jurors were somewhat sensitive to the effects of inducements, and used them to discount informant testimony, but were not influenced by the size of the incentive.[32]

One reason that jurors might ignore or discount informant incentives is the psychological phenomenon called "fundamental attribution error." It describes "the tendency for individuals to overestimate dispositional factors and underestimate situational factors when explaining other people's behavior."[33] In other words, we tend to think that other people make decisions uniformly based on their character—in which case incentives don't explain much—even though we recognize that we ourselves often make nuanced choices based on situational external pressures and incentives.

Another potential explanation lies in what researchers call "truth default theory." It refers to the fact that "people naturally exist in a truth-default state, meaning that they initially evaluate all incoming messages as truthful unless there is a reason to suspect deception."[34] As a general matter this default makes sense: we couldn't communicate or function if we did not take most people at their word most of the time. But that default is hard to overcome, and it can skew jury evaluations of informant witnesses.

Informant testimony about other people's confessions is an especially persuasive piece of evidence. Even the mere allegation of a confession—what the literature calls a "secondary confession"—exerts strong influence on juries. Psychologists have found that jurors consider secondary confessions especially powerful and that, when offered by the prosecution, have "a great impact on juror's decision-making."[35] This means that simply having an informant assert that the defendant confessed makes it more likely that the jury will convict, even when there are good reasons to think the informant is lying.

Finally, incentives turn out to be powerful and risky. Incentivizing people to implicate others both increases the likelihood that they will come forward with information and also the likelihood that they will lie about it. In one study, offering an incentive raised the general rate at which people were willing to "snitch" and report what other people had said. But the rate only went up for false reports of confessions, not true ones.[36] In other words, incentives increase the likelihood that a witness will lie in order to get them, even if jurors are insensitive to that fact.

For all these reasons, jurors are an imperfect check against lying informants. Even an informed, properly instructed jury will not necessarily be very good at figuring out whether an informant is telling the truth. The adversarial criminal system relies heavily on information-sharing and disclosure as a check on wrongful convictions. But false informant testimony is more powerful than this model acknowledges. Or as one seasoned jailhouse informant candidly explained:

> [T]he jury not knowing the system or how it works is going to believe when I get up there with all these details and facts, that this guy sat in the jail cell, or he sat on the bus, or he sat in the holding tank somewhere, or told me through a door or something, they're gonna believe me.[37]

IV. Experts

We often ask ordinary people serving as jurors to decide complicated, technical, or nonobvious issues. When jurors do not have sufficient information or training to make good decisions, our legal system turns to experts. Experts can testify about more issues than ordinary lay witnesses are allowed to by offering their expert opinions about data, research, and other materials that the jury might not get to see directly. The basic rule is that a party may call an expert witness if "the expert's scientific, technical, or other specialized knowledge will help the trier of fact to understand the evidence or to determine a fact."[38] The expert must be properly qualified, their testimony must be "based on sufficient facts or data," and their testimony must have "a reliable basis in the knowledge and experience of the relevant discipline."[39] The judge is the gatekeeper, in charge of deciding whether an expert's testimony is both relevant and reliable and therefore admissible.

In the criminal system, most experts work for the government.[40] They are forensic lab technicians, ballistics and fingerprint analysts, and even police officers. Often, such government experts are called to explain the general character of certain kinds of criminal behavior, psychology, or subcultures about which ordinary people might not have full information. For example, the government often calls gang experts to explain to juries how gangs operate, what kinds of behaviors and practices are typical, and what various words or actions might signify to other gang members. The California Supreme Court has explained that "the culture and habits of criminal street gangs" are "sufficiently beyond common experience that the opinion of an expert would assist the trier of fact," which is why "[t]he use of expert testimony in the area of gang sociology and psychology is well established."[41] The New Mexico Supreme Court likewise approved the credentials of a police detective gang-culture expert whose job was to explain to the jury, among other things, that gang-affiliated tattoos and various forms of aggressive "staring" could constitute disrespect that might cause another gang to retaliate violently.[42]

Similarly, courts routinely permit law enforcement experts to testify about the culture, habits, and practices of drug dealers. As one federal court explained it, "[t]he operations of drug dealers are generally an appropriate subject for expert testimony. Because the clandestine nature of narcotics trafficking is likely to be outside the knowledge of the average layman, law enforcement officers may testify as experts in order to assist the jury in understanding these transactions."[43] Courts have permitted law enforcement experts to testify specifically about informant culture in gangs or jails to explain, for example, the significance of the term "snitching" or the stigma associated with cooperation.[44]

The use of experts in the criminal system is lopsided in favor of the government. Courts have long accepted government forensic and policing experts; law enforcement witnesses often benefit from presumptions of reliability and admissibility. Many scholars lament that courts tend to be "lax" and "reflexively" permit the introduction of government-sponsored forensic evidence even where its reliability is unproven or highly questionable.[45] An exhaustive study by the National Academies of Sciences found that "trial judges rarely exclude or restrict expert testimony offered by prosecutors."[46]

By contrast, courts habitually prohibit criminal defendants from introducing comparable experts, and it can take years for empirically solid defense expertise to become legally acceptable. For example, it took many years for courts to let defendants use expert testimony regarding battered women's syndrome. Such expertise was first offered in the 1970s to explain the psychological science behind why battered persons might stay with abusive partners in life-threatening situations. Courts rejected it at the time, although all states and all courts now recognize the scientific value of such expertise.[47] Similarly, it took decades for courts to accept defense expertise on the fallibility of eyewitness testimony. Courts initially refused to permit behavioral psychologists and other scientists to explain to juries how commonly witnesses misidentify people and why. Today the science of false eyewitness identification is well established, and the majority of courts permit such defense experts to testify.[48]

It is against this background of resistance to defense expertise that American courts now grapple with whether to let jurors hear from informant experts called by defendants.

V. Informant Expert Testimony

There are two main reasons that courts currently give for excluding defense expert testimony regarding informants. First, that it invades the province of the jury with opinions about witness veracity. Second, that jurors already know enough about informants based on common sense and popular culture so as to render such testimony unhelpful. Neither is accurate.

No one is allowed to tell a jury whether to believe a particular witness. Evaluating credibility is the jury's job, and experts cannot opine about whether a particular informant is telling the truth. That is not, however, what proper informant experts do. Rather, they educate jurors about dynamics that are beyond most people's common experience, like the robust market for information that pervades American jails or aggressive jailhouse informant strategies for gathering information. In the Leniart case, for example, I was not there to tell the jurors whether any of the informants were lying, and on appeal the Connecticut Supreme Court agreed that my testimony would not have invaded the province of the jury.

Courts have also held that informant experts are not helpful to jurors because informant unreliability is a matter of common sense. As one federal trial court wrote, "juries already understand that jails are miserable places. Juries understand that cooperating witnesses have committed crimes and have powerful motives to say what they can to stay out of or to be released from jail."[49] The Connecticut Supreme Court similarly believed that jurors could glean enough information about informants from "popular culture" to make decisions about informant credibility.

It is true, of course, that many people possess general information about informants, much like they do about gangs or drug dealers. Popular television shows like *The Wire* or movies like *Snitch* and *Black Mass* have made the drug snitch and mafia informant into recognizable characters.[50] There have also been an increasing number of high-profile media investigations into informant-based wrongful convictions, many of which are included in this book. But select encounters with Hollywood and high-profile journalism do not mean that jurors understand how the U.S. criminal system actually deploys, pressures, and rewards informants or the many sophisticated tools and strategies that informants have at their disposal that might call their reliability into question.

For example, one common yet counterintuitive phenomenon that jurors are unlikely to learn from the movies is the problem of informant collusion. As a matter of common sense, consistent testimony from multiple informant witnesses might lead a juror to believe that each of the stories is more likely true. But that is an unsafe assumption in the world of informants. As discussed in greater detail in chapter 4, experienced or repeat informants have been known to develop sophisticated collusive strategies to procure, fabricate, share, and sell information in order to bolster their stories. Informants learn that such collusive bolstering increases the appearance of credibility and therefore the value of their information, which in turn increases their chances of getting rewarded by the government. For example, in one Louisiana wrongful-conviction case, a mother and her three sons were set up by a group of colluding prison informants. The fact that thirty-one informants came forward turned out to be evidence not of the family's guilt but rather of an information-selling network inside the federal prison.[51] In Los Angeles, jailhouse informants explained that they often shared information with each other and collectively developed fabricated stories by repeatedly running those stories past law enforcement officials until they got the desired response.[52] Counterintuitively, the existence of multiple informants presenting the same or similar evidence should itself be viewed as a potential red flag indicating unreliability. Without expert testimony, jurors are unlikely to know this.

Not only is popular culture a problematic teacher; the psychological research described above reveals that jurors sometimes need help processing the information they have, above and beyond their common-sense reactions. We now know, for example, that basic features of the human mind can make jurors overly susceptible to believing alleged secondary confessions. We also know that jurors tend to underestimate the influence of incentives. Such cognitive biases are not cured by watching Netflix.

For all these reasons, expert testimony can meaningfully assist jurors evaluate informant testimony. In a 2018 survey of laypeople and attorneys, the vast majority of participants—approximately 80 percent—agreed that it would be useful for juries to hear an expert testify about secondary confession evidence and the circumstances that make secondary confessions more or less reliable.[53]

Finally, as a matter of consistency and fairness, courts should acknowledge that defense informant experts are providing much the same sort of testimony that government gang experts, drug experts, and even the government's own snitch experts have long been permitted to provide. If "the clandestine nature of narcotics trafficking is likely to be outside the knowledge of the average layman,"[54] so is the clandestine nature of informant use. If jurors need a police expert to explain that aggressive staring between rival gang members can trigger violence,[55] then jurors should also get to hear an expert explain that a jail inmate requesting a transfer to a new cell block is evidence that they might be targeting someone in that new location. In civil cases, jurors will often get to watch a "battle of the experts" in which experts on both sides of a question offer competing analyses. Jurors in criminal cases should get to hear from both sides too.

All that said, expert testimony is far from a magical solution. At least two studies found that mock jurors underestimated the content of expert testimony and evaluated compensated informant witnesses just as favorably as other jurors did without hearing from an expert.[56] The same cognitive biases that inhibit jurors from appreciating informant incentives may also inhibit them from internalizing expert explanations. Like other procedural protections, experts are thus an incremental tool that courts can deploy in the effort to strengthen jury decision-making and to render the process more evenhanded.

VI. Juries and Experts Going Forward

The Connecticut courts flip-flopped over the expert question for years. In 2010, the trial judge in the Leniart case forbade me from testifying. In 2016, the Connecticut Court of Appeals decided that the trial judge got it wrong. The appeals court explained why my expert testimony would have helped that jury:

> Natapoff testified that even if average jurors had some limited knowledge related to the use of jailhouse informants, they did not understand the true culture of jails or the full extent to which informants could benefit in our criminal justice system. She explained that a juror could not be expected to understand the efforts informants put forth to obtain their information or the possible sources for that information. Further, according to Natapoff's research, jurors often have a misguided understanding regarding the consequences an informant likely will face if he or she lies. She explained that although perjury prosecutions of informants are rare, jurors nevertheless often believe the threat of perjury charges plays an important role in ensuring that an informant tells the truth. Natapoff testified that without access to background information, jurors are ill-equipped to assess properly an informant's credibility, even in the face of an instruction asking them to take great care in doing so. In the face of Natapoff's uncontested testimony that jurors were not fully aware of the dangers in relying on informant testimony and that expert testimony could assist jurors in properly evaluating an informant's credibility, the court abused its discretion by concluding that the substance of Natapoff's testimony was within the ken of the average juror.[57]

In 2019, the Connecticut Supreme Court split the baby. On the one hand, it held that the original trial court was within its authority to exclude my testimony. It disagreed with the appeals court, finding that jurors can generally be expected to know enough about jailhouse informants to make informed credibility decisions. "[T]he potential abuses associated with jailhouse informant testimony are generally engrained throughout popular culture," wrote the court, thus rendering my more specific expert testimony in that case unnecessary. On the other hand, the court also made clear that such expert testimony is generally admissible, that it does not invade the province of the jury, and that other defendants in other cases might be able to use it.

The Leniart case might seem like an odd choice of example, since it is not the kind of morally unambiguous wrongful conviction that scholars and advocates usually point to when seeking legal change. Maybe George Leniart was innocent, maybe he wasn't. Maybe all those informants were lying, maybe they weren't. Either way, the jury did not have all the information it needed to make a rigorous decision in a case that turned heavily on compensated informant testimony. That was a failure of the trial process, regardless of the outcome. In a system like ours, which relies on juries to safeguard its integrity and to make life-and-death decisions about reliability, we should do more to support and inform that vital decision-making process.

The Connecticut story is far from over. In 2019, the same year that the state's high court decided *State v. Leniart*, the Connecticut legislature passed informant reform legislation that now requires prosecutors to track all their informants statewide and to make greater disclosures about them to defendants. The new law also requires all courts to hold pretrial reliability hearings in murder and rape cases to screen out potentially unreliable informant witnesses before they ever get to the jury. The very next year, the Connecticut Supreme Court revisited the informant question. It expressed deep concern about informant unreliability and decided to extend the requirement that juries be given special cautionary instructions when informants testify.[58] *State v. Leniart* thus turned out to be just one chapter in a much longer story of change in which growing skepticism about the integrity of informant testimony is now giving rise to stronger legal protections.

The evolution of Connecticut law mirrors the national trend. When I wrote the first edition of this book in 2009, there were few legal challenges to informant witnesses, expert or otherwise. No courts permitted academic experts like me to testify for the defense about jailhouse or other kinds of informants, at least not in front of juries. Today, with so many more exonerations and snitch scandals on the public record, there is far greater recognition of the risks posed by informants and the failures of the adversary system—and common sense—to address them. As a result, many state courts and legislatures have decided to strengthen the trial-by-jury process. These reforms are described at greater length in chapter 8.[59]

4

Beyond Unreliable

In the 25 years I have been in this business, I have worked
with hundreds of informants. I believe that exactly one of
them was completely truthful, and there is no way to be
100% sure about him.
—John Madinger, senior special IRS agent and former narcotics agent[1]

All too often, the U.S. criminal system convicts the innocent. The now-
steady stream of exonerations is stark evidence that, even in the most
serious cases, innocent defendants may still plead guilty or be convicted
at trial despite the existence of some of the most elaborate procedural
protections in the world.[2] The sources of this disaster are complex: an
overwhelmed public defender system, long sentences, high trial conviction rates, and systemic pressures that steer defendants into guilty pleas
are just some of the reasons why innocent defendants may dread their
day in court.

Criminal informants are an important piece of the wrongful conviction puzzle. This is not merely because they often lie. After all, any witness is potentially unreliable. It is rather because informants have such
predictable and powerful inducements to lie, because law enforcement
relies heavily on their information, and because the system is not well
designed to check that information. As a result, unreliable informant
information permeates the process in ways that predictably lead to bad
results such as wrongful arrests, bad search warrants, and fabricated evidence as well as the ultimate failure: wrongful conviction.

I. Lying Informants

The groundbreaking book *Actual Innocence* estimated in 2000 that
21 percent of wrongful capital convictions are influenced by criminal

informant testimony.[3] Four years later, a study by Northwestern University Law School's Center on Wrongful Convictions traced 45.9 percent of documented wrongful capital convictions to false informant testimony, making "snitches the leading cause of wrongful convictions in U.S. capital cases."[4] Another report that same year estimated that 20 percent of all California wrongful convictions, capital or otherwise, resulted from false snitch testimony.[5] Today, the Innocence Project concludes that nearly 20 percent of all DNA exoneration cases involve a lying jailhouse snitch.[6] According to the National Registry of Exonerations, approximately 15 percent of all wrongful murder convictions involve a jailhouse informant, and 23 percent of wrongful capital convictions are due to jailhouse snitches.[7] More generally, law professor Samuel Gross's study on exonerations reports that nearly 50 percent of wrongful murder convictions involved perjury by someone such as a "jailhouse snitch or another witness who stood to gain from the false testimony."[8]

The informant tendency to lie is old and infamous. It led federal judge Stephen S. Trott, himself a former prosecutor, to warn that "[informants'] willingness to do anything includes not only truthfully spilling the beans on friends and relatives, but also lying, committing perjury, manufacturing evidence, soliciting others to corroborate their lies with more lies, and double-crossing anyone with whom they come into contact, including—and especially—the prosecutor. A drug addict can sell out his mother to get a deal, and burglars, robbers, murderers and thieves are not far behind."[9] Or as the Fifth Circuit Court of Appeals once noted, "[i]t is difficult to imagine a greater motivation to lie than the inducement of a reduced sentence."[10]

Because snitching has become so pervasive, the threat of perjured testimony goes beyond the problem of the individual bad witness. In 2006, for example, a federal jury wrongfully convicted Ann Colomb and her three sons for allegedly running one of the largest crack cocaine operations in Louisiana. The Colomb family served four months in prison awaiting sentencing before all charges were dismissed. Their wrongful convictions were based on fabricated testimony obtained from a ring of jailhouse informants who bought and sold information about the Colomb family inside the local federal prison. The ring worked by selling prisoners files of documents and photographs that would permit them to fabricate testimony in order to reduce their own sentences. The government planned to use thirty-one such informants against the Colombs.

The scheme was revealed when a disgruntled prisoner, Quinn Alex, gave $2,200 to another prisoner in order to get a file. When the file never came through, Alex wrote an angry letter to the prosecutor demanding that the other prisoner be charged with theft. The presiding judge, U.S. district judge Tucker Melancon, told a journalist afterward: "It was like revolving-door inmate testimony. The allegation was that there was in the federal justice system a network of folks trying to get relief from long sentences by ginning up information on folks being tried in drug cases. I'd heard about it before. But it all culminated in the Colomb trial." Judge Melancon ordered the U.S. Department of Justice to investigate.[11]

While all compensated criminal informants pose the risk of fabrication, jailhouse snitches are particularly pernicious. In a jaw-dropping 1989 interview with *60 Minutes*, jailhouse snitch and admitted perjurer Leslie Vernon White described how he was able to obtain information about other prisoners and fabricate their confessions, while himself in prison, and trade those fabrications for reduced sentences. The White scandal led to a grand jury investigation into the use of jailhouse snitches in Los Angeles, which concluded not only that jailhouse snitches routinely lied but also that police and prosecutors knowingly relied on and exploited unreliable informants.[12] For example, the grand jury found evidence that police and prosecutors would purposely place suspects in the "informant tank" at the jail, surrounded by snitches working with the government, "in the hope that one or more of the informants would 'come up with information' to strengthen the case against the inmate."[13]

Twenty-five years later and fifty miles south of L.A., Orange County was rocked by a massive jailhouse informant scandal. For years, the sheriff's department ran a secret jailhouse informant program, violating defendants' constitutional rights, paying violent gang members, maintaining a secret database, and lying to courts about it. The scheme unraveled when an intrepid public defender named Scott Sanders spent over a year fighting to get the secret documents that would ultimately reveal the government's misconduct.[14]

The jailhouse snitch problem is a concentrated version of a more general danger associated with criminal informant use, which is the threat to innocent suspects who happen to be incarcerated, who have criminal records, or who are otherwise associated with a criminal milieu such as illegal drug use. Innocent people with criminal associations are more susceptible to informant targeting and conviction because law enforcement and jurors alike are predisposed to believe in their guilt. Incarcerated or recidivist suspects are thus particularly vulnerable to wrongful conviction based on unreliable snitch information because it is harder for them to defend against informant lies.[15]

Of course, sometimes informants, even unreliable ones, tell the truth. In other words, the problem is not that criminal informants always lie. Rather, as we saw in the previous chapter, it can be extremely hard to tell when they do and when they don't. And unlike other kinds of witnesses, informants are deeply self-interested in their false stories. Their ability to convince the government that their information is true and valuable may mean the difference between their own freedom and incarceration or even life and death.[16]

II. Law Enforcement Dependence on Informants

Despite their known unreliability, law enforcement relies on informants, often heavily. This is not only because police and prosecutors need information to make cases but also because law enforcement success is often measured in terms of numbers of arrests and prosecutions, thereby putting pressure on police and prosecutors to use the cheapest and fastest methods rather than the most reliable. This is particularly true in drug enforcement, where the government has become profoundly reliant on informants in conducting investigations, selecting targets, making arrests, and obtaining convictions.[17]

Because law enforcement officials need to create cases, they have incentives to believe informants when they offer information that appears valuable. These incentives grow stronger once informants become trusted, cases are initiated, and the official becomes dependent on the informant for the success of the case.

This dependence can become so great that it creates a sort of perverse romance—"falling in love with your rat." A prosecutor explains the phenomenon:

You are not supposed to, of course. . . . But you spend time with this guy, you get to know him and his family. You like him. . . . [T]he reality is that the cooperator's information often becomes your mind set. . . . It's a phenomenon and the danger is that because you feel all warm and fuzzy about your cooperator, you come to believe that you do not have to spend much time or energy investigating the case and you don't. Once you become chummy with your cooperator, there is a real danger that you lose your objectivity.[18]

Another prosecutor describes how reliance on a cooperator affects numerous crucial decisions down the line. Once the government believes an informant,

it is a certainty that the information obtained from the cooperator will become part of the base of information utilized to evaluate future would-be cooperators. Moreover, the information will affect future questioning of witnesses and defendants; it will alter how investigators view the significance of witnesses and particular pieces of evidence; and it may taint the way the case is perceived by the prosecutors and agents. In other words, false information skews the ongoing investigation. The false information may prove critical to issues that have far greater import than whether to accept as true the proffer of another would-be cooperator. Rather, it might impact decisions regarding charges to be filed against other defendants, it might affect decisions related to an appropriate plea for a given defendant, and it might even influence whether the government decides to seek the death penalty.[19]

Studies show that police and prosecutors, like everyone else, tend to interpret information in ways that support their previous decisions and resist interpretations that suggest they got it wrong the first time around. Psychologists refer to this phenomenon as "confirmation" or "expectancy" bias, "belief perseverance," or "tunnel vision." Law professor Daniel Medwed explains how cognitive tunnel vision causes law enforcement officials to stick to their original theories about who is guilty even in the face of contradictory evidence. Tunnel vision can also lead law enforcement to selectively identify and seek out evidence that confirms their first impressions.[20] As a result, once law enforcement officials accept informant information, it becomes important for the government to preserve the credibility of that information and that informant, even when other evidence suggests that they may be unreliable.[21]

These psychological dynamics have troubling legal implications. The Due Process Clause of the U.S. Constitution requires prosecutors to discover and disclose to defendants impeachment material about government witnesses, namely, evidence suggesting that the witness might be lying.[22] The adversarial process depends on this disclosure to ensure that defendants can meaningfully ferret out informant lies. But police and prosecutors lack incentives to seek out such material, not only because it could literally destroy their cases but also because they have vested interests in believing their informants. Moreover, police in possession of impeachment material may be reluctant to share it with prosecutors, knowing that it will have to be disclosed to the defense. This means that the usual protections against unreliable witnesses—prosecutorial ethics and discovery—may be unavailable precisely because prosecutors themselves have limited means and incentives to discover the truth.

Sometimes police and prosecutors are taken in by their own informants. For example, prosecutors believed Marion Albert Pruett's 1982 testimony against a prisoner accused of killing Pruett's cellmate and put Pruett into the federal witness protection program. Pruett subsequently committed a string of bank robberies and murdered two convenience store clerks and eventually confessed that he had killed his cellmate himself.[23]

Sometimes government officials lack information about the risks that their source is lying. The Baltimore prosecutor in Tony Williams's 2003 murder trial was unaware that the state's key witness, a jailhouse snitch, was also on the Baltimore police payroll as an informant.[24]

Sometimes police withhold information about their informants not only from prosecutors but also from their own police supervisors. In 2009, the St. Louis Police Department initiated an investigation into its own officers to determine whether rank-and-file police were lying about their informants. Two officers, for example, had claimed to have gotten tips from informers who turned out to be dead or in jail at the time. The police union got a temporary restraining order on behalf of the officers against their own supervisors, arguing that disclosing informants' identities to police supervisors "would jeopardize informers' lives, [police] officers' careers and public safety." A judge eventually sided with the department and permitted the investigation to proceed.[25]

Sometimes prosecutorial ignorance is intentional. Tom Goldstein was wrongfully convicted of murder in 1980, spending twenty-four years in prison on the basis of testimony from jailhouse snitch Edward Fink. Although he lied about it at trial, Fink had received lenience for numerous offenses by working as an informant for the local police department for many years. However, because the Los Angeles County prosecutors' office lacked procedures to keep track of informants and their deals, the prosecutor on Goldstein's case did not know Fink's history in that office and therefore never disclosed the information to the defense.[26] In its 1990 investigation of informant abuses, the Los Angeles grand jury concluded that the Los Angeles District Attorney's Office had intentionally decided not to keep track of its informants and their unreliability. The reasons for this decision were twofold: because "the defense might discover information" if it were documented, and because "the Sheriff's Department might be deemed to be violating defendants' rights to counsel" if full information about informant practices was revealed.[27] In other words, under pressure to make cases and to shield law enforcement from scrutiny, the prosecutors' office purposely refrained from learning about and documenting its own use of unreliable snitches.

In other situations, officials may ignore or even affirmatively encourage informant mendacity, concealing informant lies from the defense as well as the court in order to obtain convictions. For example, prosecutors lied for twenty years about their key informant witness, beginning with Delma Bank's 1980 murder trial all the way through his appeal and state habeas petition. Informant Robert Farr had set up Banks in exchange for cash and lenience, a fact that the government continuously denied.[28] Similarly, James Walker spent nineteen years in prison for a 1971 murder he did not commit, on the basis of allegations of a criminal informant, John Snider. Although they had proof that Snider was lying, police and prosecutors covered up his lies and withheld evidence regarding Snider from the court and from the defense.[29] In another case, the Ninth Circuit threw out the death penalty sentence imposed on Lacey Sivak because prosecutors withheld evidence that the informants in the case were getting deals and because prosecutors knew that the informants were lying on the stand.[30]

Sometimes informant use reflects deep institutional dysfunction of which unreliability is just one aspect. Throughout the 1990s, Detroit homicide police ran an illegal snitching operation on the ninth floor of the police department. Informants received sentencing reductions in addition to food, drugs, access to sex, and special privileges from detectives in exchange for making statements against dozens of prisoners who were eventually convicted of murder. Detectives actively instructed informants to fabricate testimony. One informant reported that "detectives supplied him and other informants with prewritten statements to memorize before the preliminary hearings of the accused men. In those statements, informants would say that the accused person confessed to their crime in a way that 'filled in' the details detectives were missing to connect the suspect to their crime."[31]

The snitch ring was an ill-kept secret. Indeed, one Detroit prosecutor at the time complained about the practice to his supervisors, writing that "promises of leniency are made to these snitches without approval—or prior knowledge—which exceeds police authority and violates our policies." The prosecutor also knew about the fabrications: "I have been told," he wrote, "that snitches do lie about overhearing confessions and fabricate admissions in order to obtain police favors or obtain the deals they promised."[32] The practice nevertheless continued, resulting in dozens of convictions and, decades later, numerous exonerations.

These examples of official wrongdoing are not meant to impugn the vast majority of police and prosecutors who do not engage in such conduct. But they do illustrate the dangers and temptations with which police and prosecutors must contend. Informant witnesses represent a kind of perfect storm: deeply unreliable sources managed by officials with strong incentives to accept and defend their information. In these ways, the interdependence of law enforcement and its informant witnesses can threaten the entire fact-finding process.

III. The Corroboration Trap

Sometimes a single informant provides the central or only evidence in a case. Such scenarios are so obviously risky that a number of states now require corroboration for informant testimony. But corroboration is not foolproof. Sometimes informants are used to bolster other, equally unreliable forensic evidence, which makes that evidence look stronger than it actually is. And because informants often collude, sometimes multiple informants will provide corroboration for each other's fabrications, making all their false stories look more plausible than they actually are. In each of these cases, informant evidence is corroborated but nevertheless still unreliable.

In 2004, Texas executed Cameron Todd Willingham for allegedly murdering his three children. Willingham maintained his innocence throughout, turning down plea offers that would have saved his life. His conviction and execution are now widely believed to have been wrongful, based on discredited junk arson science. But Willingham was not convicted solely on faulty forensics. Weeks after Willingham's high-profile arrest, jailhouse informant Johnny Webb came forward and alleged that Willingham had confessed to him in the jail. Between the arson claims and the jailhouse snitch, all doubt about Willingham's guilt evaporated, even to his own lawyers. Years later, Webb—who was diagnosed as bipolar—recanted his testimony, admitting that the prosecutor had offered him an undisclosed deal in exchange for his testimony against Willingham.[33]

Other cases similarly demonstrate how jailhouse informant testimony can bolster bad forensics. In Florida, at least three men were wrongfully convicted based on the testimony of a fraudulent "dog sniff" expert who offered junk science evidence of the men's alleged guilt. In all three trials the government relied on jailhouse snitch testimony to reinforce the faulty dog sniff evidence. The three men were eventually exonerated.[34] And even though bite mark evidence has been thoroughly discredited, David Spence was convicted based on bite mark evidence and the testimony of six jailhouse informants, two of whom later recanted. Spence was executed in Texas in 1997.[35]

Put differently, bad informants can be used to corroborate bad forensics. The problem arises in part because informant testimony is not independent evidence: informants may come forward entrepreneurially to provide information about high-profile cases in the media or about other people in the jail, while police and prosecutors encourage and invite this entrepreneurship. In this way, the very existence of a high-profile case or defendant can affirmatively generate informant evidence. That evidence, in turn, is most valuable to the government when the underlying case is already weak, which means that the informant testimony is even more likely to distort the outcome and lead to wrongful conviction.

Corroboration is also misleading when multiple informants offer the same story. In a typical criminal case, the existence of multiple sources for the same evidence tends to render that evidence more reliable, in part on the assumption that each piece of evidence has been independently generated. But informants are known to proactively collaborate and collude in order to render their stories more plausible and thus more valuable to the government. As one federal court of appeals explained, "because they are aware of the low value of their credibility, criminal[] [informants] will even go so far as to create corroboration for their lies by recruiting others into the plot."[36] For example, in Ann Colomb's wrongful conviction described above, the Louisiana prosecutor planned to use thirty-one informants from the federal prison, all of whom were part of a for-profit snitch ring in which each informant corroborated the same story. A comparable informant collusion scheme operated for many years in the Atlanta jail. Prisoners bought and sold "packages of information" to each other to be offered to the government in exchange for leniency. Prices for information ran as high as $250,000, in a market that a federal judge excoriated as "abominable."[37] In the 1989 Los Angeles grand jury investigation, informants likewise reported that they shared information and tactics with each other and collectively developed fabricated stories by repeatedly running those stories past law enforcement officials until they got the desired response.[38] One experienced Los Angeles snitch even wrote a "*manual* . . . instructing other jailhouse snitches how to fabricate confessions."[39]

As a result of these dynamics, the existence of multiple informants presenting the same or similar evidence can itself, ironically, be a potential indicator of unreliability. The California legislature has formally recognized the high risk of jailhouse informant collusion by barring the use of the uncorroborated testimony of an in-custody informant. The law specifically forbids the use of another jailhouse informant to serve as corroboration unless the government can prove that the testifying informant has not communicated with other informants.[40]

IV. When the Innocent Plead Guilty

Most American defendants do not litigate or challenge the evidence of their guilt. Rather, they plead guilty. This practical reality reduces the salience of accuracy. Plea bargaining turns evidence and accuracy into commodities that are traded and negotiated along with many other inputs into the bargaining process. As a result, many innocent defendants conclude that it is in their best overall interests to plead guilty to crimes they did not actually commit. Twenty percent of the wrongful convictions listed in the National Registry of Exonerations are the result of a plea. In misdemeanor cases, hundreds of thousands of innocent people routinely plead guilty in order to get out of jail so they can go home and care for their children, keep their jobs, or avoid eviction.[41]

For the vast majority of defendants who must negotiate under these conditions, a lying informant can alter the calculus about whether to go to trial. The mere threat of an informant witness can make it more likely that an innocent defendant will take a plea rather than risk conviction and the substantially higher sentences that flow from losing at trial. In 2008, for example, fourteen men in Cleveland, Ohio, were found by a federal judge to have pled guilty to false charges levied by a DEA informant. The first defendant in the case, a mother of three, insisted on her innocence, went to trial, and was wrongfully convicted. She received a sentence of ten years. The remaining fourteen men then pled guilty in exchange for lower sentences.[42] In Hearne, Texas, several innocent defendants pled guilty after being accused by informant Derrick Megress, even though Megress was later shown to be lying. Similarly, two innocent people in Tracy City, Tennessee, pled guilty after Tina Prater alleged that she had bought drugs from them, even though she hadn't.[43]

This kind of tragic calculus occurs throughout the penal system, although the nature of plea bargaining and the appellate process make it impossible to know how often it happens. Innocent defendants plead guilty for a number of reasons. They may think that they will lose at trial and that their punishment will be heavier than the one offered in a plea. The federal sentencing guidelines expressly encourage this sort of calculation by imposing longer sentences, the "trial penalty," on defendants who do not take a plea.[44] Defendants may also plead guilty because they are being held in jail on bail that they cannot afford to pay and a plea provides the immediate freedom of probation or a sentence of time served. Or they may plead guilty because their lawyers tell them to or because they are ignorant of their rights and other options. They may even plead guilty because they think they are guilty of an offense when they are not.

Professors Samuel Gross and Barbara O'Brien conclude that it is almost impossible to determine how many innocent defendants plead guilty, because false convictions are "invisible at their inception." Most defendants who plead guilty do not appeal, and even if they do it is difficult to overturn a guilty plea, which means that "[t]he exonerations that we know about are overwhelmingly for convictions at trial."[45] Sometimes, however, wrongful pleas do make it to the public record. Writing in 2008, Gross and O'Brien described some infamous examples:

> We do know about a substantial number of exonerations of innocent defendants who pled guilty and received comparatively light sentences—in one particularly disturbing factual context. In the past decade, several systemic programs of police perjury have been uncovered, which ultimately led to exonerations of at least 135 innocent defendants who had been framed for illegal possession of drugs or guns in Los Angeles, in Dallas, and in Tulia, Texas. . . . Most of these innocent drug and gun defendants pled guilty, and had been released by the time they were exonerated two to four years later.[46]

Each of these three "particularly disturbing" examples involved criminal informants and/or undercover narcotics agents operating in the mode of an informant. In the Los Angeles Rampart scandal, officers used informants to set up innocent targets. In Dallas, police used informants to plant fake drugs on suspects. In Tulia, Texas, a single undercover narcotics officer fabricated drug evidence against dozens of African American targets.

In sum, while we do not know how many innocent defendants plead guilty, we know that it happens on a regular basis and that informants are a dangerous aspect of the problem. When a criminal informant fingers an innocent person, the pressures of the criminal system may drive that person to plead guilty rather than face worse consequences. This is especially true for defendants with prior criminal records, who are less likely to be presumed innocent by law enforcement officials and jurors. It is also especially true for defendants with overworked, underpaid public defense counsel who lack the resources to fully investigate and litigate the case.[47] Moreover, in order to avoid trial and protect the identity of the informant, prosecutors may offer reduced charges, probation, or lower sentences to persuade a defendant not to contest the case. The tragedy remains invisible because the informant's misinformation is never tested or revealed. Because the vast majority of cases are resolved through guilty pleas rather than trials, the possibilities for this sort of miscarriage of justice are both widespread and nearly impossible to discover after the fact.

V. The Important but Limited Role of Procedural Protections

Legislators increasingly recognize the unreliability of criminal informants and the inadequacy of existing procedural protections. Numerous jurisdictions have considered and implemented a variety of legislative reforms aimed at reducing the likelihood of wrongful convictions. These reforms are discussed in depth in chapter 8; they include such things as corroboration requirements, reliability hearings, and stronger discovery and disclosure requirements when the government seeks to use informants as witnesses.

Better procedural protections improve the chances that the defense will be able to uncover an informant's lies, and as such they are important tools in protecting against wrongful convictions. But such procedures are inherently limited because they do not address the underlying phenomena that drive the use of unreliable informants. First, many such procedures are applicable only at trial and therefore do not directly affect plea bargains, namely, the source of the vast majority of criminal convictions. They also do not affect the process of using informants in investigations or to obtain warrants, techniques that lead to thousands of bad searches and arrests every year. At best, they indirectly shift police and prosecutorial incentives to rely on unreliable informants in shaping basic decisions about investigations, arrests, and charging.

More fundamentally, however, procedural protections do not alter the basic structure of the informant market. They do not reduce informants' underlying incentives to lie in the first place; nor do they regulate the vast discretion that law enforcement wields in negotiating the informant deal. For all these reasons, procedural reforms are only one aspect—albeit an important one—of the larger challenges posed by unreliable informants.

5

Secret Justice

Every thing secret degenerates, even the administration of
justice; nothing is safe that does not show it can bear discussion and publicity.
—Lord Acton (1861)[1]

Informant practices are inherently secretive: snitches often need their
identities protected for safety, while the effectiveness of informant-
driven investigations turns on their clandestine nature. But the secretive
effects of using informants go far beyond protecting ongoing investigations or concealing particular informants' identities. Snitching has
altered the ways in which U.S. criminal investigations are conducted
and recorded; it affects public record keeping by police and prosecutors,
discovery practices, and what gets written down during plea negotiations. It has also shaped the informational rules prescribed by Supreme
Court doctrine, internal judicial branch information policies, and
even information-sharing between the U.S. Department of Justice and
Congress. In other words, the pressure to conceal informant practices
broadly affects the criminal system's culture of record keeping, adversarial information-sharing, public policy, and disclosure, making the
entire process less transparent and less accountable.

Sometimes informant practices make it harder for the public to access documents and processes that have traditionally been publicly
available. For example, a 2006 investigation by the Associated Press revealed the existence of widespread sealing and "secret dockets" in the
federal court system for Washington, D.C. Nearly five thousand criminal cases remained sealed long after the case was over, and for hundreds
of those cases, the system falsely indicated that there was "no such case"
if the case number was entered into the system. Most of the cases involved cooperating government witnesses.[2] In 2016, the Federal Judicial
Center conducted a survey of federal lawyers and judges on the extent

of threats to cooperators. In response to the survey, a committee of the U.S. Judicial Conference recommended additional widespread sealing, specifically the creation of a "sealed supplement" to every federal criminal case to shield all sentencing and cooperation information from the public.[3] Several federal judicial districts have already eliminated public website access to docket entries and to plea agreements in criminal cases. The purpose of the protocols is to make it impossible to discern without physically coming to the courthouse whether a defendant is cooperating. They also prevent the public from seeing whether court documents are sealed in the first place—considered a red flag that suggests cooperation.[4]

Informant use also naturally decreases transparency due to its informality. Highly regulated formal spaces tend to be better documented, informal spaces less so. Because informant law gives police and prosecutors so much informal discretion and leeway in the creation, management, and rewarding of informants, that informality inherently demands less documentation, public record keeping, and external accountability.

These are a few of the ways in which using informants curtails public access to information about how we adjudicate guilt and impose punishment. The loss is significant because we rely on such information to monitor whether the criminal system is effective and fair—in individual cases and also systemically. Taking such information off the public record thus bolsters law enforcement authority while reducing the ability of legislatures, courts, the press, and the public to evaluate executive actors and hold them accountable. This is a powerful and often troubling hallmark of informant culture and one of the dynamics that tends to go unremarked precisely because it takes place beneath the public radar. This chapter traces the depublicizing influence of informant use through several main areas of the criminal process—investigation, plea bargaining, and discovery—and its global impact on public access to information about the penal system.

I. Investigation

As a general matter, the process of investigating crime is one of the least regulated, least public aspects of the legal system.[5] Police decisions such as whether to investigate a crime or make an arrest are for the most part not subject to legal challenge or judicial review.[6] They are accordingly subject to few documentation requirements.[7] Police reports—which record police decisions and the information gathered during investigations—are notoriously partial and provide only a limited window of information, if they provide any information at all.[8] Sometimes police reporting is purposefully opaque: the police departments of Chicago and New York long maintained a system of "double files" in which publicly accessible police reports, including those given to prosecutors, contained only a partial version of the facts, while the department's internal "street files" contained fuller information.[9]

This tradition of undocumented investigative decision-making has been challenged in a variety of ways, including decades-long demands for civilian review boards.[10] For several decades, we have seen numerous attempts to require police to collect data on racial profiling practices.[11] The excitement and controversies around body camera technologies are in large part about the tantalizing possibility of greater transparency and accountability regarding day-to-day police decision-making.[12] The bitter struggles over these kinds of reforms reflect deep-seated traditions of discretionary policing, in which collecting public policing data has been a foreign and often difficult innovation.

The use of criminal informants is a paradigmatic example of this kind of discretionary, undocumented decision-making; it is also a powerful engine of its expansion. In practice, police can flip a suspect, obtain information, and maintain an ongoing relationship with an informant without ever publicly revealing the transactions. Police reports will often omit mention of informant sources, while search warrant applications typically do not reveal informant identities. If police so choose, the crimes committed by cooperating informants may never be recorded. Conversely, harms to cooperators may remain secret as well. Informant-based investigations thus slip easily beneath the radar of the criminal system's documentation processes.

The unregulated character of informant investigations is no accident. Starting with its decision in *Hoffa v. United States*, the Supreme Court has methodically exempted informant creation and deployment from the kinds of constitutional regulations that cover other investigative techniques, including Fourth Amendment rules on searches, seizures, and warrants, the Fifth Amendment requirement that suspects be given Miranda warnings and counsel, and Sixth Amendment right-to-counsel rules.[13] In turn, because police are less constrained when using informants, this naturally makes informant-based investigations easier, cheaper, and more inviting. If the police can persuade an informant to cooperate in order to obtain information about a target, that decision is hard for third parties to challenge, and if it turns up no evidence, it need never be revealed. Likewise, a wired informant can collect information whenever the police want her to, off the record. By contrast, if the police apply for a warrant or a wiretap, they must justify their requests to a court, their requests could be denied, and their justifications can be challenged later by defense counsel.

For example, instead of getting a warrant, Virginia police used convicted burglars as informants to break into a suspect's home to look for marijuana. According to one of the informants, Renaldo Turnbull, police assured them that they would be protected if they burglarized the suspect's home: "The [police] dude said he was going to look out for us, so let's go do it," he said. Turnbull also explained the general instructions that he received from his police handler: "He told me what to look for. He said, if you know of any burglaries or anything, let [him] know. He said no evidence, no pay. He said if you know where it is, go get it."[14]

When police do decide to seek a search warrant, the process becomes more regulated and requires more documentation. To get a warrant, an officer must submit a sworn affidavit containing information sufficient to find "probable cause," that is to say, enough evidence from which the judge could conclude that there is a fair probability of criminal activity or evidence. When a police officer proffers an informant tip in order to obtain a warrant, she needs to provide the judge with enough information about that informant and that tip so that the judge can independently determine whether the informant is sufficiently reliable and therefore whether probable cause exists. This process is designed to ensure that warrants issue in conformity with the Fourth Amendment, which states that "no warrant shall issue but upon probable cause supported by oath or affirmation."[15]

Even in this more regulated, documented arena, using informants erodes public transparency. In Pittsburgh, for example, a 2014 investigation identified what it called "an informant mill in which suspects became informants and helped agents to bust others, who then in turn became informants aimed at other targets." The study found that nearly

40 percent of federal prosecutions in southwestern Pennsylvania involved an affidavit based on an unnamed confidential informant, the vast majority of whom were seeking leniency for their own crimes. The majority of requests were filed by the FBI or the DEA, but they also included affidavits from the Postal Inspection Service, the ATF, Immigration and Customs Enforcement, the Food and Drug Administration, the U.S. Secret Service, the U.S. Marshals Service, the IRS, the Department of Agriculture, and Homeland Security. In all but a tiny number of cases, judges granted the request for a warrant or a wiretap without questioning the reliability or identity of the unnamed informant.[16]

In his exhaustive study of narcotics warrants issued in San Diego in 1998, law professor Lawrence Benner discovered that informant-based warrant applications involved more secrecy and demanded less rigor than warrant doctrine contemplates. For example, 64 percent of all warrant applications studied relied on a confidential informant, or "CI," and 95 percent of those warrant applications withheld the identity of the informant from the magistrate. Police justified doing so on the basis of the following generic boilerplate language contained in each warrant application:

> I desire to keep said informant anonymous because CI has requested me to do so, and because it is my experience that informants suffer physical, social and emotional retribution when their identities are revealed, because it is my experience that to reveal the identity of such informants seriously impairs their utility to law enforcement, and because it is my experience that revealing such informants' identities prevents other citizens from disclosing confidential information about criminal activities to law enforcement officers.[17]

As Benner points out, the use of such boilerplate language provides no factual or case-specific support for the proposition that the particular informant's identity needs to be withheld from the court, which violates both the rule and spirit of the warrant process:

> A public entity is granted a privilege to refuse to disclose the identity of an informant only if the public interest requires it because the "necessity for preserving the confidentiality of [the informant's identity] outweighs

the necessity for disclosure in the interests of justice." . . . The use of boilerplate . . . bypasses this entire process and indeed denies judges the very information they would be required to have in order to make a determination that the CI's identity should not be revealed.[18]

The same study also revealed the practice of using "phantom affidavits," in which the officer seeking the warrant does not know the confidential informant on whom she is relying for the information but rather swears under oath that another officer told her that the informant provided that other officer with the incriminating information. This practice means that the officer applying for the warrant does not know the identity of her source for probable cause and that, more generally, no officer ever has to swear under oath to the existence of the informant at all.[19]

Such practices do not necessarily mean that police are fabricating informants or that informants are lying. But they weaken established provisions for judicial oversight of search warrants and obscure from public view the means by which police obtain their evidence. Because informants can so easily be kept secret—even from the very police officer seeking the warrant—they become a cheap, unregulated means for police to obtain the weighty investigative and highly intrusive authority of a warrant.

Because investigative constraints tend not to apply to informant practices, this has fueled a culture of secrecy that goes beyond the lack of documentation. Using snitches has become a method of concealing investigative techniques and police decisions, a practice in which the usual disclosure rules do not apply, one in which cutting corners and breaking rules can easily be hidden. Recall from chapter 4 the St. Louis police officers who lied about their informants and then tried to enforce the culture of secrecy by refusing to disclose the identity of their informants to their own police supervisors. In a similar vein, the Brooklyn police officers who traded drugs for information from their snitches were responding to systemic incentives: to use illegal informant deals to get quick and easy drug busts. They could do so because their investigatory relationship with those snitches was discretionary, undocumented, and likely never to come to light. The same dynamic fueled the tragic death of Kathryn Johnston described at the beginning of this book, in which Atlanta police used an unreliable tip from a drug dealer to get a warrant, fabricated an informant for the warrant application, and then pressured another snitch to lie to cover up their misrepresentations. They could behave this way precisely because they knew that their use of informants—real and fabricated—would likely never be revealed, that they had tools at their disposal to prevent their misconduct from being exposed, and that if they did in fact produce drugs or a conviction the system would treat the ends as justifying the means.[20]

In sum, the discretion and secrecy associated with using criminal informants promotes a clandestine culture of secrecy that extends beyond individual cases. From constitutional rules that do not apply to police misconduct that will never be discovered, informant-based investigations ensure that much of the criminal process will remain under wraps, inaccessible to public or judicial scrutiny.

II. Plea Bargaining

Approximately 95 percent of all criminal convictions in the United States are the result of a guilty plea.[21] This means that trials and litigation are rare, while negotiated deals are overwhelmingly the norm. This fact has implications for the transparency of the criminal system. While trials and hearings are public, plea bargaining is private. Litigated facts become part of the public record, while negotiated facts remain off the record, known only to the bargaining parties. The trend toward plea bargaining has thus been accompanied by a trend toward the depublicization of the criminal system. Information gathered by the government—and the investigative methods used to get it—are increasingly difficult for the public to learn about. Public information about the kinds of crimes that are actually committed and by whom is likewise disappearing, replaced by information about the outcomes of deals struck between the government and defendants. As criminal liability is increasingly resolved privately through deals, the public loses sight of the way the system really works. As federal judge Stephanos Bibas once wrote, inside players such as prosecutors, defense attorneys, and judges have quite a bit of information about the way the system operates, but the public experiences the criminal process as "opaque, tangled, insulated, and impervious to outside scrutiny and change."[22]

The informant deal is an extreme version of the guilty plea, a kind of hyper-deregulated, extra-secretive bargain. An informant deal resembles a plea in that it resolves the informant's potential criminal liability, at least temporarily, in exchange for information. It is also like a plea bargain in that the resolution of liability is negotiated and takes place in private between the law enforcement official and the defendant or perhaps a defense attorney.

But informant deals are less regulated and more secretive than plea bargains for a number of reasons. Unlike a plea, the deal may never come to light at all. A typical informal agreement between a police officer and a street suspect—in which the suspect avoids arrest and the officer obtains information—may never be written down or revealed to anyone else. Whatever crimes the suspect committed may remain unknown to the public, to prosecutors, and even to other members of the police department.

Even if an informant is arrested, their potential liability may be handled in ways that evade regulation, documentation, or scrutiny. For example, in *United States v. White*, police officer Mike Weaver searched Shawn White's car and found a glass pipe containing what appeared to be methamphetamines. Weaver offered White a deal. Before reading White his Miranda rights,

> Weaver stated that he wanted to ask defendant some questions and see how cooperative he would be that night. . . . Weaver explained that if he sent the glass pipe to the crime lab and the lab found methamphetamine residue, he could charge defendant with a felony of possessing methamphetamine. Weaver said that the "deal" was that he could write the police report to reflect a charge of possessing drug paraphernalia, a misdemeanor, or possessing methamphetamine, a felony. Weaver advised that depending on defendant's level of cooperation, defendant could decide to "take the whole 100 yards, or deal with the small stuff." Weaver told defendant that he could help in a lot of ways, or he could "sit there like a lump on a log," which was not in his best interest. Weaver told defendant that if he did not cooperate, Weaver would simply list charge after charge and take defendant to the county jail.[23]

White cooperated and, as promised, Officer Weaver wrote the report to reflect only the possession of paraphernalia. The writing of the police report in effect constituted a plea bargain, in which White's actual criminal conduct was never fully recorded.

Prosecutors also alter criminal cases and charges to reflect a defendant's cooperation. A prosecutor may decline to indict on the understanding that the informant will start "working off" her charges. Charges may be dropped or reduced, and facts pertaining to charges and sentencing—for example, the amount of drugs at stake—may be negotiated between the parties so that the record will reflect the agreement. In other words, the court and the public will eventually see only what the parties decide to reveal.

Finally, and of great importance, the state can extract concessions in an informant deal that it could not otherwise get through a criminal sentence obtained via guilty plea. For example, informants can be required to have sex, expose themselves to illegal drug use, or even risk their lives as part of a cooperation deal—requirements that no court could legally impose as part of a formal sentence.

To be sure, informant deals vary immensely and take place along a spectrum of informality and secrecy. At the most formal and transparent end, a represented defendant will sit down with his attorney and negotiate a written agreement with the government, with relatively precise terms of cooperation in exchange for known benefits. Such deals are typical of white collar and political corruption cases.[24] The plea agreements entered into by Enron CFO Andrew Fastow and by William "Rick" Singer in the college admissions scandal are a matter of public record, as are the contours of each man's cooperation, making it possible for the public to figure out what crimes were forgiven and what benefits were exchanged.[25] By contrast, at the most secretive end of the spectrum, no one but the police officer and suspect may ever know what crimes were committed and what information was obtained. Because the bulk of informant use takes place in street-level and drug enforcement, where investigations and deals tend toward the informal, informant use as a whole tends toward the secretive.

In these ways, pervasive informant use exacerbates the trend toward the secret adjudication of crime and punishment. The greater the reliance on informant deals rather than traditional plea bargains and trials, the less the public learns about the crimes being committed and about how the criminal system resolves liability.

III. Discovery

Once a criminal case is filed, the defendant is entitled to certain kinds of information from the government. Discovery is the primary formal mechanism through which the government's evidence and investigative methods are revealed and therefore is important not only to individual defendants but also to the public interested in learning how the government does the work of criminal justice. While there are other mechanisms by which the public can sometimes obtain government records, e.g., the Freedom of Information Act,[26] defendants' ability to obtain government-generated information and place it on the public record is a crucial source of public access. Because the governmental use of informants tends to truncate defendants' access to discovery, it simultaneously restricts public access to that information as well.

As explained in chapter 2, the Supreme Court has held that impeachment material regarding the credibility of government witnesses must be disclosed to the defense.[27] Typical impeachment material includes any promises made to the informant, their criminal record, the benefits conferred on the informant by the government in exchange for information in the instant case, and the informant's history of testimony and rewards in other cases.[28] If the government wishes to withhold the identity of its informant at trial, it must justify nondisclosure against the defendant's weighty right to a fair trial and his constitutional right to confront the witnesses against him.[29]

In 2002, in *United States v. Ruiz*, the Supreme Court sharply reduced defendant entitlements to discovery regarding informants. Angela Ruiz was charged with possessing 30 kilograms of marijuana. Prosecutors offered her a so-called fast track plea bargain in which, in exchange for a recommendation of a downward departure under the U.S. Sentencing Guidelines, she would "'waive the right' to receive 'impeachment information relating to any informants or other witnesses.'"[30] Ruiz rejected the offer and eventually pled guilty without a deal. On appeal, she argued that she should not have been required to waive her rights to exculpatory impeachment material to which she was constitutionally entitled.

The Ninth Circuit Court of Appeals reversed Ruiz's conviction, deciding that the government could not constitutionally withhold that impeachment information and that therefore it could not pressure Ruiz to bargain away her right to it. It reasoned that defendants must be entitled to receive from the government the same exculpatory evidence before pleading guilty as they are before trial because "guilty pleas cannot be deemed intelligent and voluntary if entered without knowledge of material information withheld by the prosecution."[31]

The U.S. Supreme Court disagreed and reversed. It ruled that, although defendants are entitled to such information if they proceed to trial, "the Constitution does not require the Government to disclose material impeachment evidence prior to entering a plea agreement with a criminal defendant."[32] The Court worried in particular about restricting the government's use of informants, noting that disclosure "could 'disrupt ongoing investigations' and expose prospective witnesses to serious harm."[33]

Accordingly, after *Ruiz*, the government need not produce Giglio impeachment material before a guilty plea and must do so only if the defendant decides to proceed to trial. Because the majority of convictions are the result of a guilty plea, the effect of *Ruiz* is to declare a vast amount of information about informant use exempt from discovery. In practice, some prosecutors' offices provide this information to defendants anyway, even though constitutionally speaking they do not have to. Likewise, some jurisdictions have instituted local rules that require greater disclosure. But as *Ruiz* demonstrates, the government's preference will often be to withhold so as to strengthen its bargaining position. This means that a great deal of information about the government's use of criminal informants will never come to light, either for defendants or for the public.

Ironically, the very existence of discovery rules can drive police and prosecutors to act in more clandestine ways. As policing scholar Jerome Skolnick described in 1966, police truncate their written, discoverable reports to hide the existence of their informants:

> [P]olice will not say in an arrest report that they cajoled, or, in rare instances, threatened a suspect to get information. More importantly, they will not, if possible, reveal that an informant was utilized at all. Indeed, this concealment is a major task of police. [I]t almost never happens that

an informant is not used somewhere along the line in crimes involving "vice." . . . Nevertheless, of the five hundred and eight cases in the narcotics file of the Westville [California] police during [a two-year period], less than nine percent mentioned the use of an informant.[34]

More recent studies confirm that police often avoid revealing informant information in warrant applications or to prosecutors. Police may also decline to arrest informants in the first place in order to avoid a paper trail.[35] Prosecutors likewise avoid making overt promises to informants in order to escape Brady disclosure requirements.[36] In other words, both prior to discovery and during the discovery process itself, using informants tends to cloak the workings of the criminal process.

IV. Public Transparency and Executive Accountability

The culture of secrecy surrounding informant use is in tension with some fundamental aspects of American criminal justice. Our penal system promises transparency and public access to information in ways that are important not only to the adjudication of specific cases but to the democratic process itself. As Professor Gary Marx wrote in his seminal book *Undercover: Police Surveillance in America*, "[s]ecret police behavior and surveillance go to the heart of the kind of society we are or might become."[37] From the Sixth Amendment right to a public trial to the First Amendment rights of free speech and press, many aspects of our criminal system demand that cases and processes be made public so that voters, legislators, and the media can view the workings of the executive branch.

The Supreme Court explains this commitment to transparency as a form of governmental accountability. The idea that criminal processes, records, and results should be public, or what the Court has referred to as the "right to gather information,"[38] is part of a larger democratic commitment to public accountability and responsiveness. In discussing "the therapeutic value of open justice," the Court quoted the philosopher Jeremy Bentham:

> Without publicity, all other checks are insufficient: in comparison of publicity, all other checks are of small account. Recordation, appeal, whatever

other institutions might present themselves in the character of checks, would be found to operate rather as cloaks than checks; as cloaks in reality, as checks only in appearance.[39]

Information access is also connected to political and intellectual freedom. In establishing the public's right to observe criminal proceedings, the Court has said: "The First Amendment goes beyond protection of the press and the self-expression of individuals to prohibit government from limiting the stock of information from which members of the public may draw."[40]

Because transparency and public access to information are so important, they cannot be dispensed with lightly. If the government wants to keep information secret, it must justify that secrecy against a presumption of openness and the value of maintaining a public and open justice system. As the Supreme Court has written: "The presumption of openness may be overcome only by an overriding interest based on findings that closure is essential to preserve higher values and is narrowly tailored to serve that interest."[41]

For example, in a 1985 decision, then–Judge (now former Justice) Anthony Kennedy unsealed an informant's file because the government and the informant had failed to justify the need for secrecy.[42] In that case, informant William Hetrick had pled guilty to drug and tax evasion charges. The media sought access to Hetrick's request for a sentence reduction in connection with his testimony against celebrity automobile executive John DeLorean. At the request of both Hetrick and the government, the district court sealed the proceedings. The court of appeals ordered that they be unsealed. Kennedy explained as follows:

> We begin with the presumption that the public and the press have a right of access to criminal proceedings and documents filed therein. . . . The primary justifications for access to criminal proceedings [have been] first that criminal trials historically have been open to the press and to the public, and, second, that access to criminal trials plays a significant role in the functioning of the judicial process and the governmental system. . . . The interest which overrides the presumption of open procedures must be specified with particularity, and there must be findings that the closure remedy is narrowly confined to protect that interest. . . . The

penal structure is the least visible, least understood, least effective part of the justice system; and each such failure is consequent from the others. Public examination, study, and comment is essential if the corrections process is to improve.[43]

The meaning of such reasoning is that the need for informant secrecy should not be assumed; rather, it must be evaluated each time on the specific facts of each case. Even though "information relating to cooperating witnesses and criminal investigations should be kept confidential in some cases,"[44] the countervailing importance of public access must be accounted for every time. When in doubt, transparency is supposed to win. Blanket acceptance of informant anonymity, undocumented deals, or sealed case files contradicts this fundamental idea.

Another important feature of the Supreme Court's publicity jurisprudence is the critical role of the defendant in producing public information. Even as the Court recognizes the public's need to understand the way the system works, it assumes that the adversarial process produces enough information to satisfy that need.[45] As the Court puts it: "In an adversary system of criminal justice, the public interest in the administration of justice is protected by the participants in the litigation."[46] Essentially, the public gets to watch only those trials that the parties actually decide to conduct. By permitting public access to record information produced by actual cases, the Court's idea is that the public will obtain a sufficiently full and accurate picture of the way the criminal system works to satisfy underlying First Amendment free-speech and information-gathering values. In this sense, defendants function as vital proxies for the broader public interest in access to government information.

When it comes to informant use, however, this model breaks down because snitching practices undermine the Court's assumption that parties to criminal litigation will produce a robust public record. As plea bargaining and informant use curtail defendant access to information about law enforcement practices, so, too, is public information reduced. To put it another way: one of the reasons why the public lacks access to and understanding of the criminal process is that defendants who plead guilty—i.e., most defendants—lack tools to access governmental information about their own cases. Cases like *Ruiz* further handicap defendants' ability to obtain informant-related discovery, in conjunction with police and prosecutorial informant practices that evade documentation and review, rendering the entire criminal process less public.

The move toward informant secrecy affects not only public access to information but also other branches of government. When defendants lack access to informant-related data, courts lose the ability to review that information. The culture of nondisclosure affects legislative access as well. For example, in the 2004 congressional report titled "Everything Secret Degenerates: The FBI's Use of Murderers as Informants," the U.S. House of Representatives Committee on Government Reform documented its inquiry into the FBI's mishandling of its mafia informants throughout the 1970s and 1980s. During that investigation, the FBI and the U.S. Department of Justice used numerous mechanisms to withhold information from the committee, to cover up wrongdoing by government officials and their informants, and generally to stonewall the investigative process. "Throughout the committee's investigation," the report complained, "it encountered an institutional reluctance to accept oversight. Executive privilege was claimed over certain documents, redactions were used in such a way that it was difficult to understand the significance of information, and some categories of documents that should have been turned over to Congress were withheld."[47] The committee concluded that one of the central harms associated with FBI informant practices was the agency's resistance to public transparency and legislative oversight.

V. Informants in the Digital Age

Modern information technology and the internet raise new and dramatic challenges for the ancient practice of using informants. Courts are increasingly moving toward digitized dockets and public records made accessible over the internet. While such records were always technically available to the public, the ability to access them easily, remotely, and for free raises new issues about confidentiality and safety.[48] At the same time, the deployment of informants through social media makes possible an enormous set of new privacy invasions, even as those social media platforms have become sites for invidious new forms of witness intimidation.[49]

Back in 2004, the website Whosarat.com generated a national controversy over the tension between witness intimidation and the competing need for public transparency. In retrospect, Whosarat.com looks tame in comparison to today's social media environment: the site collected and posted some public court records and information about individuals who were allegedly cooperating with the government. Whosarat triggered so much anxiety at the time that the *New York Times* ran an editorial on the dilemma created by this "one odious website":

> We believe that transparency is essential to a fair judicial system and it would be a mistake to overreact to one odious Web site by pulling down plea agreements from the Internet wholesale. But Whosarat.com should serve notice that a different level of caution may be necessary in the wired age. In selective cases, where the life of the witness may be in jeopardy, courts should consider not putting the documents online.[50]

Today, anyone can post a "snitch list" on Facebook or Twitter, and the internet is awash with information about alleged cooperators. Sometimes the lists and documents are fake, sometimes the information is real.[51] With the easy sharing of case information on social media, it is increasingly difficult for the legal system to meaningfully control or protect its own records; this difficulty is in addition to the omnipresent risk that court and law enforcement data might be hacked.[52] Put differently, in much the same way that we individuals are losing our ability to maintain our privacy and protect our information against new surveillance technologies, so are courts.

These difficulties have not stopped the court system from trying. In November 2006, the U.S. Judicial Conference sent a memorandum to the entire federal bench, recommending "that judges consider sealing documents or hearing transcripts . . . in cases that involve sensitive information or in cases in which incorrect inferences may be made."[53] In its report on public access to electronic case files, the Judicial Conference recommended against making criminal court records electronically available to the public primarily because of the risk of exposing informants. Specifically, the conference reasoned as follows:

> Routine public remote electronic access to documents in criminal case files would allow defendants and others easy access to information

regarding the cooperation and other activities of defendants. Specifically, an individual could access documents filed in conjunction with a motion by the government for downward departure for substantial assistance and learn details of a defendant's involvement in the government's case. Such information could then be very easily used to intimidate, harass and possibly harm victims, defendants and their families.[54]

A decade later, a committee of the Judicial Conference again recommended greater use of sealing to shield all plea agreements and sentencing information from the public. Defense attorneys worried that universal sealing would perversely make every defendant look like a snitch: sealing "will multiply the number of inmates at risk exponentially without protecting anyone," said one chief federal public defender. The Reporters Committee for Freedom of the Press pointed out that "depriving the public of this information in all cases will prevent the public from ever knowing the reasons that a criminal defendant received the sentence he or she received. That is completely antithetical to the idea of a transparent criminal justice system."[55]

The challenge is bigger than any case-specific inquiry into whether it might be dangerous to reveal an informant's name or whether a particular investigation might be compromised by such revelations. Rather, the legal system is grappling with disruptive changes in technology and informational access in the face of our nation's historic commitment to the public adjudication of crime. In the name of witness protection, courts are moving toward wholesale policies of hiding cases, dockets, and practices, even in the face of increasing technological access. This trend stands in stark contrast with Justice Kennedy's classic constitutional analysis, in which he explained that the judicial presumption of openness must be outweighed by specific reasons for closure on a case-by-case basis. Today, the potential threat to some witnesses is seen by many courts as a reason to overcome the presumption of openness for all criminal records.

Taken together, in all of these many ways, the official practice of using informants undermines public transparency throughout the criminal system. By resolving liability in secret, it insulates investigative and prosecutorial techniques from judicial and legislative scrutiny. This reduced public access affects numerous other constituencies, making it more difficult for the press, crime victims, families, and policy analysts to obtain information about the workings of the justice system or about specific criminal cases. Informant use has thus become a powerful and destructive informational policy in its own right, reducing public transparency and obscuring the real impact of criminal practices on individuals, communities, and other institutions.

6

The Community Cost

In 1998, I taught a weekly after-school law class in West Baltimore. The class attracted a variety of kids ranging from middle-school to high-school age. Some were genuinely interested, some were hanging around the community center with nothing else to do, and some had parents, coaches, or probation officers who pressured them into attending. One afternoon, I was explaining several complex constitutional principles and clearly losing the students' attention. But a bright-eyed boy who looked to be about twelve years old raised his hand.

"I got a question," he said, leaning forward intently. "Police let dealers stay on the corner because they snitchin'. Is that legal? I mean, can the police do that?"

The question took me off guard—I was not used to hearing children explicate the working details of the criminal process. I had to think for a minute, then explained that the police did indeed have legal discretion to let drug dealers remain free. The boy's face sagged with disgust. "That ain't right," he huffed, and a number of other young people chimed in. "They ain't doing their jobs!" exclaimed one. "So all you gotta do is snitch," another concluded, "and you can keep on dealing."

The U.S. criminal system is internationally infamous for its disparate treatment of low-income communities of color and the people who live there. Mass incarceration and the war on drugs have made law enforcement a pervasive presence in these neighborhoods, especially for young African American men. Street stops and arrests are more prevalent in these spaces; police tactics are more intrusive and violent; and at every step of the way, the penal process treats Black men especially harshly.

The sheer scale of the phenomenon has become the subject of local protests and national politics. Although Black incarceration rates have been falling since 2001, they remain five times that of white incarceration rates. Younger people are especially affected: Black male teenagers ages eighteen to nineteen are over ten times as likely to be imprisoned as white males of the same ages. The chance of a Black man spending time in prison at some point in his life hovers around one-third.[1]

These damning statistics flow from numerous sources. The war on drugs has been a multidecade producer of racial inequality, although its footprint was worse twenty years ago. All racial groups use drugs at approximately the same rates, but Black people are incarcerated for drug offenses at nearly five times the rate of whites; in 2000 they were incarcerated *fifteen times* more often.[2] Of the 176,300 people imprisoned nationwide for a state drug offense in 2018, 45 percent were African American or Latinx, although the two groups represent only 30 percent of the U.S. population. Even after decriminalization and other recent reforms, racial disparities in drug arrest rates persist and in some places have been exacerbated.[3]

The racial skew of the criminal system also results from the overpolicing of communities and people of color. In numerous jurisdictions, police use their broad discretion to stop and arrest Black people at higher rates for low-level offenses such as trespassing, disorderly conduct, and jaywalking.[4] Civil rights litigation around the country has revealed that African American and Latinx men are disproportionately stopped, frisked, searched, and arrested pursuant to what are known as "broken windows" and "order maintenance" policing policies.[5] And as the Black Lives Matter movement and the police killings of George Floyd, Eric Garner, Michael Brown, and so many others have made painfully visible, police tactics used against Black people are more violent: Black Americans are three times more likely than white Americans to be killed during a police encounter.[6]

In the poorest communities of color, these statistics are embedded in a bleak socioeconomic context. Not only do such neighborhoods suffer from overpolicing; they also endure high rates of crime and victimization, with Black homicide victimization rates nearly seven times that of whites.[7] Poor neighborhoods simultaneously suffer from pervasive joblessness, substandard housing, and racially segregated schools of low quality.[8] The challenges of economic survival mean that gray-market or illegal work activities are inextricably intertwined with the legal economy and with everyday experiences.[9] High levels of criminal conduct and victimization thus take place within a larger framework of poverty and social insecurity.[10]

For these socially fragile, heavily policed communities, law enforcement policies have special significance. In many ways, criminal enforcement is the most palpable form of governance to make itself felt in these neighborhoods. Not only do criminal policies affect individuals and their families who are touched by crime; routine experiences with police, prosecutors, probation officers, and courts alter the ways that residents perceive the entire governmental apparatus. In communities where the penal system plays such a large role, law enforcement practices influence people's more general perceptions of the legitimacy, effectiveness, and fairness of the government, above and beyond its narrow crime-fighting function.[11] When those practices are persistently debilitating or exclusionary, they can, as legal scholar Monica Bell puts it, "operate to effectively banish whole communities from the body politic."[12]

As my Baltimore students made clear, informant use is one of these normatively influential practices. Drug enforcement has focused its resources in these neighborhoods, resulting in some of the heaviest concentrations of drug-related arrests and convictions in the country.[13] Central to this pervasive drug enforcement presence is the creation and maintenance of criminal informants. These already vulnerable communities thus experience the consequences of snitching to a higher and more extreme degree. This confluence has important implications.

First, there will be more criminal informants in these communities than elsewhere, in some neighborhoods many more. This is detrimental to families, personal relationships, and social networks. Second, pervasive snitching exacerbates certain kinds of crime and violence, worsening the very neighborhood conditions that law enforcement is ostensibly tasked with remedying. Third, using informants is a racial focusing mechanism, exacerbating overpolicing and imposing the costs of informant use disproportionately on communities of color. And fourth, the widespread use of criminal informants alters the role and authority of the legal system itself: it shapes police interactions with suspects, deforms police relationships with residents, and worsens the community's experiences and perceptions of being policed.

I. More Snitches

How many criminal informants might be active in low-income, heavily policed neighborhoods? This is a tough question because no one, not even the officials who use them, knows how many informants exist in the entire system. Even without direct data, however, we can extrapolate. In a nutshell, based on overall cooperation rates and the prevalence of drug enforcement in the most heavily policed communities of color, it is reasonable to infer that as many as 4 percent of the young Black male population in these particular communities might be actively cooperating with police at any given time.

The federal system provides the most information. The U.S. Sentencing Commission reports that, in 2019, approximately 10 percent of all federal defendants received a sentencing departure for cooperation and 22.6 percent of drug defendants did.[14] An early report by Sentencing Commission researchers estimates that less than half of all cooperating defendants receive a recorded sentencing benefit.[15] Conservatively, if only half of all cooperating defendants get sentencing credit, this would suggest that about 20 percent of all federal offenders and 45 percent of federal drug defendants cooperate in some way even if their sentences do not publicly reflect it. These cooperating defendants do not include the approximately 30,000 confidential informants—who also often commit crimes—who work for the FBI and the DEA.[16]

While illuminating, federal statistics are of limited value in assessing the national state of affairs. First, the federal criminal system is small, comprising less than 5 percent of U.S. felony cases. Furthermore, as described above, the federal sentencing guidelines and U.S. criminal code are expressly designed to promote cooperation through the mechanics of mandatory minimum sentences and constraints on judicial discretion. State criminal systems often treat these issues differently. Accordingly, while the federal picture of pervasive cooperation is relatively clear, it is only one piece of a larger puzzle.

At the state and local levels, we have far less direct information. Unlike the federal system, most states lack systemic record keeping to track defendants who benefit from having cooperated, either at sentencing or at earlier stages in a case. Nevertheless, while local law enforcement does not directly reveal how often it uses or rewards informants, we can still deduce the probable impact of informant use on heavily policed Black communities.

First of all, we know that drug arrests and prosecutions are concentrated in Black neighborhoods and populations: African Americans account for approximately 13 percent of the national population but 32 percent of national drug arrests and approximately 30 percent of drug convictions.[17] In particular, Black people are nearly four times more likely to be arrested for marijuana possession, which represents over 40 percent of all drug arrests.[18] Criminal informants are staple features of such investigations and cases. All by itself, therefore, the scale of drug enforcement against the Black population indicates that the scale of criminal informant use will be similarly and disproportionately large.

We also know that drug enforcement is not evenly distributed. In certain states and counties, Black arrest rates are especially high, even though drug use is evenly distributed throughout the population. For example, in Pickens County, Georgia, about an hour north of Atlanta, Black people are almost *a hundred times* more likely to be arrested for marijuana possession compared to white people.[19]

Criminal system involvement is also heavily concentrated in certain cities and neighborhoods, placing a staggering proportion of young African American men under criminal supervision at any given time. For example, in Maryland, approximately 30 percent of the young African American men in the entire state are under the control of the criminal system on any given day, which is to say, in prison or jail or on probation or parole; approximately 10 percent are actually behind bars. In Baltimore, the numbers are even higher: over half of the young Black men between the ages of twenty and thirty are under criminal justice control, and nearly one in five are in custody on any given day.[20] Similarly, in one neighborhood in Milwaukee, an estimated 42 percent of Black males between the ages of twenty-five and thirty-four were either incarcerated or under criminal justice supervision in 2013. In North Nashville, Tennessee, in 2012, the incarceration rate alone—not including supervision—for Black men of that age was 28 percent.[21]

Cities and neighborhoods with high levels of criminal-system involvement are deeply intertwined with state carceral institutions. Fourteen percent of all people released from Maryland prisons in 2001, nearly 40 percent of whom were convicted of drug offenses, returned to a mere six Baltimore neighborhoods.[22] Similarly, in 2003, half of all released prisoners in Illinois returned to Chicago, and 34 percent of those returned to just six neighborhoods.[23] In all these ways, criminal-system involvement is often highly localized in specific neighborhoods in ways that national statistics and averages obscure.

Finally, we can ask the question that brought us here: How much of this highly localized involvement in the criminal system implicates snitching in communities of color? One way of approximating an answer is to ask how much of this criminal involvement involves drug offenses, substance use, or other crimes that law enforcement typically handles by creating or using informants. The answer is probably about one-third. Approximately 30 percent of all state felony caseloads are drug offenses, and approximately 30 percent of state felony drug prisoners are African American.[24] Of the 10 million arrests made in 2019, 1.5 million were drug arrests, and 26 percent of those drug arrests were of Black people. Conversely, 15 percent of all arrests of Black people are for drug offenses.[25]

Drug enforcement is not the only high-snitch arena. Burglary, for example, is an arena in which police traditionally rely on informants, representing a little over 8 percent of all state felony convictions.[26]

Widespread substance use among the criminally involved population also plays a crucial role. Many people commit crimes such as burglary, theft, and other property offenses in order to support an addiction. For example, from 2007–2009, 40 percent of all jailed defendants in the United States reported that they committed their offenses while under the influence of drugs, and 40 percent of people jailed for a property offense reported committing the offense in order to get money for drugs.[27] More broadly, approximately 60 percent of people in prisons and jails meet medically established criteria for drug dependence or abuse.[28] A large percentage of property crimes and other offenses are thus "drug-related," in the sense that the defendant commits the crime because of a substance use disorder. Because such defendants have knowledge of and connections to the drug economy, they are prime candidates to become informants. The pervasiveness of substance use in the criminal justice population—and the law enforcement predilection for turning such individuals into snitches—therefore suggests that pressure to inform is being brought to bear in a wide range of cases.

Taken together, we can infer that at least one-third of the entire U.S. criminal justice population is facing drug or drug-related charges and/or has a substance use disorder and therefore is likely to experience strong pressure to cooperate. More than one-third of African Americans in the criminal system will likely fall into this category because they make up a higher proportion of drug cases. The system naturally puts pressure on this segment of the population to become informants by virtue of the nature of their offenses, their substance use problems, and the increasingly heavy sentences that drug and recidivist defendants face.

But pressure is one thing, and snitching is quite another. How many suspects actually bend to the pressure and provide information? Again, we need to extrapolate. Federal statistics suggest a general cooperation rate of 20 percent, and 45 percent for drug offenses, but that will not hold true for all state or local jurisdictions. The pressure to cooperate is probably higher for federal drug crimes than it is in jurisdictions that lack high minimum sentences, mandatory sentencing guidelines, or that generally sentence at a lower threshold, although some states imitate the federal cooperation incentive structure.[29] On the other hand, the federal system deals less with the kinds of petty drug offenses that are ripe for snitching, and the kinds of informal street deals described throughout this book are more likely to occur between local substance users and beat cops than with the FBI.

For the sake of argument, let us assume that state and local drug suspects snitch at half the rate of federal drug defendants. In other words, assume that 22 percent of this high-risk group actually cooperates with law enforcement, providing information about accomplices, acquaintances, friends, neighbors, or family.

The implications of this estimate are potentially dramatic. In those localized highly policed neighborhoods in which as many as half of the Black men between the ages of twenty and thirty are under criminal supervision, one-third of *those* fall into the high-risk, drug-related snitching group. If as many as 22 percent of *those* individuals are actually informants, that would mean that, in some of these neighborhoods, one in twenty-five Black men in this age group—or about 4 percent—could actually be giving the government information at any given time.

In 2009, using these same types of data, I estimated the scale of informant use to be higher, closer to 6 percent of the young Black male population in heavily policed neighborhoods. Since then, drug enforcement has receded as a percentage of national criminal dockets and Black drug incarceration rates have fallen, so it stands to reason that informant use would also decline. Remember these are all extrapolations—we have no more direct data on the phenomenon today than we did in 2009. But 4 percent would still be a lot. It would implicate many extended families, apartment complexes, neighborhood events, and congregations. It would make it likely that someone—maybe more than one someone—within that institution or social network would have already given information to the police or might actively be trying to find incriminating information about others and would have the police's ear when they do.

To be sure, this estimate may still be too high. In some districts, police and prosecutors indicate that they do not routinely rely on criminal informants, even in drug cases. Alternatively, this estimate may still be too low. Many observers of the criminal system, from judges to sociologists, conclude that drug cases almost always involve snitches, that street-level criminal suspects routinely cooperate with the police, and that informing is pervasive.

In sum, we simply do not know directly or with any certainty how many people are actually working criminal informants or how many young African American men are under pressure to inform. Given the persistent lack of data, we cannot know. And the most serious manifestation of the phenomenon will be limited to those neighborhoods with the highest concentrations of crime, police presence, and social vulnerability. But we do know that the structure of the penal system, with its continuous deep penetration into poor Black communities, together with the habits of law enforcement, make it likely that in our most economically distressed neighborhoods a significant proportion of the young Black male population is under heavy governmental pressure to provide information about others in order to avoid arrest and incarceration.

Answering the empirical question of how many snitches there are does not, of course, answer the normative question: What's wrong with a lot of snitching? After all, residents of vulnerable communities have a deep interest in crime control, not least because high crime rates can mean high victimization rates. Such communities need police with the tools to prevent and solve crimes. Using criminal informants can be one way for police to get such information.

Numbers alone also cannot explain what is problematic about living around snitches. It is sometimes said that only the guilty should fear informants because only the guilty have something to hide. If the practice successfully disrupts criminal activity, law-abiding citizens should benefit.

There is some truth in both these propositions. High-crime communities need better crime control, better relations between police and residents, and more safety and security. The tricky question is whether those goals are promoted by creating and deploying criminal informants in the ways that we currently do. And although the criminal process resists disclosure on this subject, the limited evidence indicates that snitching practices may be counterproductive in precisely this regard. Not only do informants exacerbate crime, violence, and other destructive phenomena; even for the innocent, the pervasive presence of criminals trying to work off their charges can create fear, distrust, and social dysfunction. These problems are explored below.

II. More Crime

Criminal informants commit crimes. This is true both by definition and in practice. First, by definition, an informant provides information in order to escape the consequences of having already committed, or at least being suspected of committing, a crime. That means that every snitch deal inherently involves a governmental decision not to pursue and punish those crimes. Active criminal informants also typically commit new crimes or help others do so while they are cooperating with the government. Those new crimes impact the communities in which they take place.

For example, in Mount Vernon, New York, officers protected and supported drug dealers who served as their informants. According to secret tapes made by a police whistleblower, "the department's narcotics unit allowed favored drug dealers to sell with impunity, get deliveries, and control territory. In exchange, . . . the dealers, serving as confidential informants, gave [police] information leading to the arrests of their own low-level clients."[30] Similarly, as part of its investigation into a fencing ring in Portland, Oregon, the FBI promoted the ongoing theft of retail merchandise from local stores in order to collect evidence against illegal secondhand sellers. The shoplifting ringleaders—Lorie Brewster and David Pankratz—were given immunity from prosecution and permitted to keep hundreds of thousands of dollars in proceeds from the goods they stole.[31]

Above and beyond such authorized crimes, informants also routinely commit unauthorized crimes. As the stories throughout this book demonstrate, once a criminal actor agrees to provide information to the government, he or she may continue to commit new offenses on their own initiative to which police and prosecutors may turn a blind eye. The fact that law enforcement tolerates some unchecked criminality by its informants constitutes one of the practice's major dangers and poses a special threat to communities in which this conduct takes place. For example, the Seattle ATF used Joshua Allan Jackson as an informant even though he had a long history of violence against women. His prison records revealed him to be a mentally unstable person who had been arrested in forty-three states. In 2012, he held an eighteen-year-old woman as a sexual prisoner in a motel room paid for by the ATF.[32] In Pittsburgh, Robert Harper robbed a grocery store worker with an AK-47 after local police and prosecutors released him from jail in exchange for his grand jury testimony about jailhouse drug dealing. At the time, Harper was incarcerated and awaiting sentencing for six prior armed robberies. While on release, he committed an additional sixteen armed robberies and shot two people.[33]

Informants who expect to be forgiven for their crimes can pose special threats to friends and families. In Tampa, Florida, police permitted their informant to use his government-issued cell phone to "scheme[] to steal property and beat up his friends. While his police handlers listened in and looked the other way, he threatened to beat the mother of his child so badly 'that her brain will seep from her ears.'"[34] One of the dealer-informants in Mount Vernon had a string of domestic violence convictions for choking and assault, even as police let him evade arrest for his drug business. A former prosecutor flagged the risks of using informants involved in domestic violence. "It's natural to feel that you're emboldened by this because you have the backing of the police and they're going to help you if you get stuck in a situation," he said. "It's potentially very dangerous for everyone in that household or in that relationship."[35]

In his classic study of police practices in a typical midsized American city, Professor Jerome Skolnick concluded that, as a general matter, "burglary detectives permit informants to commit narcotics offenses, while narcotics detectives allow informants to steal."[36] More generally, sociological studies find that police assume and know that their informants commit unauthorized crimes. One study described a St. Louis street snitch who "stayed out of sight for several days after giving information to the police," since snitching had permitted him to escape his "third weapons charge [and] he reasoned [that his] quick appearance almost certainly would indicate that he had snitched in exchange for his freedom."[37]

Finally, every time police reward a person with a substance use disorder with cash for drugs (or sometimes actual drugs), they enable that informant's continued illegal drug use and dependence. As one officer acknowledged:

> Payment to addict-informants puts the officer in something of a moral quandary. We can be reasonably certain that monies given to an addicted person are going to be used to support that addiction. Because the addiction can only be maintained by violating the law, this places the officer in the position of tolerating or at least knowing of ongoing criminal activity—something we are paid to stop.[38]

Of course not all informants commit new crimes, authorized or unauthorized. Some simply provide information about past crimes and hope for reduced punishment for what they've already done. But active informants populate a gray world of continuing criminal activity, in which some crime is openly encouraged by the government, some crime is tolerated or ignored, and some is never discovered. These new crimes typically occur in the communities in which informants live, forcing friends, families, residents, and businesses to contend with higher incidents of drug use and drug dealing, violence, weapons, thefts, and the myriad other offenses that informants commit while working for the government.

III. More Violence

In 1996, the criminologist Dr. Jerome Miller explained how using informants exacerbates violence in urban communities. Not only do snitches commit crimes themselves, but they erode social mechanisms for keeping the peace by creating distrust and inviting retaliation. As Dr. Miller put it:

> No single tactic of law enforcement has contributed more to violence in the inner city than the practice of seeding the streets with informers and offering deals to "snitches." . . . [R]elying on informers threatens and eventually cripples much more than criminal enterprise. It erodes whatever social bonds exist in families, in the community, or on the streets—loyalties which, in past years, kept violence within bounds.[39]

Ten years later, sociologists confirmed this observation. Richard Rosenfeld, Bruce Jacobs, and Richard Wright wrote that police snitching tactics "contribute to the violence in already dangerous communities." Their street-level studies of police and informant behavior revealed that, because criminals cannot trust each other, "dependence on firearms is likely to rise; without accomplices, guns become the backup." More generally, "[t]he practice undermines trust and breaks apart communities. It erodes faith in official authorities. It foments retaliation, which ignites the street-level microstructure in potentially deadly conflict spirals." They concluded that "snitching is a pervasive element of inner-city street life that poses dangers for street criminals and law-abiding residents alike."[40]

  Gangs and other criminal organizations famously use violence to deter snitching. Researchers in organizational science have long recognized that deploying informants in any organization can be expected to lead to violence, as the organization responds by trying to police itself more firmly.[41] Government studies found that the spike in witness intimidation in the mid-1990s was directly linked to increased gang activity and was most prevalent in connection with violent crime.[42] Even more specifically, studies of violence in the drug trade identify the "elimination of informers" as a structural source of ongoing violence.[43]

  The death of sixteen-year-old Martha Puebla exemplifies the violent side effects of snitching policies. In an effort to obtain a confession, Los

Angeles police lied to a gang member and told him that Puebla was informing on him. This misrepresentation led not to a confession but to Puebla's murder.[44] Likewise, when police in Brea, California, turned seventeen-year-old Chad MacDonald into an informant, it led not only to MacDonald's death but also to the rape and shooting of his sixteen-year-old girlfriend by gang members against whom MacDonald was informing.[45] This book contains numerous stories in which the government's decision to use informants has meant tolerating violence against others—from the death of Kathryn Johnston in Atlanta to Karen Parker's childhood of sexual abuse at the hands of con man Paul Skalnik. In other words, when government officials turn to criminal informants as a law enforcement tool, they should expect to provoke more violence in the communities most affected by those tactics. Because fear and violence constitute some of the most devastating aspects of impoverished urban life, this particular effect of snitching policies is one of the most costly.

IV. Racial Focusing and Inequality

Another underappreciated collateral consequence of informant use is that it focuses law enforcement attention on the communities in which informants live. Snitches tend to snitch on the people with whom they live and interact. When police rely on informants to direct new investigations, police resources will naturally be channeled back into the communities from which the informants come.

This phenomenon has special significance for heavily policed urban communities to which drug enforcement resources are already disproportionately devoted. It suggests that the use of informants is part of the reason why communities of color are overrepresented in drug enforcement efforts. For example, the San Diego Search Warrant Project concluded that search warrants were issued disproportionately against Black and Latinx residences in neighborhoods that were predominantly of color. Although Black and Latinx people represent less than one-third of the San Diego population, over 80 percent of all warrants—and 98 percent of all warrants seeking cocaine—targeted Black and Latinx households. The majority of those warrants turned up no evidence, while two-thirds of warrants directed at white homes produced contraband.

One reason for the disparity is that 80 percent of warrants were based on confidential informants. Because informants tend to give information about individuals in their own racial groups, the study hypothesized that disproportionate arrests of African American and Latinx people would lead to disproportionate—and inaccurate—targeting of Black and Latinx homes.[46]

The racial focusing phenomenon also means that communities of color and their residents are overexposed to the unreliability, crime, and violence associated with informants. False accusations, mistaken warrants, erroneous raids, and wrongful convictions associated with snitches will be more frequent in communities in which the practice is prevalent.[47] The official toleration of crime and violence committed by informants means that the communities in which they live pay the price. All of these costs—crime, violence, loss of privacy—are themselves contributors to social disadvantage, making it more difficult for people to thrive personally, socially, and economically. The use of informants can thus be understood as one of the concrete mechanisms through which the criminal system contributes to racial and communal inequality.

V. More Tension between Police and Community

Distrust of the police is a long-standing legacy in poor communities of color. The history of policing in African American neighborhoods remains famously fraught with official violence and racism as well as the tolerance of victimization and Black-on-Black crime.[48] Policies like stop-and-frisk and order maintenance arrests disproportionately impact people of color. Racial profiling remains a nationwide problem.[49] The police murder of George Floyd in Minneapolis in 2020 was part of a long history of police killings of unarmed Black people. Indeed, many of the largest and most famous protests in urban American history have been triggered by police brutality against Black men.[50]

Distrust of police is also socioeconomic and personal, flowing from local economic and policing policies. As sociologist Robert Sampson puts it, "inner city contexts of racial segregation and concentrated disadvantage, where inability to influence the structures of power that constrain lives is greatest, also breed cynicism and perceptions of legal injustice."[51] Or as Professor Bell explains:

Sociologists studying poverty and community life have long provided evidence that even when people rely on each other to survive poverty and social marginality, those relationships are generally not sanguine, trusting relationships. Those relationships are often unstable and destabilizing. The resultant distrust extends to police, to other institutions, to neighbors, family members, and intimates. It is born of concentrated disadvantage, which co-occurs with racial segregation and marginality.[52]

The problem of police distrust has been recognized at the highest levels of governance. In 1999, U.S. Attorney General Janet Reno acknowledged that "the perception of too many Americans is that police officers cannot be trusted. . . . Especially in minority communities residents believe the police have used excessive force, that law enforcement is too aggressive, that law enforcement is biased, disrespectful and unfair."[53] In the aftermath of the 2014 police killing of Michael Brown, U.S. Attorney General Eric Holder shared his own experiences with police:

> I understand that mistrust. I am the Attorney General of the United States. But I am also a black man. I can remember being stopped on the New Jersey turnpike on two occasions and accused of speeding. Pulled over. . . . "Let me search your car." . . . Go through the trunk of my car, look under the seats and all this kind of stuff. I remember how humiliating that was and how angry I was and the impact it had on me.[54]

Personal experiences with racial profiling, violence, and victimization exert a strong influence on African American relationships with police. After Milwaukee police brutally beat Frank Jude, and pictures of his battered face appeared in the newspaper, 911 calls plummeted 17 percent. The study's authors concluded that "many members of the black community stopped calling 911, their trust in the justice system in tatters."[55]

The heavy deployment of criminal informants is one more ingredient in this already volatile matrix. Snitching represents a visible, official disregard of criminal legal rules that generates more crime and additional violence, and alters many dynamics between police and community residents. As such, it can function as an invitation to residents to rethink their relationships to police. For example, in 2005, NBA basketball star Carmelo Anthony was a forward for the

Denver Nuggets. That year, Anthony appeared briefly in a homemade "Stop Snitching" video filmed in his hometown of Baltimore. Although 'Melo said nothing untoward, other people in the video talked openly about the culture of drug dealing and suggested that snitches might come to harm. Lambasted by the press for his appearance in the video, Anthony gave an interview to *ESPN The Magazine* in which he described his own conflicted relationship to the police growing up in Baltimore. Police, for example, beat him up. "Nothing major," he said. "They'd just choke me, drag me around." As a result, Anthony was leery of cooperating. "I would never snitch," he said to ESPN. "I would never testify on anything. That's just the street code. If you snitch, you're talking about someone's life."[56] Anthony grew up in Baltimore in the 1980s and 1990s. A decade later, my young Baltimore students concluded in a similar spirit that police who let snitching drug dealers stay on the corners were not doing their jobs.

Urban America has been living with drug informants for the duration of the war on drugs—since the 1980s. That represents decades of living around criminal defendants who remain active, or receive reduced sentences in exchange for turning in others, and decades of the kinds of unreliability and violence that we now know to be associated with informant use. For residents of those communities, it has also meant decades of watching friends and family members, girlfriends and boyfriends, people with substance use disorders, and other vulnerable acquaintances succumb to police pressure to provide information under threat of increasingly severe sentences. Such experiences erode trust in the law enforcement function. As criminologist and policing expert David Kennedy mourned, "[t]his is the reward we have reaped for [thirty-plus] years of profligate drug enforcement in these communities."[57]

Snitching is thus part of the larger challenge of police legitimacy in the age of racialized mass incarceration and pervasive surveillance. That challenge has generated an enormous literature.[58] One especially influential approach to the problem has been psychological. Psychologist Tom Tyler is a leading theorist of why people do or do not cooperate with police.[59] He concludes that, although people help the police fight crime in part because they think it is in their self-interest to do so, a much more powerful motivation is that they consider the police to be legitimate, deserving of deference and cooperation. This legitimacy depends heavily on the procedures that police use. Together with Professor Jeffrey Fagan, Tyler writes:

> For the police to be successful . . . they must have active public coop-eration. . . . Cooperation increases not only when the public views the police as effective in controlling crime and maintaining social order, but also when citizens see the police as legitimate authorities who are entitled to be obeyed. Such legitimacy judgments, in turn, are shaped by public views about procedural justice—the fairness of the processes the police use when dealing with members of the public.[60]

By "procedural justice," Tyler and other scholars mean all the ways in which police handle people and decisions, regardless of the outcome. "It includes judgments about the quality of decision-making, which includes neutrality: making decisions based on facts, and applying rules consistently. It also involves judgments about the quality of interper-sonal treatment: respect, politeness, consideration of one's views."[61] In this scheme, mistrust fuels a vicious cycle because the legitimacy and efficacy of law enforcement practices depend heavily on public percep-tion. When people perceive law enforcement as racially biased, unfair, or unprincipled, they are less likely to cede legitimacy and authority to the police.[62]

The use of criminal informants is a powerful example of procedural justice failure. By its very nature, informant use is based on shaky facts and the inconsistent and nonneutral application of rules. Procedural justice theory helps explain how informant practices can undermine public perception of police legitimacy, thereby discouraging trust and cooperation.

A final contributor to the distrust problem flows from the more gen-eral fear that the police cannot or will not protect residents from crime in general and from witness intimidation in particular.[63] Urban America is famously underprotected, with understaffed police departments, slow 911 responses, and high official tolerance for offenses like car theft and assault. African Americans often suffer from higher crime victimization rates than other populations.[64]

In those "hardest-hit neighborhoods, people describe how fear, and the conviction that serious crimes are not solved, make them reluctant to confront homicide, unwilling to cooperate with authorities or act as witnesses, and disinclined to place their faith in the police."[65] "We know no one will protect us," explains one Los Angeles resident. "We have to protect ourselves."[66] Potential victims—disproportionately Black and Latino young men—see police as "unreliable and hostile" and conclude that they will not be protected, leading to an escalation of the cycle of violence. Scholars conclude that residents of cities like Los Angeles, Chicago, New York, and Baltimore often experience "police injustices and indifference, persistent and unresolved cases of violence, and residents' cynicism and withdrawal." In these communities, "citizens fear retribution if they cooperate with police, and police are unable to provide protection."[67] Local residents' unwillingness to talk to police is thus directly connected to their perception that police are insufficiently responsive.[68]

This public reluctance, in turn, makes it harder for police to do their jobs. Police describe their alienation from residents, their own fear of going into high-crime areas,[69] and their conviction that "the people here hate us."[70] As residents lose confidence in police, police lose confidence in their ability to solve crime.

The widespread use of informants contributes to this vicious cycle, distorting the public's relationship to police in numerous ways. It erodes the appearance of fairness because it represents the open toleration of crime by the very people charged with enforcing it. Residents who see police tolerating drug dealing, or failing to arrest other kinds of offenders, or releasing dangerous arrestees, are likely to lose faith in the enforcement process. Victims of crime also learn that their victimization will be tolerated. When people have personal connections to individuals who commit crimes with impunity, or to crime victims who go unrecognized, their sense of law enforcement commitment and efficacy is bound to suffer.

Criminal informants also make the legal process more secret and unpredictable, governed by personal relationships between police and criminals rather than by public rules.[71] Crime and punishment can be negotiated off the record, under the table, subject only to the vagaries of the informant marketplace. For communities in which the criminal system is often the most visible manifestation of the government itself, this kind of governance is a persistent reminder that power, not law, is the name of the game.

Finally, snitching teaches a destructive lesson in civics: that the law is for sale. Criminals who escape punishment by informing have in effect bought their freedom. The government's willingness to trade away liability even for violent and destructive crimes sends the public message that the law can be broken under the right circumstances and that people can get away with murder if they know how to play the game. When police tolerate new criminality from their informants, the message is even worse. It says that the government prizes its informers over the safety and well-being of the communities in which they operate.

Taken together, informant practices in heavily policed communities of color represent a deep hypocrisy. It is the residents of these communities who suffer the most from mass incarceration and criminal law's inflexible harshness: intrusive policing, long sentences, and the many devastating collateral consequences of convictions including disenfranchisement, unemployment, and worsened poverty. The very same people who are punished most harshly for breaking the law are simultaneously told by snitching that the law is negotiable, contingent, a matter of power and luck, and sometimes not enforced at all. Put differently, the normative and public safety principles that have been used for decades to justify intrusive policing and harsh punishment are routinely waived or ignored with respect to the people, crimes, and cases that populate the massive informant marketplace. Apparently this hypocrisy is so obvious on the ground that twelve-year-old children have figured it out.

VI. More Social Instability

The final sort of toll exacted by informant policies is social and psychological in nature. What is it like to live in a community in which as many as one in twenty-five young men might be criminal informants? What is it like to know that people around you may be committing crimes and working with the police at the same time? Recall that these are already heavily policed, economically unstable, socially vulnerable neighborhoods in which many families are dependent on governmental services, many individuals are already on probation or parole, and social networks are already fragile.

In Mobile, Alabama, Pastor Elaine Alford worried about the human destruction. "What bothers me the most," she said, "is that the law puts these young men in a position to snitch on each other. And they'll make them say things, put such fear in them and make them say things, you know, cause them to snitch on people that have been friends and family. That's, I guess, the most profound thing . . . that family members are telling lies on family members in order to save themselves."[72]

Pervasive informing can distort the most intimate of relationships. When Paulyn Miller was arrested on forgery charges, she volunteered to police that she had information implicating her son in a murder case. She agreed to wear a wire and testify against him, in exchange for which she received a sentence of probation.[73] By contrast, Lula May Smith served seven years in federal prison because she refused to testify against her son Darren. The prosecutor on her case admitted that Smith was prosecuted only to get to her son, that he "kept hoping [and] pray[ing]" that she would be acquitted, and that even at the time of her trial he believed that she should not have gone to jail.[74]

The caustic effects of such arrangements are not limited to individuals or even families. Interpersonal trust is a crucial ingredient for community survival, and studies show that poor urban neighborhoods are particularly dependent on social trust networks. Because such communities typically lack strong economic and public institutions, people rely on family and informal networks for jobs, income, shelter, child care, and other vital resources.[75] Social networks also play a vital role in preventing crime in the first place. According to Professor Sampson, crime and disorder directly correlate with a neighborhood's ability to maintain cohesive social networks. Strong networks facilitate order; weak ties permit disorder.[76]

Poorer neighborhoods are especially vulnerable to criminal informants because social networks are more disorganized and people's lives and spaces are less private. As numerous scholars have noted, "conditions of structural poverty strain a community's ability to develop informal social controls."[77] This strain has implications for law enforcement practices. Professor Michael Tonry writes:

> For a variety of reasons, it is easier to make arrests in socially disorganized neighborhoods. . . . [Specifically,] it is easier for undercover narcotics officers to penetrate networks of friends and acquaintances in poor urban minority neighborhoods than in more stable and closely knit working-class and middle-class neighborhoods.[78]

This means that personal relationships in poor, high-crime communities are more fragile and vulnerable, making intrusive law enforcement tactics such as snitching simultaneously more potent and more devastating.

VII. Snitching as Counterproductive Social Policy

The potential implications of informant use for socially disadvantaged, heavily policed communities are formidable: more snitches, more crime, more violence, more police-community dysfunction, and less social cohesion. Taken together, they tell us that informant use is not merely a law enforcement tactic but an important and often counterproductive social policy in its own right, affecting families, social networks, and public perceptions of the legal system itself.

To be sure, the most dramatic impact of snitching will be limited to a small number of neighborhoods. For most U.S. communities and institutions, snitching is not a quality-of-life issue. There are not enough informants to impact the everyday experiences of residents, and those informants who do exist remain largely invisible. Not so for our poorest neighborhoods of color already grappling with high rates of criminal system involvement and victimization. In these concentrated areas, there are likely to be many informants, enough so that residents live with the knowledge of their presence and the threats of informant-related crime and violence. Although these communities may be limited in number, they constitute the most troubling subjects of the penal system, both because they are home to so many people enmeshed in the criminal process and because they pay the highest price when our justice policies go awry. An official practice that threatens them with special harms thus deserves our closest scrutiny.

The special circumstances of extreme neighborhood poverty also alter the cost-benefit analysis of informant use. First and foremost, the harms of the policy are greater in these economically unstable neighborhoods.[79] But second, the benefits may also be smaller due to the flexible nature of the drug economy and the fungibility of individual players. Analysts from across the political spectrum have concluded that decades of harsh law enforcement tactics have been largely ineffective against the illegal drug economy: the United States maintains record rates of drug use, and illegal drugs remain cheap and easily accessible.[80] This means that using informants as part of an overall drug enforcement strategy does not produce the kinds of long-term benefits that it may in other arenas. For example, the FBI's use of mafia informants over the years helped to capture influential high-level bosses and to destabilize the organizational strength of the mob.[81] By contrast, when police use criminal snitches to bust a midlevel drug dealer or shut down a drug house, new dealers and houses spring up to take their places.[82] This means that even as the harms associated with informants persist, any benefits of their deployment may quickly dissipate. The tragedy is that, in the poorest neighborhoods most in need of better law enforcement, pervasive criminal snitching could be making things worse.

7

How the Other Half Lives

In 2007, David Slaine was a hedge fund manager and a multimillionaire Wall Street success story. Then the FBI approached him with a deal: become an informant to avoid prosecution for his own illegal stock trades worth millions of dollars. For the next two years, Slaine provided the FBI with dozens of tips and incriminating evidence about other traders, including taped conversations that he made wearing a secret recording device. In 2011, he testified in a case that was part of the high-profile investigation of hedge fund tycoon Raj Rajaratnam, who eventually pled guilty to insider trading. Slaine's information helped produce at least ten additional convictions.

Slaine himself pled guilty to securities fraud, admitting that he made more than twenty trades in his own account based on illegal tips, personally profiting by more than $500,000 and producing total illegal gains between $2.5 million and $7 million. At his sentencing, federal prosecutors called Slaine's cooperation "nothing short of extraordinary." The judge called him "a good person" who had committed a "serious crime" and sentenced him to probation, community service, and a large fine. Slaine was never arrested or incarcerated. Not everyone thought this was the right result. "Insider trading snitch got off too lightly," proclaimed one Reuters headline. Pointing out that Slaine faced up to twenty-five years of incarceration for his own crimes, commentators worried that "his deal is exactly the kind that can lead to problems. . . . [E]ven for the best information, letting confessed felons like him essentially off the hook is too high a price to pay."[1]

While informants are common in street- and drug-crime enforcement, the government deploys informants in many other types of investigations as well, most prominently against corporate fraud, organized crime, political corruption, and terrorism. With the notable exception of terrorism, the use of informants in these non–drug crime, non–street crime arenas is characterized by greater regulation and oversight, better protections for suspects, greater involvement of defense counsel, and more public transparency and accountability. While these realms experience their share of corruption and crises, debacles can trigger substantial public attention and efforts at reform.

These strengths flow from a panoply of facts: suspects tend to be wealthier, whiter, and better educated, with more personal resources and better access to counsel, while target institutions such as corporations or political associations have legitimate functions in society that law enforcement may be loath to undermine by more aggressive tactics.[2] The resulting cultures of investigation and prosecution are thus more sensitive to the possibility of harm, litigation, and public exposure. Or as the sociologist Gary Marx wrote bluntly in 1988, "When lower-status drug dealers and users or prostitutes were the main targets [of covert operations,] the tactic tended to be ignored, but when congressmen and business executives who can afford the best legal counsel became targets, congressional inquiries and editorials urging caution appeared."[3] All these factors add up to significantly differing informant practices, creating a kind of rich man's version of the informant experience.

At the same time, snitching is still snitching. So-called white collar crime, organized crime, and other types of informant use share many of the fundamental characteristics and dangers of their street and drug counterparts: loosely negotiated deals trading lenience for information in which culpable offenders are let off the hook; relaxed criminal procedure rules and a weakened role for defense counsel; increased secrecy and lessened public accountability; and, perhaps most important, the vast discretionary power that accrues to the government when suspects agree to cooperate. In other words, the rich man's version of snitching still looks a lot like the poor man's version.

In this chapter, I survey the most prominent arenas of non–drug related informant use: organized crime, business crime, politics, and terrorism. Numerically speaking, such cases represent a relatively small share of criminal investigations: only about 10 percent of federal cases involve fraud, organized crime, or terrorism.[4] Nevertheless, these categories exert outsized influence due to the power and prominence of the people and institutions involved and the serious nature of the criminal activities at stake. While each arena is in many ways unique, taken together they complete the picture of the varied and influential role of informant use throughout the American criminal system. Their relative strengths further suggest that the heightened transparency, better regulation, and the central role of counsel in these arenas could profitably be imported into the less regulated world of street and drug snitching to ameliorate some of its most dangerous and inequitable features.

I. FBI Informants and Organized Crime

Without informants, we're nothing.
—Clarence Kelley, FBI Director (1973–1978)[5]

The FBI is the primary general law enforcement agency for the U.S. government. In its 2008 budgetary request, the agency stated that it maintains over fifteen thousand "confidential human sources."[6] The hallmark of a typical FBI confidential human source (CHS) or confidential informant (CI) is a person identified and cultivated by a particular FBI "handler." Approximately 20 percent of CHSs are "long-term," meaning that they have been working for the FBI for five years or more. Some informants are members of organizations, either criminal or legitimate; the job is to provide the FBI with ongoing information about that entity and its other members. Some informants take the opportunity to exit a criminal organization by becoming a witness against it. Informants are rewarded in various standard ways, including with money, lenience for past crimes, and the ability to continue committing criminal offenses.[7]

The FBI uses informants in all sorts of cases, including gang investigations, financial crimes, and espionage. But many of its highest-profile informant successes have come in connection with its multidecade efforts to break up La Cosa Nostra, the Italian mafia. Mafia assassin Aladena Fratianno, a.k.a. "Jimmy the Weasel," became an informant and spent the 1980s in witness protection: he helped convict numerous mafia members.[8] And in 2018, eighty-four-year-old Francis P. Salemme was convicted of the 1993 murder of a federal witness. Salemme, better known as "Cadillac Frank" and the fearsome former head of the New England La Cosa Nostra family, had himself been in witness protection for years until the remains of the dead witness were discovered. Multiple mob informants testified against him, including Stephen "The Rifleman" Flemmi himself, who by this time was serving a life sentence for ten murders. The Salemme prosecution was described as a last vestige of the mafia's once-formidable power. As one lawyer put it, "everybody's been burned to a crisp here by informants."[9]

Other informant-driven successes disclosed by the FBI include: a three-year grand jury investigation of organized crime that led to six convictions; the investigation of three violent gangs in a city in the Northeast that led to thirty-five cases involving fifty-four gang members; and a two-year undercover operation that led to the indictment of four Houston City Council members.[10]

But the FBI's use of high-ranking criminal informants has generated both costs and critics over the years. For example, Salvatore "Sammy the Bull" Gravano was one of the FBI's most infamous, productive, and problematic informants. A mafia hit man who confessed to nineteen murders, his 1992 testimony helped the FBI obtain nearly forty convictions, most notably that of John Gotti. The government then relocated Gravano to Arizona in the witness protection program. There he rejoined organized crime and, in 2001, pled guilty to running a multimillion-dollar ecstasy drug ring. In 2003, he was charged with ordering the killing of Detective Peter Calabro, but charges were dismissed when the government's sole witness died.[11]

In 2004, Congress issued a scathing report titled "Everything Secret Degenerates: The FBI Use of Murderers as Informants."[12] The report documented not only numerous FBI informants who had committed multiple murders and other serious crimes but also the cover-ups, perjury, and other malfeasance committed by FBI and other law enforcement officials in connection with their informant relationships. In response to such scandals, the U.S. Department of Justice (DOJ) strengthened its informant guidelines to impose new restrictions on the FBI aimed at creating more accountability and preventing the FBI from authorizing and tolerating unchecked informant crime.[13] Those guidelines were revised and strengthened again in 2006 under the new title "The Attorney General's Guidelines Regarding the Use of FBI Confidential Human Sources"—they are still in effect today.[14]

The DOJ guidelines are one of the primary mechanisms through which the federal government regulates its own informant use. One of the challenges is that the FBI does not always follow them. In 2005, the DOJ's Office of the Inspector General (OIG) issued a report concluding that the FBI did not fully comply with the strengthened guidelines, finding full compliance in only 13 percent of cases examined.[15] In 2019, another OIG audit concluded that the FBI was out of compliance with the guidelines with regard to the validation of informants and monitoring long-term informants and that the process generally lacked resources, training, and oversight.[16]

Although the 2002 and 2006 guideline revisions were specifically a response to the mafia informant debacles of the 1980s, old practices apparently persisted. In 2011, documents filed in another Boston case indicated that mafia leader Mark Rossetti, indicted on state drug trafficking, gambling, and loan sharking charges, had been working for years as a federal FBI informant. Boston congressman Stephen Lynch wrote to Attorney General Eric Holder calling the Rossetti allegations "disturbing" and calling for further congressional investigation.[17]

These persistent problems remind us that internal guidelines alone cannot cure the dangers of informant use, and there is always a risk of noncompliance. Nevertheless, the DOJ efforts represent a strong model for internal law enforcement regulation. The FBI guidelines create documentation, authorization, and ongoing evaluation requirements for agents who want to create or use a confidential informant. They require any agent who wants to create a CI to submit a comprehensive "validation report" to her field manager and, if approved, to register that CI in a file containing, among other things, documentation of any promises or benefits offered to the CI. The CI must be formally informed of the terms of the cooperation, including the fact that the CI must be truthful and that the CI may not engage in any additional criminal activities other than those officially authorized by the agency. Certain types of high-level informants require additional written approvals from the FBI's Human Source Review Committee. The agency must conduct annual suitability reviews. The guidelines also limit investigative officials in other ways: for example, agents lack authority to confer immunity from prosecution on any informant—only a prosecutor can do that. Agents also may not socialize with informants or exchange gifts.[18] These kinds of important accountability tools are often lacking in other investigative agencies at the state and local levels.

Another challenge of informant use arises when law enforcement agents and prosecutors do not share information about their informants with other agencies; as a result, the left hand does not know what the right hand is doing. Starting in 1982, for example, Jackie Presser, president of the International Brotherhood of Teamsters labor union, was under investigation by federal prosecutors for stealing union money through the creation of nonexistent "phantom" employees, or so-called no-shows. It turned out that Presser had been an FBI informant for ten years and that the FBI had authorized him to hire the no-shows. Charges against Presser were dropped, and Presser's FBI handler was indicted for lying to protect Presser.[19] In 2012, Congress investigated the failed ATF effort known as "Operation Fast and Furious," through which the ATF permitted hundreds of illegal assault weapons to be smuggled out of the United States to Mexican drug cartel members. Two of the target cartel members turned out to be FBI informants, unbeknownst to the ATF agents running the operation against them. As Congressman Darryl Issa and Senator Charles Grassley complained to Attorney General Holder, this debacle represented "a serious lack of information-sharing among the major law enforcement agency components of the Department of Justice."[20]

These examples illustrate a few of the now-familiar dangers in using informants to infiltrate criminal or corrupt organizations. Such dangers include the ongoing criminal activity of the informants themselves, the close ties developed between agents and informants, and the lack of information-sharing within the government. All too often, the extent of the informants' criminal activities is known only to a few.

At the same time, these violent, corrupt informants often provided extremely valuable and accurate information. Unlike the informal encounters that so often characterize street snitching, FBI informants typically have ongoing relationships with their handlers, and the handlers themselves often know a great deal about their informants' misdeeds. The revised DOJ guidelines are premised on this model: they are designed to preserve valuable information sources while strengthening the accountability and oversight of handlers and informants alike in the face of substantial and well-known risks.

Another way to improve accountability is through the checks and balances of the political process. As we saw in chapter 2, other branches have historically taken a deferential, hands-off approach regarding executive branch informant decisions. As currently written, DOJ guidelines require only that informant-related information be shared within the executive branch: the FBI reports its informants' crimes, if it does so at all, only to DOJ prosecutors. As more informant murders and other law enforcement debacles have come to light, however, some legislators have concluded that the executive branch needs to share information more broadly.

In July 2007, the U.S. House Judiciary Committee held a congressional hearing on law enforcement use of confidential informants. The hearing addressed numerous concerns, one of them being the FBI's continued mishandling of its CIs. Congressmen Daniel Lungren and William Delahunt separately lambasted FBI assistant director Wayne Murphy for the agency's failure to control its informants, in particular the agency's failure to inform state and local law enforcement when FBI informants commit additional crimes. Representative Lungren, formerly California's attorney general, was particularly concerned about the impact on state law enforcement.

> LUNGREN: [I]s there a policy in the FBI to share information with local and state law enforcement officials when you have become aware, that is, the FBI, that your confidential informants have engaged in serious violent felony activity, not all criminal activity, serious violent felony activity in the jurisdiction of the local or the state authorities[?]
>
> MURPHY: It is my understanding, Congressman, that there is not a specific documented policy, directly to answer your question, sir. . . . Our process and approach is to take onboard criticism and observations about how we conduct our procedures and to consider whether or not we have appropriate measures in place to ensure and preserve the integrity of our process.
>
> LUNGREN: Yes, all I can say is if I were still a law enforcement officer in the state of California and you were to tell me that the FBI was reserving judgment as to whether you could tell me that you have C.I.s in my jurisdiction that are committing serious violent felonies, I would be more than offended.[21]

Representatives Lungren and Delahunt introduced a bill that would have required the FBI to report to state law enforcement serious violent felonies committed by its informants and would have imposed criminal penalties on agents who failed to do so.[22] In a radio interview, Representative Delahunt stated his concerns: "What is totally unacceptable is having violent criminals out on the street, preying on American citizens everywhere, while there is information that isn't being disclosed to local and state law enforcement authorities that have the primary responsibility in this country to protect us from violent crime." The FBI's general counsel at the time, Valerie Caproni, responded that the bill would severely hamper the FBI's ability to deploy informants: "I don't think if [this bill] was passed we could get agents to run informants," she argued.[23] The bill failed.

In 2011, in the throes of the Rossetti scandal, Representative Stephen Lynch introduced the Confidential Informant Accountability Act (CIAA), which would require all federal investigative agencies to report the serious crimes committed by their informants to Congress. Unlike the Lungren/Delahunt bill, the CIAA has no penalty provision for agents who do not comply. As Representative Lynch wrote to Attorney General Holder, the bill aims to increase interbranch accountability, as current DOJ guidelines "significantly limit the ability of Congress to fulfill its proper oversight role and examine the extent and specific types of crimes committed by FBI confidential informants."[24] Lynch has reintroduced the CIAA several times.[25]

This brief overview of FBI informant use in select high-level federal investigations presents a picture that differs in important respects from typical street-crime and drug informant practices. This is an arena characterized by documentation, regulations, and internal oversight of individual agent decision-making, albeit imperfect. It is a smaller, more focused arena, with higher-level crimes and sophisticated investigations. It is also characterized by a different kind of informant, often with resources and leverage that make them formidable players in their own right.

The problems that plague this law enforcement world are also different. Wrongful convictions still occur, crime is still tolerated, and informant–handler relationships still sometimes lead to corruption. But it is harder for such miscarriages of justice to slip beneath the radar. And when they do surface, the high-profile nature of the cases and players has generated serious public and legislative attention.

II. White Collar Crime and Cooperation

So-called white collar or business crime has always been treated differently from street crime. Encompassing such offenses as fraud, embezzlement, money laundering, tax evasion, and other nonviolent economic offenses, the white collar category has its own culture and poses its own challenges. For one thing, the federal government is central to white collar enforcement. Although federal cases make up less than one-tenth of the entire American criminal system and, numerically speaking, there are more state fraud prosecutions than federal ones, federal law enforcement dominates this arena, especially with respect to large companies and high-profile cases.[26] Federal prosecutions tend to be complex and resource-intensive and often have national ramifications, setting the tone in the business community for future practices.

White collar criminal enforcement also takes place against a backdrop of extensive civil regulation and large administrative agencies that have their own enforcement mechanisms. Most wrongful business conduct may be treated either civilly or criminally. As law professor Darryl Brown points out: "Parallel statutory regimes providing civil and criminal sanctions for essentially the same conduct exist in virtually every area of white-collar wrongdoing, including health care fraud, environmental harms, workplace safety, and securities law."[27] Business organizations thus typically spend more time negotiating compliance with civil regulatory agencies than they do confronting criminal prosecutors. As a result, business activities take place in a highly regulated atmosphere that is already heavily layered with expectations about civil compliance and cooperation and in which civil liability is often routinely substituted for criminal sanctions.

The long-standing and persistent criticism of white collar criminal enforcement is that it is too lenient, that white collar offenses are not vigorously pursued, and that offenders receive punishments that are too light. In 2002, *Forbes* magazine ran a cover story titled "White Collar Criminals: They Lie, They Cheat, They Steal, and They've Been Getting Away With It for Too Long: Enough Is Enough."[28] The story revealed that, from 1992 to 2001, enforcement attorneys from the Securities and Exchange Commission referred 609 cases to the Justice Department for potential criminal charges. Of that number, only 187 cases were actually prosecuted, 142 individuals were found guilty, and 87 went to jail. Even the highest-profile wrongdoers served relatively low sentences. In 1986, Michael Milken was sentenced to ten years for an illegal insider trading scheme worth upward of $100 million. He was released after serving just two years because he agreed to cooperate.[29] Charles Keating was convicted of fraud and racketeering for destroying the savings of 23,000 bank customers and fueling the $150 billion savings and loan crisis in the 1980s: he served four and a half years, approximately the same sentence he would have received for selling two tablespoons of crack cocaine.[30]

There was an uptick in corporate prosecutions during the so-called post–Enron era in response to the high-profile collapse of firms like Enron and WorldCom. The DOJ created the Corporate Fraud Task Force, while Congress and the U.S. Sentencing Commission increased penalties for white collar crimes.[31] The new wave of high-profile prosecutions included the massive accounting firms KPMG and Arthur Andersen, while a few executives received record-setting sentences—Enron's Jeffrey Skilling received twenty-four years, and WorldCom's Bernard Ebbers received twenty-five.[32] But that enforcement culture has ebbed and flowed. Most prominently, the 2008 collapse of the financial sector generated almost no individual prosecutions, and DOJ has been widely excoriated for treating powerful corporations and their CEOs as "too big to jail." As federal Judge Jed Rakoff complained, the "'too big to jail' excuse . . . is disturbing, frankly, in what it says about the [DOJ's] apparent disregard for equality under the law."[33]

Critics have long argued that the differential treatment between white collar and street crime reflects social biases; because white collar defendants tend to be whiter, wealthier, better educated, and socially connected to other elites, they receive better treatment and more sympathy from the criminal system's decision makers than do poorer, politically powerless defendants who are also more likely to be people of color.[34] Recall the federal judge's conclusion that inside trader David Slaine was still "a good person." Even though business crime can impose substantial social harms, stripping innocent victims of their wealth and costing the nation literally billions of dollars, white collar offenders are often deemed less culpable than street crime offenders, even though the latter collectively steal less money and harm a fewer number of people.[35] Or as Rhode Island justice Stephen J. Fortunato wrote more dramatically: "The gentle and genteel treatment by prosecutors (with occasional notable exceptions) of corporate thieves, swindlers, polluters, tax evaders, and hustlers is proof positive that there are two separate and distinct criminal justice systems operating in this country."[36] To be sure, white collar defendants themselves may still experience race and wealth discrimination: one study found that, among federal white collar offenders, Black and Latinx defendants are incarcerated more often and for longer than their white counterparts.[37] But as compared to street and drug crime, the culture of white collar prosecution has tended to be more lenient and restrained.[38]

Cooperating informants are an important part of white collar investigations and prosecutions. Because many financial or paper crimes are hard to detect, the industry is what the FBI calls "undercover resistant": it often requires cooperation on the part of a knowledgeable insider to bring crimes to light. Conversely, the threat of cooperation can serve as an informal check on wrongdoing. After the prosecution of Rajaratnam and dozens of other Wall Street traders, the FBI asserted that its investigations had "sent a chill" through the hedge fund industry and that the agency "ha[d] enough informants lined up to keep its investigations of suspected illegal insider trading at hedge funds going for at least five more years."[39]

White collar cooperation takes two main forms. One is the now-familiar individual cooperator who, in exchange for lenience for his or her own crimes, provides information about others' wrongdoings. In addition, the white collar arena has produced a distinct phenomenon: cooperation by the corporation itself. When a corporate entity becomes a "snitch," it raises unique issues for law enforcement and for the entity's individual employees. Both forms of white collar cooperation (individual and corporate) are discussed below.

A. Individual White Collar Cooperators

The typical white collar informant is a participant in a larger scheme to steal or defraud. For example, the government's financial fraud cases against Enron's chief officers Kenneth Lay and Jeffrey Skilling were built on the testimony of numerous informants, including accountants and managers in addition to CFO Andrew Fastow. Many of these witnesses were also guilty but received reduced sentences in exchange for their cooperation.[40]

When the government suspects a white collar offender, a number of things may happen that distinguish this arena from street and drug crime enforcement. First, the government may approach the suspect or their attorney, or send them a "target letter" revealing that they are under investigation, prior to any arrest or charges being filed. If the suspect does not already have counsel, this gives them the opportunity to get it.[41] Some companies actually provide counsel for employees facing employment-related criminal charges. The fact that white collar defendants have better and earlier access to counsel than do street or drug crime suspects radically improves defendant options in this arena.

Over three decades ago in his landmark book on white collar defense, Kenneth Mann described the pre-indictment process as the most important service a defense attorney can provide her client. Counsel's ability to control information early on means that a defendant can shape the direction of a case and even potentially avoid indictment altogether.[42] Cooperation makes this pre-indictment process a time of even greater opportunity and potential negotiation for represented defendants.

White collar offenders depend heavily on their attorneys during the cooperation process. A good defense attorney can evaluate the strength of the government's case, advise her client about the likelihood of success, and ensure that her client receives the greatest benefit from his cooperation. If the government eventually charges the defendant with a crime, the attorney remains the defendant's most important guarantee that the government will keep its promises and that the defendant will get maximum credit for his cooperation.[43]

Professor Daniel Richman points out that law enforcement's ability to obtain cooperation depends in part on its reputation for keeping its promises. If the government breaks its promise, the defense attorney may be the only witness who can publicize the breach. Richman tells the story of one attorney who took out a public advertisement in a national legal publication, castigating the U.S. Attorney's Office for having broken its promises to his cooperating client. The attorney wrote:

During the sentence proceedings I stated that I was going to tell every defense lawyer in our nation not to enter any plea agreement with your office. Your office cannot be trusted. Your office cares nothing about promises and agreements. I am surprised that the eagle in the Great Seal of the United States didn't fly from the wall in horror.

. . .

Like some sleazy insurance company who refuses to pay the widow because it wants the premiums but doesn't want to honor its obligations, your office will go to any length to renege on its solemn promises.[44]

By way of contrast, when police break their promises to a street-corner snitch, no one is likely to find out. In such ways, the pervasive presence of white collar defense counsel significantly levels the playing field between suspects and the government.

Once a white collar defendant decides to become an informant, cooperation and benefits can take a number of forms. Typically the cooperation will involve proffer sessions with the government in which the defendant, with their attorney, will provide information about the scheme and others' wrongdoings. They may also be required to testify before a grand jury or at the trial of others. In addition to providing information about past wrongdoings, they may help investigate ongoing crimes by wearing a wire or otherwise engaging in proactive investigation. For example, while investigating Richard Scrushy, former CEO of HealthSouth, investigators wired a financial officer's necktie to covertly record conversations.[45]

Benefits may include avoiding indictment for some or all crimes that the informant has committed. The informant may also get immunity for crimes that they admit to but the government did not already know about and/or crimes that the government subsequently discovers as a result of the cooperation. Finally, if they plead guilty, they typically receive sentence reductions.[46]

White collar cooperation agreements tend to be complex, formal, and written. They may involve careful descriptions of the kinds of immunity that a defendant is or is not entitled to, the kinds of work he or she is expected to do, and recommendations that the government may make at sentencing. Because these agreements are executed over time, sometimes long stretches of time, they must provide for the waiver or elimination of some bedrock rules of criminal procedure such as double jeopardy, speedy trial rights, self-incrimination rights, and others. As Professor Graham Hughes wrote in 1992, "deals involving promises to cooperate are sharply different from the general phenomenon of plea bargaining. They are exotic plants that can survive only in an environment from which some of the familiar features of the criminal procedure landscape have been expunged."[47]

Another important aspect of white collar cooperation, which is true for drug and other conspiracies as well, is that the earlier a defendant cooperates, the better the deal. This "first in the door" phenomenon reflects a number of considerations. The government wants people to cooperate and therefore tends to reward those who do it early, saving the government time and effort. Early cooperators also influence the way the case itself develops, identifying new defendants, becoming witnesses, and shaping the government's investigative and litigation strategies.[48] Accordingly, having good legal advice and an attorney who knows how to navigate the system can make a big difference for cooperators at this stage.[49]

In sum, individual white collar informants look something like street crime informants—but with significant differences. Both provide information about wrongdoing, and both receive lenience for their crimes. But white collar informants tend to be passive rather than proactive, revealing wrongdoing rather than continuing to engage in criminal activities themselves. They tend to have counsel from a very early stage with the concomitant ability to get better deals. They also tend to have more formal agreements with the government with respect to their obligations and expected rewards. Finally, the public is more likely to learn about them when the investigation becomes public, when they testify, or when they are sentenced. In other words, because white collar defendants are better able to defend themselves and the cooperation process is better regulated, white collar cooperation is less likely to succumb to some big dangers of the snitch deal—unreliability, ongoing criminality, total secrecy, and the victimization of innocent bystanders as well as vulnerable informants.

B. Corporate Cooperation

When a business entity engages in illegal conduct, the entity itself may be prosecuted. This practice was thrust into the spotlight during the 2002 prosecution of accounting firm Arthur Andersen for its obstruction of justice during the SEC investigation of Enron. Although the conviction was overturned on appeal by the U.S. Supreme Court,[50] the company had already gone out of business, sending a wave of anxiety through the business community.

Federal prosecutions are governed by the "Filip Memo" (2008) and the "Yates Memo" (2015), named for the deputy AGs at DOJ who issued them. The Filip Memo outlines the considerations and procedures that prosecutors must follow when developing a case against a business organization.[51] Specifically, in deciding whether to indict a company, prosecutors must consider a list of nine factors that include "the corporation's timely and voluntary disclosure of wrongdoing and its willingness to cooperate in the investigation of its agents" and "the corporation's remedial actions, including any efforts to . . . cooperate with the relevant government agencies." The Filip Memo expressly permits cooperating corporations to avoid prosecution altogether: "[T]he corporation's timely and voluntary disclosure of wrongdoing and its cooperation with the government's investigation may be relevant factors" in deciding whether to file charges.[52] The Yates Memo, by contrast, emphasizes the importance of prosecuting individuals as well as corporate entities and to "strengthen [the] pursuit of individual corporate wrongdoing." In pursuit of that goal, the Yates Memo conditions corporate cooperation on the institutional disclosure of individual wrongdoing: "[I]n order to qualify for any cooperation credit, corporations must provide to the Department all relevant facts relating to the individuals responsible for the misconduct."[53]

Different divisions within DOJ may also have their own individualized cooperation policies. For example, "the Antitrust division has established a firm policy . . . that amnesty is available only to the first corporation to make full disclosure to the government."[54]

Corporate prosecutions and cooperation are heavily shaped by the U.S. Sentencing Guidelines, which provide that a cooperating corporate entity, like an individual, may receive a reduced sentence, which is to say, a smaller fine. Every corporate defendant entity receives a "culpability score," which can be favorably reduced through its cooperation. For example, the guidelines provide for a lower culpability score if "the organization had in place at the time of the offense an effective compliance and ethics program" and if the corporation's cooperation regarding its own wrongdoing was both "timely" and "thorough."[55] Like individual defendants, corporations can seek additional departures from the guidelines by providing substantial assistance in the investigation or prosecution of another organization.[56]

Two controversial features of corporate cooperation bear further elaboration. The first is the increasingly common decision to refrain from prosecuting cooperating corporations altogether. The second is the situation in which a corporation cooperates by investigating and turning in its own employees.

1. NONPROSECUTION AND DEFERRED PROSECUTION AGREEMENTS

Cooperation has become the central means by which a corporate defendant can avoid prosecution and, as with the demise of accounting giant Arthur Andersen, the threat of economic death. Because a criminal conviction can ruin a business, companies will go to great lengths to avoid it. For a company under criminal investigation, cooperation can earn a nonprosecution agreement (NPA) or a deferred prosecution agreement (DPA), under which the corporation is not prosecuted at all. Hundreds of companies including Chipotle, Google, Johnson & Johnson, Pfizer, Ralph Lauren, United Airlines, Walmart, and dozens of banks have all avoided prosecution by entering into NPAs and DPAs. In 2020, the Department of Justice entered into thirty-nine DPAs and eleven NPAs.[57]

NPAs and DPAs are agreements between the government and the business organization in which the organization agrees to engage in remedial, cooperative measures in exchange for which the government promises not to file charges or to drop charges already filed. The comparable arrangement for individual defendants is referred to as "pretrial diversion," which at the federal level is typically available only to a limited category of minor or first-time offenders.[58] By contrast, corporate NPAs and DPAs are routinely used to resolve high-level frauds and widespread corporate malfeasance.

The benefits of the practice are significant: an offending company can stay in business, preserving jobs and economic stability in the market, while the government can force the company to change its practices. The practice is also controversial on many fronts: some argue that it gives the government too much power over businesses, while others maintain that it lets too many criminal corporations off the hook.[59]

An NPA or DPA may require a corporation to do any number of things, including cooperate with the ongoing investigation, pay fines or penalties or make restitution, hire a monitor, and admit and accept responsibility for wrongdoing. Businesses are typically willing to go to great lengths in order to comply and avoid prosecution. Or as *Forbes* magazine once described it: in response to "the mere threat of indictment, [companies are] handing over internal documents, waiving the privilege that normally shields attorney-client communications and ratting out individual employees as targets for prosecution."[60]

Because NPAs and DPAs require admissions, it is difficult if not impossible for a corporation to change its mind and subsequently defend against the allegations. This gives the government a great deal of power over the course and details of corporate cooperation. As one court put it in the KPMG case: "Anything the government regards as a failure to cooperate . . . almost certainly will result in the criminal conviction that KPMG has labored so mightily to avoid, as the admissions that KPMG now has made would foreclose a successful defense."[61] In other words, once a corporation decides to cooperate, it effectively hands the government a great deal of authority over its operations, even operations that may not bear directly on the alleged wrongdoing.

Law professor Lisa Griffin, a former federal prosecutor, has concluded that the government's reliance on DPAs suffers from a variety of flaws. She contends, for example, that prosecutors use DPAs to meddle in corporate governance far beyond the needs of the criminal investigation, engaging in forms of "corporate-wide behavior modification" that may not represent good business practices. She also notes the lack of judicial review of such agreements, under which the government obtains effective control over these entities with little external check or scrutiny.[62]

Over the past decade or so, the government has responded to at least two criticisms of its white collar cooperation policies. The Yates Memo (2015) was an effort to reduce the impression that corporate cooperation had become a way of letting individuals corporate actors off the hook. The memo emphasizes the importance of individual prosecutions as part of corporate cooperation deals, although law professor Brandon Garrett observes that, even after the Yates Memo, individual prosecutions do not appear to have meaningfully increased.[63]

Second, prior to the issuance of the Filip Memo in 2008, DPAs routinely pressured cooperating companies to waive attorney-client privileges and work-product protections in order to provide the government with full access to company records. In a conventional prosecution, an individual or corporation cannot be forced to reveal to the government confidential communications with counsel. But corporate cooperation agreements routinely required "voluntary waivers" of such privileges. In practice, this meant that corporate counsel might share confidential information with the prosecution about company practices and documents or even conversations with individual employees.[64] It also led to a number of high-profile prosecutions of corporate actors including Sanjay Kumar, CEO of Computer Associates, who lied to their own corporate counsel during internal investigations.[65]

The elite public outcry over these "compelled voluntary waivers" led the government to change its policies. Numerous critics, including members of Congress and one appellate court, found it unethical and contrary to established adversarial procedures for the government to deprive corporations of their attorney-client and work-product privileges as the price of cooperation. The Filip Memo disavowed these features of corporate cooperation deals. In revising the cooperation guidelines, Filip based his decision expressly on the fact that

> a wide range of commentators and members of the American legal community and criminal justice system have asserted that the Department's [previous] policies have been used . . . to coerce business entities into waiving attorney-client privilege and work-product protection. . . . [T]he contention from a broad array of voices is that the Department's position . . . has promoted an environment in which those protections are being unfairly eroded to the detriment of all.[66]

By taking the waiver tool off the table, the Filip Memo stands out as a rare instance of law enforcement self-restraint in the cooperation arena.

Like street crime cooperation, white collar cooperation gives the government largely unfettered authority. And like street informing, corporate cooperation offers its own temptations to government officials. In 2008, the House Judiciary Committee summoned former U.S. Attorney General John Ashcroft to explain how he received a no-bid contract worth between $28 million and $52 million to serve as the monitor for a DPA involving the medical supply company Zimmer Holdings. Zimmer hired Ashcroft at the suggestion of Chris Christie, who at the time was the U.S. Attorney in New Jersey investigating the company and had formerly worked under Ashcroft at DOJ. The week prior to Ashcroft's testimony, the department announced revised guidelines to prevent the appearance of this sort of conflict of interest. Under the new guidelines, DPA monitors must be selected by committee and approved in Washington by the deputy attorney general.[67]

Corporate cooperation is thus characterized by an increasingly powerful government that can send companies scrambling to comply with their DPAs. In this sense, despite the vast differences, corporate snitches have something in common with their individual counterparts: the decision to cooperate cedes enormous power to the government and permits law enforcement to control aspects of an individual's or a company's existence that would otherwise be beyond the reach of the criminal law.

Corporate cooperation shares another core, troublesome feature with its street counterpart: by permitting companies to cooperate, the government forgives their wrongdoing and forgoes the option of criminal punishment. As with individual informants, the routine use of corporate cooperation can suggest that the government is less serious about punishing white collar malfeasance. It may also encourage additional wrongdoing, on the theory that companies know that they will be able to cut a deal, creating what the nonprofit watchdog Public Citizen has excoriated as "an environment of corporate impunity."[68] Others agree that the increased use of DPAs has these kinds of negative effects:

> Some lawyers suggest that companies may be willing to take more risks because they know that, if they are caught, the chances of getting a deferred prosecution are good. "Some companies may bear the risk" of le-

gally questionable business practices if they believe they can cut a deal to defer their prosecution indefinitely, [law professor Vikramaditya] Khanna said. Legal experts say the tactic [of using DPAs] may have sent the wrong signal to corporations—the promise, in effect, of a get-out-of-jail-free card.[69]

Such concerns are common in the world of street crime and drug enforcement. Pervasive snitching deals have inculcated the idea that drug dealers can stay in business as long as they remain useful to the government. It was a murder case that prompted Judge Stephen Trott to make his oft-quoted lament: "Never has it been more true than it is now that a criminal charged with a serious crime understands that a fast and easy way out of trouble with the law is . . . to cut a deal at someone else's expense."[70] These destructive lessons of informant culture have worked their way into the elite world of corporate crime.

2. THE EMPLOYER-EMPLOYEE PROBLEM

A set of separate concerns unique to organizational cooperation has to do with the relationship between corporations and their employees. On the one hand, part of corporate cooperation involves identifying individual wrongdoers in the organization and revealing them to the government. The Yates Memo specifically demands that a corporation disclose wrongdoing by its officers and employees before it can receive cooperation credit: "[I]n order to qualify for any cooperation credit, corporations must provide to the Department [of Justice] all relevant facts relating to the individuals responsible for the misconduct."[71]

On the other hand, corporations may be tempted to fulfill their obligations to prosecutors by sacrificing individual employees and/ or selectively sacrificing some while protecting others. This permits scapegoating—blaming individuals for company-wide practices.[72] It also creates potential unfairness to individual employees. Because companies have significant power over their workers—particularly the ability to discipline or fire them—they can pressure workers to cooperate or provide information in ways that the state could not do directly without implicating the individuals' constitutional rights. Individual employees may have few means of defending themselves against the joint forces of their employer and the government.[73]

For example, in its investigation of KPMG for abusing tax shelters, the government indicated that, in deciding whether to indict the company, it would consider the company's long-standing practice of providing employees with legal fees in connection with legal matters arising out of their employment. In its effort to avoid indictment, the company changed its practice, informing employees that it would not pay their legal fees unless they cooperated with the government. The district court described what followed:

> The government took full advantage. It sought interviews with many KPMG employees and encouraged KPMG to press the employees to cooperate. Indeed, it urged KPMG to tell employees to disclose any personal criminal wrongdoing. When individuals balked, the prosecutors told KPMG. In each case, KPMG reiterated its threat to cut off payment of legal fees unless the government [was] satisfied with the individual's cooperation. In some cases, it told the employees to cooperate with prosecutors or be fired.[74]

In 2006, the court concluded that the government's tactics interfered with KPMG employees' right to counsel, requiring the dismissal of some of the indictments. The court also found that some of the statements taken from some employees under these circumstances were coerced and therefore inadmissible.[75] The Filip Memo subsequently disavowed the use of such tactics.[76]

The ability of cooperating corporations to direct governmental attention toward particular employees also creates the risk that individual employees will take the fall for corporatewide or high-level wrongdoing. In effect, by sacrificing vulnerable lower-level employees, the corporation can protect itself or higher-level decision makers who might otherwise be personally liable.[77] This dynamic mirrors the same, well-known problem with informants in drug organizations. High-level operatives are better able to leverage cooperation to protect themselves, while low-level dealers and users who have little information and less protection may be sacrificed. This dynamic ensures that, while cooperation in either realm often produces convictions, culpable organizations and their leadership—whether corporate or criminal—may be able to manipulate cooperation to evade responsibility.

C. White Collar versus Street Snitching

The foregoing picture reveals a set of white collar cooperation practices that differ significantly from street crime and drug informing. First and foremost, the bulk of corporate activity is perfectly legal. Unlike drug cartels, society has an interest in protecting productive business organizations, even those that have committed crimes. As the Filip Memo points out, one of the factors that prosecutors must consider in initiating a corporate prosecution includes "collateral consequences, including whether there is disproportionate harm to shareholders, pension holders, employees, and others not proven personally culpable, as well as impact on the public arising from the prosecution."[78] Moreover, the activities that constitute fraud or other crimes may look very similar to legal operations and are therefore hard to distinguish and punish. This fact shapes all law enforcement practices in the business arena, including strategies for and the significance of cooperation.

Another important set of differences flows from the fact that white collar investigations and cooperation tend to be well documented, involving lawyers on all sides. The existence of witnesses, experts, and paper trails helps to eliminate unreliability, rule-breaking, and reneging. It also enables courts and the public to figure out what happened afterward. These attributes are in stark contrast with the secretive, informal, unwitnessed negotiations that so often characterize street and drug informing.

Importantly, white collar defendants, be they corporate entities or individuals, tend to be wealthier, better educated, and better able to defend themselves against government demands compared street crime defendants.[79] This ability goes above and beyond the individual defendant's ability to fully litigate their own case. As illustrated by the uproar over compelled voluntary waivers, white collar defendants and their defense bar can muster significant public and institutional support. As a result, government strategies are likely to be more cognizant of legal rules because those rules are more likely to be challenged and litigated. These strengths—better documentation, accountability, and counsel—inspire some of the reforms proposed in chapter 8. They also remind us how informant policies can discriminate against the poor and people of color. They reflect the broader phenomenon, as law professor David Cole once put it, that we have at least two working versions of criminal justice, "one for the more privileged and educated, the other for the poor and less educated. . . . [P]olice officers routinely use methods of investigation and interrogation against members of racial minorities and the poor that would be deemed unacceptable if applied to more privileged members of the community."[80]

And yet, white collar informing shares important characteristics with its street and drug counterparts. Both confer a vast amount of discretionary, unreviewable authority on law enforcement. Both exacerbate power inequalities among potential offenders and between vulnerable offenders and the government. In both arenas, the decision to permit cooperation means that the government is tolerating and forgiving crime and sometimes even creating an atmosphere in which crime may flourish. And both deprive courts and the public of significant amounts of power over and information about the operations of the executive.

Finally, the pressure to cooperate in the corporate context risks fraying the networks of trust on which business entities depend for success. Like a neighborhood, "a corporation is a collective enterprise"[81] that can be weakened by the specter of informant use. In the same way that heavy concentrations of informants threaten social networks in heavily policed communities, the fear that corporate entities or individual employees may turn on each other can erode the trust and loyalty that businesses need in order to flourish.[82] Despite their significant differences, therefore, white collar and street crime cooperation involve many of the same dangers.

III. Political Informants

In addition to business entities, the government also deploys informants to investigate political groups and individual politicians. The use of informants in the political sphere raises especially thorny democratic governance issues. When the government incentivizes an informant to provide information about their own civic association or to infiltrate an existing political organization, it may threaten the First Amendment rights of other members of that organization. Moreover, the very choice to investigate a political association can mask partisan political motives, or even outright hostility, on the part of prosecuting authorities.

Similarly, when the state uses its considerable criminal investigative powers to go after a sitting politician, we worry that the government may be interfering with foundational democratic processes. We nevertheless permit the state to walk these fine lines because of the concomitant risk that a group or an individual elected official may themselves be committing criminal acts harmful to our democracy. The following sections explore these two varieties of political informant and the somewhat different values and problems that they implicate.

A. Infiltrators and the First Amendment

The U.S. government has a long and problematic history of using informants to infiltrate and undermine political groups and associations. Over the years, the FBI has deployed informants to surveil and penetrate the Communist Party, civil rights organizations, Students for a Democratic Society (SDS), the Black Panther Party, Occupy Wall Street, environmental groups, and Black Lives Matter, in addition to the Ku Klux Klan and other white supremacist groups. These informants not only gathered information but also sometimes provided their host organizations with resources and/or intentionally instigated actions likely to result in arrests or violence.[83] Sometimes these tactics had historic consequences. FBI informant William O'Neal, recruited by the agency from the Cook County Jail, infiltrated the Black Panthers in Chicago and helped instigate the 1969 police raid that killed Panther leader Fred Hampton.[84]

The use of informants in connection with the U.S. civil rights movement past and present has sparked special and historic concerns. Information from two FBI informants recruited from the Communist Party was used to obtain a wiretap of Dr. Martin Luther King Jr.[85] FBI informant Gary Rowe was a Klan member implicated in the murder of civil rights worker Viola Liuzzo in 1965.[86]

In 2006, FBI informant David Gletty organized a neo-Nazi march through a predominantly Black neighborhood in Orlando, Florida. The march, for which Gletty obtained the permits and was listed as the "on scene event manager," generated deep anxiety in the Black community; fears of racial unrest triggered a major police mobilization. Local leaders complained. As city councilwoman Daisy Lynum put it: "To come into a predominantly black community which could have resulted in great harm to the black community? I would hate to be part of a game. It's a mockery to the community for someone else to be playing a game with the community." The FBI later issued a statement denying that it played any role in the rally.[87] In 2019, the ACLU and MediaJustice filed a lawsuit seeking records regarding the FBI's creation of a "Black Identity Extremist" threat classification aimed at Black activists and Black-led organizations, which the complaint describes as part of the FBI's long history of "surveillance, infiltration, and disruption" of racial justice advocacy groups.[88]

Even when informants do not actively participate in criminal activity or undermine organizations, the official infiltration of political groups and other associations can disturb democratic activities. The City of New York Police Department used undercover officers and informants to infiltrate numerous groups—including "street theater companies, church groups, antiwar activists, environmentalists, and people opposed to the death penalty"—in preparation for the 2004 Republican National Convention.[89] In 2009, a national coalition of Islamic organizations expressed alarm that the FBI was persistently infiltrating mosques and using "agent provocateurs to trap unsuspecting Muslim youth."[90] A few years later, members of the Islamic Center of Irvine sued the FBI for paying an informant to infiltrate and surveil the mosque and its members.[91]

Such governmental practices can have constitutional dimensions. When the state uses informants to infiltrate and surveil political, religious, or other legitimate groups, it can constitute interference with members' First Amendment rights of free speech and association. "[I]ndividuals maintain a first amendment right to associate for lawful political purposes free from government intrusion."[92] This right, however, does not preclude legitimate law enforcement efforts. The Supreme Court has made clear that when the government merely gathers otherwise public information and intelligence about free speech activities and organizations, it does not infringe the subjects' First Amendment rights.[93] More specifically, lower courts have held that "[t]he use of informers and infiltrators by itself does not give rise to any claim of violation of [First Amendment] constitutional rights."[94]

But when the government becomes more active—going beyond mere data-gathering or the planting of a passive informant—free speech rights may be impermissibly chilled or violated. For example, in *Handschu v. Special Services Division*, New York City police used informants to infiltrate anti–Vietnam War and other political groups in the early 1970s. Those informants were used not only to collect information but also, as alleged by group members, to provoke illegal activities such as armed robbery in order to disrupt and undermine the organizations themselves. The group members sued the city to stop the practice, alleging that government "informers and infiltrators provoked, solicited, and induced members of lawful political and social groups to engage in unlawful activities[,] . . . provided funds and equipment to further that purpose," and otherwise engaged in "excesses and abusive tactics and activities with the purpose and effect of sowing distrust and suspicion among plaintiffs and other[s] who espouse unorthodox or dissenting political and social views, thereby discouraging them from associating for that purpose."[95] The court concluded that, if the allegations were true, such official practices would violate the First Amendment.

During that same period, a socialist political organization in Detroit brought suit, alleging that a paid FBI informant sought to sow distrust within the organization and to discourage others from joining by, among other things, publicly misrepresenting the party's goals, inciting violence, making racist remarks, stealing mail, and letting the informant's name be placed on the ballot for state representation as a party candidate. The federal court concluded, in *Ghandi v. Police Department of the City of Detroit*, that the informant's "conduct, if reported accurately, strikes at the very heart of a free society. It amounts to a government informer making a direct attack upon the right of a fellow citizen to publicly express his political views while campaigning for public office."[96] In 1989, the Ninth Circuit found that when immigration officials recorded church services, thereby driving congregants away, they sufficiently harmed the churches' and congregants' interests in freedom of association to support a First Amendment claim.[97] In *FBI v. Fazaga*, members of the Islamic Center of Irvine maintained that the FBI unconstitutionally used its informant to target them based on their religion. Most of their claims were dismissed on national security grounds, based on the FBI's contention that the litigation risked disclosure of sensitive counter-terrorism information.[98]

Infiltration also raises a political selectivity problem, which is the official identification of civic groups as dangerous or potentially criminal. When the government deems a political or religious or environmental group dangerous, thereby justifying the decision to recruit or plant an informant, we worry that the government is expressing a political bias under cover of the criminal system. In 1974, Professor Marx studied thirty-four cases in which information was publicly available regarding informant infiltration of political groups. Of all the groups selected for infiltration, only two were politically conservative. During the 1960s and 1970s, J. Edgar Hoover infamously used FBI informants and agents to undermine left-leaning political organizations. In an internal agency memo, Hoover explicitly instructed his agents that "[t]he purpose of this [counterintelligence] program is to expose, disrupt, and otherwise neutralize the new Left organizations, their Leadership and adherents."[99] More recently, members of the Congressional Black Caucus expressed concern that the FBI's 2017 "Black Identity Extremists" report represented a similar kind of hostility.[100] Several studies likewise conclude that the FBI uses informants and undercover operations against right-wing threats less extensively and aggressively than it does against Muslims.[101]

In these ways, using informants for political purposes raises an additional set of concerns above and beyond those triggered by traditional crime control. Fears about First Amendment infringement are at their height. Not only can the government's power to choose its targets represent a kind of thumb-on-the-scales favoritism; the proactive investigative techniques associated with informants and provocateurs may undermine the political process itself. Because of the history of governmental interference with left-wing and civil rights groups, the legacy of this sort of informant has left an important mark on the public understanding and history of snitching.

At the same time, some of the universal problems with informant use affect this arena as well. Infiltrating informants may get away with wrongdoing in exchange for their usefulness. They may finger the innocent or entrap those who would not otherwise commit a crime. When they are exposed, informants may undermine public perceptions of law enforcement legitimacy. In other words, even in this unique arena, political informants carry many of the same challenges and risks as their more conventional criminal counterparts.

B. Political Corruption

Sometimes informants are used to catch corrupt politicians. Informants can be used proactively to set up illegal transactions, or they may themselves be corrupt political operatives who turn in their former associates in exchange for lenience. That first strategy—the "sting"—has long generated concerns about selection bias and law enforcement infiltration of the political process, similar to the concerns that plague the use of the political agent provocateur. In 1978, the FBI ran one of its most famous and contentious political sting operations, known as "Abscam." FBI agents, along with criminal informant and con man Melvin Weinberg, posed as representatives of wealthy sheiks looking for investment opportunities and approached numerous political figures with bribes. The strategy netted twenty-five indictments, including the convictions of a U.S. senator, four congressmen, and several local Pennsylvania and New Jersey politicians.[102]

The defendants argued that they had been entrapped. Although two district courts agreed, eventually all the convictions were upheld on appeal. Some of the defendants argued further that the use of Weinberg, a criminal who received lenience for his mail fraud charges in exchange for organizing the sting, was improper. This argument also failed. As the U.S. Court of Appeals for the District of Columbia put it:

> Successful creation of an "elaborate hoax" such as Abscam may well require employment of "experts" such as Weinberg to give the operation an aura of "credibility" and "contacts" with criminal elements. The employment of a convicted confidence man in Abscam is analogous to the entirely proper employment of a convicted seller of drugs to purchase drugs from a suspected distributor. As the Second Circuit stated: "[U] se of dishonest and deceitful informants like Weinberg creates risks to which the attention of juries must be forcefully called, but the Due Process Clause does not forbid their employment, detail their supervision, nor specify their compensation."[103]

Although the Abscam convictions were deemed legally sound, deep concerns lingered that the government had crossed an inappropriate line by creating criminal opportunities to lure politicians about whom the government had no other incriminating evidence. As Professor Paul Chevigny wrote at the time, "the power to offer a temptation to crime is the power to decide who shall be tempted. It can be and often has been used as a way for the Government to eliminate its enemies, or for one faction in Government to get rid of another."[104]

The second strategy involves corrupt political operatives who turn on former associates in order to avoid harsher penalties themselves. Unlike the sting, this more conventional use of informants involves flipping existing offenders to reveal wrongdoing that has already occurred. This is essentially the same model as the white collar snitch, and it has the same basic strengths. Deals tend not to involve the proactive instigation or toleration of new criminal conduct; they are fully vetted by attorneys on both sides; and the public usually learns about them as well as the underlying criminal conduct at issue. But like all snitching deals, they carry risks.

Corrupt lobbyist Jack Abramoff is the poster child for this form of political cooperation, embodying both its best and worst implications. For over a decade, Abramoff bribed politicians and their staffers, accepting illegal kickbacks and lying to clients and to the government; he also bilked several Native American tribes for millions of dollars. As part of his 2006 guilty plea, he agreed to cooperate.[105] His assistance made possible the successful prosecution of a sitting congressman and numerous other high-level political officials.[106]

In exchange for his cooperation, Abramoff served three and half years in prison, although he faced as many as thirty years for his corruption and fraud cases taken together.[107] Despite Abramoff's massive wrongdoing and the heavy attention paid to his case, the public record at the time was practically devoid of complaints about his relatively light punishment. Rather, commentators focused on the high-level elected officials and widespread corrupt practices in Washington that were exposed as a result.[108] This acceptance reflected the intuition that the Abramoff case represented a strong version of the snitch compromise—although Abramoff evaded full punishment for his own serious crimes, a greater public good was served.

After the Abramoff scandal, Congress amended the Lobbying Disclosure Act to create greater transparency around lobbying activities.[109] In 2017, seven years after his release from prison, Abramoff committed a series of brand-new criminal offenses that included the failure to disclose lobbying activities in violation of the provisions of the new law. In other words, he violated the very law that his previous criminal conduct had inspired. A frustrated Congress amended the lobbying laws *again*, this time to require lobbyists to disclose any prior conviction for "bribery, extortion, embezzlement, an illegal kickback, tax evasion, fraud, a conflict of interest, making a false statement, perjury, or money laundering." The new law is called "The JACK Act."[110]

Jack Abramoff pled guilty, again, in 2020 to criminal lobbying violations and conspiracy to commit wire fraud. His on-the-nose recidivism makes the story an object lesson in snitching irony—the poster child for political corruption cooperates, escapes decades in prison, only to return to his corrupt ways. But the irony isn't over. Abramoff's new plea agreement specifically contemplates the possibility of a lesser sentence if he cooperates. He potentially faces up to five years of incarceration, but at the time of publication he is free on his own recognizance, he is not under pretrial supervision, and no sentencing date has been set. And yes, he is expected to testify against one of his co-conspirators.[111]

Jack Abramoff's impunity illuminates the risk inherent in all snitching deals: letting serious offenders negotiate their way out of liability for past crimes can encourage their continued wrongdoing. Sophisticated offenders like Abramoff have clearly received the message sent by the informant market: everything is negotiable, even when we intentionally strengthen the law, and even for the most egregious repeat offenders. Of all the costs of the informant deal, this blow to the integrity of the justice system may be the greatest one of all.

IV. Terrorism

terrorism = "activities that . . . involve acts dangerous to human life that are a violation of the criminal laws of the United States or of any State, [that] appear to be intended—(i) to intimidate or coerce a civilian population; (ii) to influence the policy of a government by intimidation or coercion; or (iii)

to affect the conduct of a government by mass destruction, assassination, or kidnapping."
—United States Criminal Code, chapter 113B—Terrorism, Definitions[112]

The terrorist attacks of September 11, 2001, affected many aspects of the U.S. legal system. In particular, it increased both the demand for and tolerance of executive authority and secrecy: from the airport intrusions of the TSA to heightened immigration restrictions and ever-widening surveillance, the so-called war on terror continues to shape the legal and criminal landscape.

An important feature of that landscape is the centrality of informants and other forms of undercover operations. The tactic is an old one: it was paid informant Emad Salem who infiltrated a group of terrorists planning the bombing of numerous New York buildings, including the United Nations, and whose tapings and testimony enabled the 1995 prosecution of the group's leader, Sheik Omar Abdel Rahman.[113] Since 9/11, however, there has been an explosion of attention, funding, and organizational commitment to developing informants in international terror and national security investigations.[114]

Any discussion of terrorism informants must begin with a caveat: many of the government's activities in this area are classified or otherwise nonpublic. In addition, terror investigations place a premium on ongoing data collection and prevention rather than generating criminal cases. Therefore, general statements about how the government uses informants, or what the costs and benefits have been, must be tempered by the acknowledgment that a lot of data are simply unavailable, although there is substantially more public information and scholarship today than there was when I published the first edition of this book in 2009.[115] Moreover, the preventative effects of informant use are difficult to measure by their very nature: we do not know what would have happened had the government not intervened. Accordingly, this section does not try to describe or evaluate terrorism informant use and practices with any comprehensiveness. Rather, it attempts a more modest task: outlining the general rules governing informants in this area, perusing the public record for the kinds of data that have become available, and thinking about useful parallels between terrorism-related informant use and other kinds of informants about which we have more information.

A final caveat is that this section focuses on so-called international terrorism investigations, which historically have been the federal government's priority. Domestic events—most prominently the January 6, 2021, attack on the U.S. Capitol—may change that: the FBI and the National Security Council have promised a new focus on domestic terrorism.[116]

The basic rules governing terrorism informants are familiar. As a general matter, law enforcement has wide discretion to create, deploy, and reward informants and to keep much of that process off the public record. These standard characteristics, however, are heightened for terrorism informants, who can be created and used by their handlers in a variety of ways, across jurisdictions and countries, often over many years, with few constraints. The rewards for such informants are also familiar: they include money, lenience for crimes committed, material support for political or economic activities, preferential immigration treatment, witness protection, and, more elusively, the freedom and power that can come with having a relationship with the U.S. government. The U.S. State Department, for example, runs a Rewards for Justice Program that can pay up to $25 million for information leading to the arrest or conviction of any individual for the commission of an act of international terrorism.[117] The Responsible Cooperators Program provides incentives for noncitizens to give information about terrorism activities, including the S-visa—sometimes referred to as the "snitch visa"—for immigrants who provide "critical reliable information" regarding terrorist or criminal activity.[118]

Above and beyond these general similarities, some special rules govern terrorism informants that make their use more flexible and clandestine than conventional informants. This additional flexibility flows from deep sources, primarily the greater authority vested in the executive when national security matters are at stake. The Supreme Court has been particularly protective of executive authority to keep national security matters confidential, noting that such executive decisions should be given the "utmost deference."[119] Moreover, terrorism investigations and cases are not always handled as criminal matters but instead may be treated as military or foreign intelligence investigations to which traditional criminal procedure protections do not apply.[120] For example, the Fourth Amendment's warrant requirement may not cover noncriminal national security investigations regarding foreign powers, organizations, or individuals at all.[121] Likewise, national security–related and classified information is more protected and therefore more difficult to discover.[122]

Surveillance in the terrorism or national security context is governed primarily by statute and by executive guidelines. The Foreign Intelligence Surveillance Act (FISA) governs national security–related electronic surveillance, wiretaps, and other processes for obtaining information.[123] FISA created the Foreign Intelligence Surveillance Court (FISC), a confidential court to which the government can apply for warrants and wiretaps in national security cases. In addition, the USA PATRIOT Act expanded the government's authority to use "national security letters" to obtain information from third parties such as phone companies.[124] These national security investigative techniques are heavily used: in 2016, the FISC issued nearly 9,000 national security letters, approximately triple the number of traditional wiretaps issued nationwide.[125]

A variety of federal agencies use informants to investigate terrorism and other national security threats. They include the Pentagon, the CIA, Treasury, Customs, the FBI, and the DEA. Information regarding the ways in which intelligence agencies, both civilian and military, use and reward informants is often classified.[126] Public information therefore tends to pertain to the FBI and, to a lesser extent, the DEA. This is because these agencies primarily investigate traditional criminal offenses and their informant practices are thus more publicly regulated than those of agencies whose primary missions are national security related. FBI and DEA informants may also start off as drug or other kinds of informants, and then morph into terrorism sources, and are thus subject to greater controls and disclosures.

Several sets of guidelines govern the FBI. The first is "The Attorney General's Guidelines for FBI National Security Investigations and Foreign Intelligence Collection." These guidelines cover the general parameters of national security investigations, data collection, and threat assessment. They include a variety of rules such as the requirement that the Attorney General's Office be apprised of investigations, internal reporting requirements, and guidelines for dealing with foreign, state, and local governments. In particular, the guidelines authorize the "[t]asking of previously established assets, informants, and cooperating witnesses, and recruitment of new assets, informants, and cooperating witnesses."[127]

The second set is "The Attorney General's Guidelines on General Crimes, Racketeering Enterprise, and Terrorism Enterprise Investigations," promulgated in May 2002 by Attorney General John Ashcroft.[128] While these guidelines require compliance with the more specific "Guidelines Regarding the Use of Confidential Informants," they make at least one important change with respect to informant use: they authorize the development of informants and other investigative tactics at the earliest stages of suspicion. Previous guidelines had required more evidence and further investigation before such tactics could be used.[129]

The attorney general's 2006 guidelines govern the use of all FBI confidential human sources, including investigations using domestic terrorism informants. They do not apply to the development of informants in foreign countries. The guidelines contain a few special reporting and confidentiality rules. For example, terrorism-related sources are not vetted by the Human Source Review Committee but instead are referred to a special national security division. In addition, the identities of those informants are typically not revealed, even to federal prosecutors and reviewers.[130]

As this brief overview makes clear, the FBI and other law enforcement agencies have a great deal of flexibility in the ways in which they can use informants to obtain terrorism-related information. Because of the increased secrecy and ongoing nature of investigations, there is even less public data on the ways in which terrorism informants are used than there is for traditional criminal informants. Nevertheless, press and public attention to the phenomenon has produced a few cases that suggest the contours of some common practices.

The FBI considers informants central to its efforts to investigate and prevent terrorist violence. According to one former FBI operative, "you can't get from A to B without an informant."[131] Over 40 percent of terrorism prosecutions since 9/11 have involved informants.[132] But the wide variety of practices defy clear categorization. Some terrorism informants are foreign nationals who have long-standing—and sometimes on-again, off-again—relationships with the U.S. government. Some are drug dealers who turn into informants to escape traditional criminal liability.

Some are U.S. residents who live in communities that the FBI wants to investigate. Some are in it for the money. And some are all of the above.

Results likewise defy easy evaluation. Some informants produce critical, reliable information that permits the government to prevent terrorist activities. Some take the government for a ride, earning money and/or lenience while producing information of little value. Some work so hard to generate cases and information that the resulting prosecutions look more like entrapment than prevention. And some do all of the above.

There have been a number of successful investigations and prosecutions, although even these have been controversial, largely because of the difficulty in discerning the true extent of the thwarted threat. For example, it was a convicted drug dealer-turned-informant who posed as a terrorist and prevented a plot to blow up fuel tanks at John F. Kennedy Airport in New York. Although many hailed this as an excellent example of preventative investigation, some criticized the case because it appeared that the main suspect lacked the resources or ability to actually carry out the plot.[133]

For some terrorism suspects, it is difficult to discern whether they would actually have proceeded without the instigation or support of the informant. In 2006, for example, informant testimony led to the conviction of a man plotting to blow up a busy New York subway station. Critics charged that the young man, who had an IQ of 78, was not a real threat and that the informant goaded him into making incriminating statements. The informant, Osama Eldawoody, earned over $100,000, including rent and relocation costs; he is now in hiding.[134]

Similarly, tapes played at a 2006 hearing revealed the large role of an FBI informant in developing the case against seven men accused of plotting to blow up the Sears Tower in Chicago. The suspects were taped reciting oaths to al-Qaeda, using words given to them by the informant, leading some to worry that the informant exaggerated the threat posed by the men.[135] Since then, the growing list of terror cases in which informants appear to do most of the work has led investigative journalist Trevor Aaronson to contend that the FBI "is hunting an enemy largely of its own creation."[136]

Like traditional criminal informants, active terrorism informants pose the threat of ongoing criminal activities. For example, Ali Mohamed, an Egyptian-born U.S. citizen, pled guilty to terrorism charges in 2000 after having served as a double agent. He worked briefly for the CIA and then spent years providing information to the FBI, even as he continued his own deep involvement in al-Qaeda training, fundraising, and support. His connections to the FBI gave him freedom to pursue his al-Qaeda–related goals, including the planning of the 1998 bombing of the U.S. embassy in Nairobi. It also gave him insight into the U.S. government's antiterrorist efforts. A former State Department official called the case "a study in incompetence, in how not to run an agent."[137] In 2009, a Jordanian CIA informant, whom agents considered to be a "golden source," turned out to be a suicide bomber who killed nine people at a CIA base in Afghanistan.[138]

Terrorism informants also raise the familiar specter of unreliability. After winning two high-profile terrorism convictions and claiming that it had thwarted a sleeper terrorism cell in Detroit, the Department of Justice took the highly unusual step of repudiating its own case and having the charges thrown out. The cases were based on bad evidence obtained from a single informant who was attempting to avoid fraud charges in another case. Although recognizing that their case rested on weak evidence, prosecutors had hoped to leverage the prosecution in order to get additional suspects to cooperate.[139]

An additional problem with terrorism informants appears to be the perception that the U.S. government doesn't keep its promises. In a 2002 article, U.S. News & World Report reported that numerous informants had complained that the government had mistreated them; they even sued in civil court to try to get promised benefits, including health care, immigration status, and money.[140] One valuable Yemeni informant, Mohamed Alanssi, who helped the United States investigate over twenty cases, set himself on fire in front of the White House to protest his treatment by the FBI.[141]

Finally, informant practices exacerbate the racial and religious profiling that has plagued antiterrorism enforcement. Since 9/11, racial and religious discrimination against Muslims has increased at airports, in immigration, and in politics.[142] As Professor Wadie Said writes, the FBI's use of informants to infiltrate mosques in the absence of any suspicion of criminal activity is consistent with "widespread support for or tolerance of the racial profiling of Arab- and Muslim-Americans for national security purposes."[143] Professor Shirin Sinnar points out that the FBI uses its "vast network of confidential informants [to] identif[y] [Muslim] individuals deemed prone to 'radicalization' and offers them ostensible opportunities to engage in violence. If individuals take the bait—sometimes after intense prodding from informants—federal prosecutors indict them for federal offenses including material support to terrorism."[144] Human rights attorney Diala Shamas worries that this kind of "categorical suspicion" against Muslim Americans and the heavy pressure to become informants "has had chilling consequences on speech, religious practice, and many other aspects of Muslim life in America."[145] In 2020, the Supreme Court unanimously held that three Muslim men could sue the FBI for placing them on the No Fly List in retaliation for their refusal to become informants.[146]

This brief sketch indicates that, despite their special character, terrorism informants present many of the same benefits and challenges as do criminal informants. On the one hand, they offer unique information and access that is often impossible to get in other ways. On the other, they pose threats of unreliability, further crime, corruption, discrimination, and the danger that they may continue to operate as criminals even as they cooperate with the government.

Some of the risks of informant use are actually heightened in this arena. Handlers may be less able to track, control, or even understand the behavior of their international operatives. Secrecy is at its height, so the opportunity for abuses—by government agents as well as informants—is correspondingly greater. Moreover, with respect to international investigations, the handling or mishandling of such individuals can implicate diplomatic and international relations and crimes committed in other countries.[147]

While terrorism informants are shrouded in secrecy and thus difficult to evaluate, the insights that we glean from traditional informants can help us think about informant use in this even more clandestine, less regulated world. Indeed, the 2007 congressional hearing on informants reflected this connection: the joint hearing was held by the House Subcommittee on the Constitution, Civil Rights, and Civil Liberties and the House Subcommittee on Crime, Terrorism, and Homeland Security in recognition of the fact that both domestic and national security interests are implicated by informant practices. Noting several instances in which informants were used to thwart terrorist attacks, Representative Lungren cited the need to improve terrorism informant practices as an important reason for additional hearings and new legislation.[148]

The central lesson from the world of traditional criminal investigation is that informants are at their most dangerous when the government permits them to commit new crimes, off the record, without regulation or public transparency. The pressure for such compromises is at its height in terror investigations because active informants provide such potentially valuable information. Experiences with criminal informants suggest, however, that these compromises are the most expensive and deserve to be resisted. While many of the reforms described in chapter 8 may be inappropriate in the terrorism context, the principles behind them—the need for more reliability and accountability and less violence and crime—are equally present. In a sense, fostering these principles in the antiterrorism arena is even more vital because the stakes are so high.

Regulation and Reform

Crime is contagious. If the government becomes a law-breaker, it breeds contempt for law; it invites every man to become a law unto himself; it invites anarchy. To declare that in the administration of the criminal law the end justi-fies the means—to declare that the government may commit crimes in order to secure the conviction of a private criminal—would bring terrible retribution.
—Justice Louis Brandeis[1]

When I published the first edition of this book in 2009, informant reform was just getting started in the United States. It was scattered and piecemeal and relatively obscure. I predicted that would change, and it has. Today, nearly half of all states have considered or implemented significant informant reform legislation. Around the country, local, state, and federal officials are grappling with different facets of informant use and have proposed or instituted a variety of new rules. For the first time in its history, the prestigious American Law Institute has issued a set of principles and guidelines for informant use.[2] Many of these reforms address the ways in which informants are used as witnesses; others take aim at the problematic role of informants in the war on drugs. Still others focus on vulnerable informants such as minors, immigrants, or people with mental health or substance use challenges. Almost all reforms involve greater data collection and transparency. Taken together, these efforts represent a robust and expanding public policy dialogue about criminal informants, their benefits and dangers, and the appropriate extent of restrictions on and public scrutiny of law enforcement practices.

This turnaround is the result of numerous forces. Those include decades of work by the innocence movement, hundreds of exonerations involving lying informants, and the 2012 founding of the Nat'l Registry of Exonerations, which makes it easier to identify and study when informants cause wrongful convictions. We have also seen an unrelenting series of high-profile snitch scandals, from Orange County to Detroit, that have brought the risks of official informant use into dramatic view. Heightened media attention has produced rigorous investigations from many outlets including the *New York Times* and the popular podcast series *In the Dark*. More broadly, openness to informant reform is part of a new penal zeitgeist: a national willingness to reconsider mass incarceration, to challenge problematic policing practices, and to question the unfettered exercise of prosecutorial discretion.

Because using informants is complicated, reform is complicated too. Informant deals implicate core features of American law enforcement culture, part and parcel of the long-standing dominance of plea bargaining itself. Informant practices ebb and flow with social inequalities, and they reflect systemic economic, racial, and institutional biases. Their impact is simultaneously legal, cultural, historical, and personal. Because informant use and its problems are rooted in so many of our social institutions, they cannot be fixed solely by changing legal rules. Conversely, efforts to change those rules often implicate deep features of the criminal system that are not easily revised.

This complexity characterizes many challenges facing the criminal system. The justice process is not controlled by law alone. Rather, it is shaped by social forces and economic realities; the local habits of police, prosecutors, and judges when they apply the law; and ineffable matters like the public perception of crime and justice. As a national community, we understand better today than we did a decade ago that the criminal system is driven not only by evidence and crime rates but by money and race. This is as true for informant use as it is for any other staple practice of American law enforcement.

Another reason that informant reform is complicated is that stricter legal rules do not always improve the actual outcomes of the criminal process. This is not only because rules can be evaded but also because 'rict rules in one arena can drive officials toward less regulated, more 'retive practices. For example, the existence of strong criminal pro-
c\re protections at trial incentivizes prosecutors to avoid trials altoge⸱ in favor of plea bargaining, over which they have more control.[3]
Sot⸱cholars have argued that U.S. law enforcement relies more heav-

ily on covert operations compared to its European counterparts in part because other American police activities are more stringently regulated.[4] Accordingly, while stricter rules can improve some features of informant use, they may counterproductively drive other informant practices even further underground.

These are not arguments against regulation or for accepting the status quo but for thoughtful changes sensitive to the realities of the American criminal landscape. More than any other nation, the United States relies heavily on the criminal process to intervene in people's lives and to regulate the workings of communities and institutions. Not only do we famously incarcerate more people than any other country, we subject tens of millions of people every year to law enforcement interventions including stops, arrests, incarceration, and convictions. This heavy reliance makes the legal rules of criminal governance especially significant. Such rules, and the commitments behind them, influence not only the experiences of criminal suspects and the outcomes of criminal cases but our collective experiences of being governed.

Accordingly, even though legal reform can be only a partial response to the complex challenges of informant use, reform is vital, not only to improve the criminal process but also for its social influence and the principles for which it stands. Because informant use engages so many aspects of the larger criminal justice project, efforts to improve the accuracy, fairness, and transparency of informant use are also steps toward a fairer, more responsive legal system and democracy.

Since I first started writing about snitching, many people—including a sitting U.S. congressman—have asked me why I do not propose a complete ban on all informants. The answer is that informant use is not a stand-alone phenomenon that can be neatly excised from the rest of the system. Rather, it is a function of entrenched features of the U.S. criminal process: the state's ability to negotiate criminal liability through plea bargaining and broad law enforcement discretion to pick and choose among potential suspects. As I explain in the introduction, as long as this negotiation and selection authority remains in place, it will permit some version of the informant deal. Conversely, we cannot eliminate snitching without substantially curtailing these broader characteristics of our criminal process, an enormous undertaking that would far exceed the scope of the problems raised by informant use. But precisely because plea bargaining is bigger than the snitching problem, we do not need to do away with the former in order to meaningfully address the latter. Put differently: we can substantially improve how we permit the state to wield the informant deal short of upending the entire criminal system as we currently know it.

Regulating the Informant Market

The major dysfunctions of the informant market are formidable: its secretive lack of accountability, the harms it inflicts on the vulnerable, and its unprincipled, instrumental toleration of crime, victimization, inaccuracy, and inequality. No single reform can fix these things, but we can change our minds about how much of them we will tolerate. The key to regulating the informant market is to reject the culture of secrecy and impunity that generates so many of its harmful consequences and to insist on principled legal limits to the ways in which the state can deploy the informant deal. The central aim of such changes is protective: to protect vulnerable informants and defendants, to protect the public, and to protect the integrity of the criminal process itself. Such changes may seem basic, but they are not simple. They contradict decades of informant law and practice in which police and prosecutors have been permitted to evade core legal rules and principles, and to inflict crime and violence on the vulnerable, all in relative secrecy.

This chapter thus proposes a comprehensive approach to regulating and reigning in the state's power to create, use, reward, and penalize informants. Some of the proposals below have been adopted in numerous jurisdictions, while others have yet to be considered. Some proposals would be straightforward to implement, while others would require significant changes. Some are likely to be immediately effective, while others are admittedly partial and imperfect. Taken together, they provide a framework not only for changing existing laws but for entirely rethinking the appropriate role of informant use and the informant deal within the American criminal process.

I. Defining Informants

Proposal: Define "criminal informant" as any criminal suspect or defendant who provides information in exchange for
or in anticipation of any benefit, including lenience, money,
or other benefit for themselves or someone else.

Laws pertaining to "informants" must first define the term. Different people give information to the government for different reasons;
these include victims, whistleblowers, experts, investigators, and
citizen bystanders. The definition above zeroes in on the government-
conferred benefit as the defining characteristic of the informant deal
while excluding other, less problematic types of information sources.
Such a definition includes all suspects and defendants with whom the
government negotiates informant deals and who thus have strong incentives to accept personal risk and/or fabricate evidence in exchange for
benefits.

Some jurisdictions already take this type of comprehensive approach.
The state of Washington, for example, defines "informant" as any person
who:

> (a) Was previously unconnected with the criminal case as either a wit-
> ness or a codefendant; (b) claims to have relevant information about the
> crime; (c) is currently charged with a crime or is facing potential criminal
> charges or is in custody; and (d) at any time receives consideration in
> exchange for providing the information or testimony.[5]

In 2008, Nebraska similarly amended its criminal code to broaden its
definition of "informant" to include any criminal suspect, whether or
not they are detained or incarcerated, who "received a deal, promise,
inducement, or benefit." The legislature reasoned that "[t]here is a compelling state interest in providing safeguards against the admission of
testimony the reliability of which may be or has been compromised
through improper inducements."[6]

In some other states, by contrast, informant reforms have been limited to a subcategory of criminal informant: in-custody informants, or
so-called jailhouse snitches. This is due in part to the high-profile nature

of jailhouse informant unreliability, which has focused legislative attention on this particular class. While jailhouse snitches have strong incentives to fabricate evidence, however, they are far from the only category
of informant that does. The same motivations that lead in-custody informants to lie also create the risk of fabrication by suspects who remain
at large. Moreover, many types of informants, not only those who are
incarcerated, may be subject to coercive and unfair pressures to cooperate. By adopting a comprehensive definition of "informant," legislatures
can ensure that reliability, fairness, and accountability reforms apply to
the entire problematic class of criminal informants, not just those who
happen to be incarcerated at the time they provide information to the
government.

II. Aggregate Data Collection on Informant Creation and Deployment

Proposal: Law enforcement agencies should collect aggregate
data on the number of informants they create, the crimes
those informants help solve, the crimes those informants
themselves commit, and the benefits conferred on those
informants in exchange for their information. Data should
include the age, gender, race, ethnicity, and location of informants so that the differential impact on particular groups and
communities can be tracked. When shared, like public tax
data, such aggregate informant data should exclude information that could be used to identity individual informants.

While the use of criminal informants is pervasive throughout state and
local law enforcement, most jurisdictions lack any mechanism for keeping track of the number of informants used by the government, their
productivity, and/or their criminality. This makes it impossible to evaluate whether informant use actually makes communities safer, how
many crimes informants help solve, and how many crimes they commit themselves. This is a particularly pressing problem for poor, heavily
policed neighborhoods in which drug informants and their harms are
concentrated. These communities and their representatives deserve
access to data on the law enforcement policies that impact them.[7] Such

data would also permit courts, legislatures, and other policy makers to make better policy decisions about informant use. Finally, aggregate data would let the public see how law enforcement actually operates and permit a more informed public dialogue about the full costs and benefits of law enforcement tactics.

Informant data collection builds on existing laws and regulations. States and localities are required to provide the FBI with a wide array of crime statistics in order to obtain federal funding. These existing reporting requirements can be expanded to include informant-related information.

The FBI already has in place an approximation of this mandate. FBI informants are tracked and evaluated along a variety of metrics, including their value to investigations and the crimes they commit. According to the Office of Inspector General:

> The FBI tracks the productivity of its [confidential informants] by aggregating their "statistical accomplishments," i.e., the number of indictments, convictions, search warrants, Title III applications, and other contributions to investigative objectives for which the CI is credited.[8]

The FBI is separately required to report annually to the Department of Justice "the total number of times each FBI Field Office authorized a Confidential Human Source to engage in Otherwise Illegal Activity, and the overall nationwide total."[9] States have begun to follow suit. As described below, several states have instituted informant data tracking requirements that would make aggregate data collection straightforward.

The purpose of such data collection and sharing is to permit a better public and governmental understanding of informant use, to identity its true costs and benefits, and to inspire public debate. The purpose is not to endanger individual informants or officers or to impede law enforcement investigations. For that reason, public data should be reported in the aggregate without the inclusion of individual identifying information.

III. Informant Crime Control

The central compromise and danger of the criminal informant market is the official toleration of crime. This danger can be mitigated in a number of ways.

A. *Legislative Limits on Crimes for Which Cooperation Credit Can Be Earned or Used or Offered*

Proposal: Legislatures should restrict cooperation benefits in connection with serious crimes such as murder and rape, so that offenders who commit particularly heinous or otherwise problematic crimes cannot anticipate working off their liability by becoming informants. Conversely, with respect to minor offenses, centrally traffic violations, legislatures should prohibit police from pressuring violators into becoming informants. Legislatures should also ban the use of informants in capital cases.

As the law currently stands, there is no crime for which punishment cannot be mitigated through cooperation, from speeding to murder, and no type of case in which informants cannot be used. In practice, criminal offenses of every stripe are worked off or tolerated in exchange for cooperation, and informant witnesses are used in a wide array of prosecutions.

In 2008, a bill was proposed in the New York Assembly that would limit the ability of defendants to trade testimony for lenience for certain crimes. The proposed bill would have mandated that "no prosecuting attorney shall offer a dismissal of or refuse to bring charges for the crimes of murder, manslaughter, rape, or kidnapping, in exchange for the testimony of a person."[10]

Limiting serious crimes for which cooperation can be earned could have two salutary effects. The first is that offenders in that class would no longer be able to anticipate sentence reductions for turning in their accomplices or acquaintances and therefore might be less likely to commit the offense in the first place. The second is a more general message sent by elected representatives to the public and law enforcement alike: the law means what it says. Such a limitation could ameliorate the public impression created by widespread snitching that liability—even for the most serious crimes—is negotiable and contingent.

To be clear, this approach does not solve deeper systemic problems with informant use. Indeed, the caustic effects of street snitching suggest that low-level deals for petty crimes may be the most problematic in the aggregate. At the very least, however, legislatures should affirmatively limit cooperation as the omnipresent exception to every criminal law and close the snitching loophole to those who commit the most serious crimes.

At the other end of the spectrum, very minor crimes should not open the door to the risks of the informant deal. Most important, legislatures should prohibit police from pressuring traffic offenders into becoming drug informants. As we saw in chapter 1, police in Attica, New York, stopped Bianca Hervey for driving on a suspended license. They threatened her with jail unless she became a drug informant, even though she had no contact with drugs or the drug economy.[11] With over 20 million traffic stops every year, that vast traffic enforcement apparatus should not be converted into an opportunity to draft ordinary people into the war on drugs.

Finally, legislatures should ban the use of informant testimony in capital cases. Given the unreliability of the evidence, the strong incentives for its fabrication and misuse, and the finality of the punishment, informant-generated evidence is too inherently and demonstrably risky to use as a basis for the death penalty. In 2015, a bill to this effect was introduced in the Texas legislature. It read in part:

> [I]n a capital case in which the state seeks the death penalty . . . testimony of an informant or of an alleged accomplice of the defendant is not admissible if the testimony is given in exchange for a grant or promise by the attorney representing the state or by another of immunity from prosecution, reduction of sentence, or any other form of leniency or special treatment.[12]

B. Limits on Crimes That Can Be Committed by Active Informants

Proposal: No informant should be authorized, before or after the fact, to commit a crime of violence against another person.

Violent crimes committed by informants impose particularly heavy costs because they victimize other people who are then deprived of the full protection of the law. Many of the stories in this book describe informants whose handlers looked the other way when their sources committed crimes of sexual assault, domestic violence, and child abuse. The FBI Confidential Informant Guidelines already stipulate that no agent can authorize an informant to commit a crime of violence. The District of Columbia has a similar statutory requirement that informants shall be "directed to refrain . . . from participating in unlawful acts or threats of violence."[13] Such an express requirement should be widely adopted and enforced. As described below, informants who harm others through violence should also be identified, reported, and prosecuted.

C. Reporting Informant Crimes

Proposal: Investigative agents who know that their informant has committed a serious or violent crime should be required to report that crime to state or local law enforcement authorities in that jurisdiction; agencies should be required to report the number and extent of their informants' crimes to the relevant legislature.

One of the challenges of informant criminality is the secrecy with which it is treated by law enforcement. Legislators and courts, or even law enforcement in other agencies or jurisdictions, will typically never learn about the extent of crimes committed by informants. In an effort to redress this kind of interbranch secrecy, U.S. representative Stephen Lynch introduced the 2017 Confidential Informant Accountability Act, which would require all federal investigative agencies to report to Congress all serious crimes committed by their informants. A predecessor bill would have required FBI agents to report their informants' serious violent felonies to local law enforcement. Such bills provide potential models for all agencies and jurisdictions. Such reporting would not only help check informant criminality but also reestablish public safety as a priority over the maintenance of information sources.

D. Prosecuting Informant Perjury

Proposal: Prosecutors should enforce perjury laws against informants.

Prosecutors rarely enforce perjury laws against their own informants, even when they know that their informants have been untruthful or produced wrongful convictions. This is simultaneously a dereliction of prosecutorial duty, an invitation to informants to fabricate, and mis-leading, since juries often assume that lying informants risk prosecution. Prosecutor offices should establish special units to enforce truthful informant testimony, in the same way that many offices have established conviction integrity units.

IV. Protecting Informants

Informants themselves are often vulnerable to physical threats and psychological exploitation. They may be afraid to testify, but they may also be afraid not to cooperate. They may not understand their rights or the full implications and risks of being an informant. Such pressures and ignorance undermine not only their reliability and availability as witnesses but also their personal autonomy and security. There are a variety of ways to increase informant protections. These include, first and foremost, limiting the use of especially vulnerable informants in the first place. Second, people deciding whether to enter a cooperation deal should have access to counsel. Finally, those who choose to incur the risks of cooperation should receive improved protection.

A. Limit the Use of Vulnerable Informants

Proposal: Ban or limit the use of especially vulnerable informants such as children, immigrants at risk of deporta-tion, transgendered individuals who face heightened threats when incarcerated, individuals with mental disabilities, and people suffering from substance use disorders.

Vulnerable informants raise troubling problems. They are more subject to coercion, less likely to be able to make good decisions on their own behalf, and as a result more likely to enter into bad deals or to get hurt as a result of their cooperation. For these reasons, their information may also be more unreliable. Pressuring vulnerable suspects to cooperate can also be unfairly coercive or, in some cases, deadly for the informant.

All states should ban the use of all child informants. Only two states currently limit the use of juvenile informants by law. California prohibits the use of informants under the age of thirteen and requires court permission for the use of informants under the age of eighteen.[14] This reform was prompted by the 1998 gang murder of juvenile informant Chad MacDonald.[15] North Dakota, in the wake of the death of college student Andrew Sadek in 2014, passed "Andrew's Law," which bans the use of informants under sixteen, restricts the use of informants between the ages of sixteen and eighteen, and bars college police from using students as informants.[16] Several state legislatures including Pennsylvania, Minnesota, and Mississippi have introduced legislation that would ban the use of child informants. All states should follow suit. The U.S. Supreme Court has decided that children cannot constitutionally be punished like adults, in part because "juveniles are more vulnerable or susceptible to negative influences and outside pressures."[17] For the same kinds of reasons, law enforcement should not be permitted to use minors as informants.[18]

Immigrants have little or no protection when they are faced with the choice between cooperation or deportation. As described in previous chapters, this lack of regulation has permitted significant coercion, especially of young people, and racial profiling, especially of Muslims. Greater restraint and regulation are needed here as well.

Transgendered individuals face heightened threats when incarcerated and may therefore be more likely to cooperate, even when it is not in their interests to do so. Like other vulnerable classes of people, their special risks should be taken into consideration before they are pressured into cooperating.[19]

Somewhat more attention has been paid to reforming the use of informants with mental illness or a substance use disorder (SUD), which often go hand in hand. Because it is so common to use informants with SUD in drug investigations, regulating their use represents a thorny challenge. Some police rely heavily on the practice, and decreasing their use would require changing some ingrained investigation habits. These habits, however, are worth changing. It is, of course, illegal to provide informants with drugs for personal use, but police routinely provide cash or even drugs to people with SUD, thereby exacerbating the very problem that drug enforcement is supposed to combat. Informants with

SUD have been at the heart of numerous debacles, from the Los Angeles Rampart scandal to the drugs-for-information revelations in Brooklyn. The practice of giving drugs—or cash for drugs—to people who suffer from a substance use disorder should be halted. In the same vein, no one in a drug rehabilitation program should be used as an informant in a way that will threaten their rehabilitation.

Some states and law enforcement institutions already expressly disfavor the use of informants with SUD. Florida's "Rachel's Law" requires police to consider whether the person has a history of substance use before using them as an informant; "Matthew's Law" in Minnesota discourages the use of people in substance use treatment programs.[20]

Other policing institutions have instituted reforms that indirectly reduce reliance on informants with substance use histories. After the Tulia debacle, for example, the Texas legislature and Texas Department of Public Safety established new procedures and performance measures for drug investigations and enforcement. The new performance measures heavily disfavored the arrest of drug users while promoting and rewarding the investigation and arrest of high-level traffickers. In testimony before the U.S. House Judiciary Committee, Deputy Commander Patrick O'Burke of the Texas Department of Public Safety explained the effects of the restructuring. Previously, police performance was measured by arrests, which created incentives to use snitches to produce a high volume of arrests but had little impact on the drug trade. The new performance measures shifted police priorities away from the cultivation and arrest of low-level users and toward higher-level traffickers. O'Burke testified at the time that this shift in priorities permitted police to interdict more drugs even as they conducted fewer arrests.[21]

B. Counsel

Proposal: Provide legal counsel for uncharged suspects who are considering cooperation.

The informal, secretive, one-on-one negotiations between police and suspects are the source of many problems with informant use. Often characterized by unreliability, ongoing criminality, rule-breaking, and coercion, the power struggles and imbalances between suspects and

192 | REGULATION AND REFORM

police are rife with danger and irregularity. The traditional way in which the U.S. criminal system handles such dangers is by giving people a lawyer. This not only reduces the coercive aspects of police pressure but also regularizes the exchange of information and benefits to make it more reliable, fair, and rule-bound. In the wake of the death of Rachel Hoffman—the twenty-three-year-old informant who was killed during a controlled buy—Florida passed Rachel's Law, which requires, among other things, that the government must "[p]rovide a person who is requested to serve as a confidential informant with an opportunity to consult with legal counsel upon request before the person agrees to perform any activities as a confidential informant." Rachel's Law does not require the state to actually provide counsel; it should.[22]

In federal white collar practice, it is already common for the government to provide counsel to uncharged potential cooperators. Because they are not yet charged with a crime, such suspects do not yet have the constitutional right to a lawyer. Nevertheless, as described in chapter 7, U.S. attorneys may inform suspects that they are potential targets of an investigation, or even sometimes ask the court to appoint counsel so that the suspect can discuss his or her options with a lawyer and so the process of cooperation can proceed fairly and smoothly. More broadly, wealthy, well-resourced white collar defendants are likely to have ready access to counsel and thus escape the pressures to make an uninformed decision. Making counsel available to the many cooperating suspects who do not have lawyers would thus improve the fairness and regularity of the process.

To be clear, the realities of street and drug crime differ significantly from white collar investigations, and the interpolation of counsel into the now-routine dynamic between police and suspects would be disruptive. It would mean that, at some point, police could no longer get quick, informal information from suspects who fear arrest or criminal charges. It might mean that fewer suspects would cooperate, and more might end up being charged with crimes. The point at which counsel is made available would have to be early enough to make a difference in the quality of information provided and the fairness of the negotiation, but not so early as to hamstring police in their investigative functions.

Nevertheless, courts, legislatures, and prosecutors' offices should make counsel available to avoid the irregularity, inaccuracy, and unfairness that plague direct negotiations between suspects and the government. The need for counsel is particularly strong for high-risk suspects, for example, vulnerable individuals, those who are being asked to engage in violent or otherwise risky operations, or suspects who the government may ultimately use at a public trial.

C. Witness Protection

Proposal: Strengthen state witness protection programs.

The federal government's Witness Security Program (known as "WITSEC") is the witness protection model for the rest of the country. Affording short- and long-term protection for cooperating witnesses, it is comprehensive and well resourced, having provided protection for thousands of witnesses and their families since 1970.[23] Most state and local law enforcement agencies, however, have few or no such resources.[24] Local witness protection may consist of as little as a couple of nights in a hotel before trial. For informants who live in close proximity to the people against whom they are testifying, such protection is ineffective. Part of informant reform thus requires increased physical protection of testifying informants at the state and local levels along the lines of the federal WITSEC program.

Several states, including Maryland and Massachusetts, have passed additional measures such as increased penalties for witness intimidation. Others have created or beefed up their witness protection programs. The Maryland legislature has also made it easier to introduce into evidence statements made by witnesses who are rendered unavailable due to a defendant's misconduct. In other words, if a witness fails to show up in court, her previous statements made out of court can be used as evidence if the defendant threatened that witness or otherwise rendered her unavailable.[25]

V. Defense Informants

Proposal: Create an independent authority to award cooperation benefits to informants who provide exculpatory information or who testify on behalf of the defense.

The informant market is inherently lopsided: a prosecutor can reward an information source with lenience or money, whereas a defendant who tries to pay or otherwise reward a potential witness will be accused of bribery or witness tampering. As Chief Justice Earl Warren once observed, "if a criminal defendant insinuated his informer into the prosecution's camp in [the same] manner he would be guilty of obstructing justice."[26] Because the government rewards only those informants who provide evidence supporting the government's case, there is a strong disincentive for informants to reveal information that might help the defense, as well as strong incentives to fabricate inculpatory evidence.

To remedy this imbalance, jurisdictions should create a mechanism for rewarding defense informants who possess exculpatory information so they can receive charging or sentencing credit in the same way that government-sponsored informants currently do. For example, the state could create an independent prosecutor whose job is to field such requests. Alternatively, many individual prosecutor offices now maintain conviction integrity units that review their own convictions for error; offices could create comparable, independent internal units to consider defense requests for informant leniency. In a similar vein, Professor George Harris has proposed that potential defense informants should be permitted to apply directly to the court for the status of "cooperating for compensation."[27]

To be sure, rewarding defense informants would have its challenges. Potential informants might be reluctant to disclose information to or negotiate with prosecutors and thus expose themselves to the risk of prosecution or retaliation. Courts cannot award cooperation credit to the same extent that prosecutors can, since judges do not control the filing of criminal charges. The current culture of cooperation is entirely dominated by law enforcement priorities, and it would take work to expand that culture to invite exculpatory evidence.

But such difficulties are logistical, not principled. There needs to be greater parity between the government's ability to pay for information with the most valuable currency—lenience—and the defense's complete inability to access this powerful tool. Defense informants are also an obvious counterbalance to the one-sided incentives currently faced by informants to fabricate inculpatory evidence that helps only the government. Creating a reward mechanism for defense informants would thus advance accuracy and structural equity.

VI. Police Guidelines

Proposal: All police departments should establish comprehensive internal guidelines governing the creation, deployment, reward, protection, and documentation of criminal informants.

The frontline controls on police use of informants are self-regulatory: police departments' internal regulations governing the creation and use of informants.

There are two basic models currently available for police departments crafting internal guidelines: the International Association of Chiefs of Police (IACP) Model Policy, and the FBI's Confidential Informant Guidelines. The IACP Model Policy requires, for example, that police document their proposed informants, obtain supervisor permission before using them, and periodically review their suitability. The policy states that informants are to be arrested when they commit crimes "beyond what is authorized by the agency."[28] In a similar vein, the U.S. Department of Justice has engaged in ongoing revisions of its guidelines for informant use that bind the FBI, DEA, and other federal investigative agencies.[29] Such guidelines reflect DOJ's conclusion that effective informant use requires greater documentation, more internal review, and better-organized relationships among the various authorities that use informants and their information.

Some local police departments already regulate informant use through internal guidelines. They may require documentation and/or prohibit the use of informants who are violent offenders, substance users, juveniles, or who have outstanding warrants. The Las Vegas Police Department, for example, promulgated detailed written guidelines that, among other things, require officers to create informant files; the guidelines also mandate that informants "must be in a position to measurably assist in a present or future investigation" before they can be deployed. In addition, "officers having knowledge of crime committed by an informant must notify their immediate supervisor to report the crimes to the section handling those cases."[30] Similarly, the Deschutes County Sheriff's Office in Oregon discourages the use of juvenile informants and bars the use of mentally ill informants.[31] When I wrote the first edition of this book in 2009, neither the Stanislaus County Sheriff's Office nor the Lake County Sheriff's Department in California had informant policies, even though both used informants in dozens of cases. Today, both offices do.[32] While not all police departments will need guidelines as detailed as the FBI's, all departments should have written guidelines appropriate to their informant use in addition to training for officers to master them.

VII. Prosecutorial Guidelines

Proposal: All prosecutorial offices should establish internal guidelines that control the creation, deployment, reward, protection, and documentation of informants.

The federal government already has various guidelines prescribing the considerations that should go into creating an informant. The official manual for United States Attorneys, for example, which governs federal prosecutorial decisions, states that prosecutors should consider the following factors before entering into a nonprosecution agreement with a cooperating defendant:

1. The importance of the investigation or prosecution to an effective program of law enforcement, or consideration of other national security or governmental interests;
2. The value of the person's cooperation to the investigation or prosecution;
3. The person's relative culpability in connection with the offense or offenses being investigated or prosecuted and his/her history with respect to criminal activity; and
4. The interests of any victims.[33]

As described in detail in chapter 7, in prosecuting corporate crime the Department of Justice follows the Filip Memo and Yates Memo, which prescribe internal rules for entering into deferred prosecution agreements.

In 2008, the American Bar Association (ABA) approved new standards for prosecutorial investigations. Although they are not binding on any particular office, the legal profession often follows ABA standards, and the Supreme Court routinely cites them as guidance in determining best practices or ethical rules. These new standards contain ten factors that prosecutors should consider in "deciding whether to offer a cooperator significant benefits, including a limit on criminal liability, immunity, or a recommendation for reduction of sentence." Those factors include whether "the cooperator has biases or personal motives that might result in false, incomplete, or misleading information"; whether "leniency or immunity for the criminal activity of the cooperator is warranted by the goals of the investigation and the public interest, including appropriate consideration for victim(s) interests"; and whether "providing leniency, immunity or other benefits would be seen as offensive by the public or cause a reasonable juror to doubt the veracity of the cooperator's testimony."[34]

Once prosecutors decide to enter into an informant deal, the office should have guidelines to regulate how such cooperators can be deployed and what sorts of information should be obtained. Prosecutor offices should also maintain data systems to keep track of informants, the cases they are involved in, the deals they make, and the offenses they commit. Several states, including Connecticut, Nebraska, Oklahoma, and Texas, now require all state prosecutors to maintain data on and to track their use of jailhouse informants.[35]

Prosecutorial guidelines are primarily a matter of internal self-regulation. While state and local prosecutor offices have widely varying approaches to informants, their policies—where they exist—are typically not publicly accessible. In response to a 2006 public records request made by the ACLU, for example, forty-seven California prosecutor offices declined to provide information regarding informant policies.[36] Moreover, such internal regulatory policies are not enforceable by outsiders. In other words, there is no legal remedy for the violation of such regulations or guidelines, except internal disciplinary actions that might follow. Nevertheless, such guidelines and internal rules are crucial to improving informant practices, since so much of informant use is delegated to the discretion and judgment of such law enforcement actors.[37]

VIII. Heightened Judicial Scrutiny

Proposal: Courts should exercise their existing supervisory
authority to improve accuracy and fairness in informant
practices.

Although informant practices are largely a function of the executive
branch, the judiciary has a great deal of influence in this arena. Presiding over warrant requests, motions, pleas, trials, and sentencing, judicial
officers oversee crucial aspects of the informant process. While specific
procedural reforms are proposed below, there is a general need for
courts to take their oversight role more seriously.

For example, magistrate judges issuing warrants based on allegations
from informants should stop accepting boilerplate assertions of reliability and the need for anonymity. Rather, magistrates should require specific facts from police to establish the reliability of their sources. Judges
should also halt the widespread practice of issuing warrants without
asking police to produce the live informant. While informants need not
appear in every case, the current expectation that police will never have
to produce an actual snitch in court contributes to the culture of the
invisible informant who can be switched around or even fabricated, a
culture tragically illustrated by Kathryn Johnston's death. The realistic
possibility that a judge might demand to meet the informant, even once
in a while, would help prevent such practices.

Trial judges should vet informants under their inherent authority to
screen unreliable or prejudicial witnesses. Although the establishment
of a formal, informant-specific "reliability hearing" process is proposed
below, trial judges already have the authority to hold pretrial hearings:
to screen out unfair, harmful, or prejudicial evidence and to establish
"whether a witness is qualified";[38] where it appears that the probative
value of an informant witness might be "substantially outweighed by the
danger of . . . unfair prejudice, confusing the issues, or misleading the
jury";[39] or, more generally, "if justice so requires."[40]

At sentencing, courts should strive for more transparency and consistency in the awarding of cooperation credit so that the bases for rewards are more clearly visible and so that like defendants are treated

alike. Federal cooperation sentencing departures currently reflect racial disparities for which judges are largely responsible.[41] While prosecutors still retain primary authority to make charging decisions and to recommend sentencing credit, trial courts have the opportunity to establish fairer and more evenhanded approaches to the question of sentence reduction.

IX. Criminal Procedure Reforms

Over half of all states have now considered or engaged in some type of legislative informant reform. The dominant categories include heightened discovery and disclosure rules, data collection and tracking requirements, reliability hearings, cautionary jury instructions, notification to victims of informants when those informants receive sentencing leniency, and increased protections for vulnerable classes of informants.

This section discusses a subset of those reforms aimed at strengthening the adjudicatory process: discovery, reliability hearings, corroboration requirements, and jury instructions. They are crucial tools in the effort to reduce wrongful conviction and to increase fairness to defendants who face allegations from compensated informant witnesses. However, because trials constitute such a small proportion of U.S. criminal dockets—on the order of 5 percent—such reforms can only ever represent only one piece in the reform puzzle. The larger informal penal market in information and leniency requires greater regulation and transparency whether or not defendants happen to go to trial, and those kinds of broader regulatory proposals are discussed above. To be sure, important regulatory effects will flow from the threat of trial-based disclosures and hearings, since police, prosecutors, and defense attorneys often operate in the shadow of trial.[42] But in a world where trials are rare, such protections are necessary but not sufficient to bring the informant market into better compliance with legal and democratic norms.

A. Tracking, Discovery, and Disclosure

Proposal: Prosecutors should collect and disclose to defendants all pertinent impeachment information regarding
criminal informants used in the case, prior to the entry of
any guilty plea or the beginning of a trial.

An increasing number of jurisdictions have passed heightened tracking and discovery requirements for informants whom the government
intends to use as witnesses. Sometimes these requirements are limited
to jailhouse informants; sometimes they include all potential witnesses
providing information in exchange for a benefit. Connecticut and
Nebraska, for example, require prosecutors to track the use of their
informants and to put the data in a statewide database.[43] The statutory
language regarding jailhouse informants below is from Connecticut,
and Florida, Illinois, Maryland, Minnesota, Nebraska, Oklahoma, Texas,
and Washington have all passed comparable laws.[44] These laws require
prosecutors to collect and disclose:

(1) The complete criminal history of any such jailhouse witness, including
   any charges pending against such witness, or which were reduced or
   dismissed as part of a plea bargain;
(2) The jailhouse witness's cooperation agreement with the prosecutorial official and any benefit that the official has provided, offered or may offer
   in the future to any such jailhouse witness;
(3) The substance, time and place of any statement allegedly given by the
   defendant to a jailhouse witness, and the substance, time and place of
   any statement given by a jailhouse witness implicating the defendant
   in an offense for which the defendant is indicted;
(4) Whether at any time the jailhouse witness recanted any testimony subject
   to the disclosure and, if so, the time and place of the recantation, the
   nature of the recantation and the name of any person present at the
   recantation; and
(5) Information concerning any other criminal prosecution in which the jailhouse witness testified, or offered to testify, against a person suspected
   as the perpetrator of an offense or defendant with whom the jailhouse
   witness was imprisoned or otherwise confined, including any coop-

eration agreement with a prosecutorial official or any benefit provided or offered to such witness by a prosecutorial official.[45]

Sometimes these discovery reforms apply only when the state intends to use the informant as a trial witness, that is to say, in a small subset of cases. Such disclosures, however, should be routinely made in all cases, regardless of whether the defendant goes to trial. Specifically, legislatures should ensure that all defendants receive comprehensive impeachment material to be considered during plea negotiations. This would reduce the temptation for the government to use the plea process to hide information about informants, particularly when they are demonstrably unreliable or have committed additional bad acts. It is also fairer to defendants because it permits more fully informed plea decisions. Finally, such a requirement would increase general transparency by disclosing the use of informants in cases resolved by guilty plea, namely, the overwhelming majority of U.S. cases.

B. Reliability Hearings

Proposal: Upon a defendant's request, courts should hold a
pretrial reliability hearing requiring the government to establish the reliability of any informant witness or statements
made by that informant.

A powerful mechanism for increasing informant reliability is to give courts a greater role in screening such witnesses and their information before they ever get to the jury. Requiring courts to establish the reliability of informant witnesses can prevent wrongful convictions, increase fairness to defendants, and provide better oversight of the use of unreliable criminal witnesses.

Several states now require reliability hearings in one form or another. Illinois was an early leader and has mandated reliability hearings for jailhouse snitch witnesses since 2003.[46] Connecticut requires reliability hearings in all murder and rape cases. Oklahoma and Nevada courts have also required reliability hearings.[47] Reliability hearings have been legislatively proposed in Colorado, Kansas, Massachusetts, Mississippi, Montana, North Carolina, Pennsylvania, and Washington.

Courts have long performed this kind of gatekeeping function when it comes to expert witnesses, holding hearings to determine whether such witnesses are sufficiently reliable to be permitted to testify. As the Supreme Court explained in *Daubert v. Merrell Dow*: "Expert evidence can be both powerful and quite misleading because of the difficulty in evaluating it."[48] Jurors are less effective than courts at screening out technical or specialized testimony, in part because experts carry a powerful aura of knowledge that can be particularly persuasive. Courts therefore step in to screen such witnesses to avoid confusing and misleading jurors and to ensure fair and accurate trials.

Informant reliability hearings proceed on the same premise. Informants resemble experts in that they purport to know things that others do not know, and they have an aura of special—albeit criminal— knowledge that is highly influential with juries.[49] In addition, courts are better positioned to evaluate informant reliability because judges understand the incentive structures of the criminal system and will be more familiar with the tendencies of such witnesses to lie.

As Professor Harris points out, there are other similarities between informant and expert witnesses.[50] Both are "paid" by one party, which makes them more one-sided than the typical witness. Their testimony is coached and prepared by the side that calls them, making them more difficult to cross-examine. Moreover, where theirs is the central evidence against the defendant, informants' stories are hard to corroborate or contradict. This makes their testimony even more difficult to challenge on cross-examination, particularly since their own lives or liberty hang in the balance. Having courts scrutinize these witnesses outside the presence of the jury would alleviate many of these problems.

C. Corroboration

Proposal: All information from compensated criminal informants should be strongly corroborated. Corroboration should not come from another compensated criminal informant.

Corroboration requirements have deep roots. Under biblical law and English common law tradition, the "two witness" rule prohibited conviction on the basis of a single witness. In the United States, at least fifteen states require corroboration for accomplices. Such rules also affect informants because accomplices often become key witnesses against each other in exchange for lenience.[51]

In 1999, in Tulia, Texas, an undercover narcotics agent falsely charged dozens of African American residents with drug dealing, charging approximately 16 percent of the town's Black population. With no corroboration or physical evidence, the government obtained numerous convictions and guilty pleas. Governor Rick Perry eventually pardoned the Tulia residents, but only after many of them had already served four years in prison. The agent, Tom Coleman, was eventually convicted of perjury.[52]

In the wake of the Tulia scandal, Texas passed legislation requiring corroboration for all undercover drug operatives who are not themselves police officers. The law reads as follows:

(a) A defendant may not be convicted of [a drug] offense . . . on the testimony of a person who is not a licensed peace officer or a special investigator but who is acting covertly on behalf of a law enforcement agency or under the color of law enforcement unless the testimony is corroborated by other evidence tending to connect the defendant with the offense committed. (b) Corroboration is not sufficient for the purposes of this article if the corroboration only shows the commission of the offense.[53]

In 2005, federal legislation was introduced titled "No More Tulias: Drug Law Enforcement Evidentiary Standards Improvement Act." Among other things, the bill would have established that no person could be convicted of a drug offense on the basis of the uncorroborated testimony of a single law enforcement officer or an informant working on behalf of law enforcement.[54]

There is a robust national consensus that corroboration should be required for all jailhouse snitches. The American Bar Association voted in 2005 to urge all states to require corroboration for jailhouse informant testimony.[55] Likewise, in its 2007 policy review, the Washington, D.C.–based Justice Project recommended that all states adopt a jailhouse informant corroboration requirement. Pursuant to the recommendation of the California Commission on the Fair Administration of Justice, California now requires corroboration for in-custody informant witnesses. Moreover, that corroboration cannot come from another jailhouse snitch. In response to the well-known problem of jailhouse informant collusion, California law specifically states that "[c]orroboration of an in-custody informant shall not be provided by the testimony of another in-custody informant unless the party calling the in-custody informant as a witness establishes by a preponderance of the evidence that the in-custody informant has not communicated with another in-custody informant on the subject of the testimony."[56]

D. Jury Instructions

Proposal: Whenever a criminal informant testifies at trial,
the jury should be instructed to be especially cautious
before believing that testimony and warned to be suspicious
of witnesses who anticipate or receive benefits for their
cooperation.

Some states handle the problem of informant unreliability by giving the jury special instructions. A typical instruction regarding jailhouse informants, this one from California, reads as follows:

> The testimony of an in-custody informant should be viewed with caution and close scrutiny. In evaluating this testimony, you should consider the extent to which it may have been influenced by the receipt of, or expectation of, any benefits from the party calling that witness. This does not mean that you may arbitrarily disregard this testimony, but you should give it the weight to which you find it to be entitled in the light of all the evidence in this case.[57]

Other jurisdictions requiring such instructions include Connecticut, Colorado, Illinois, Montana, Ohio, Oklahoma, Utah, and Wisconsin.[58]

Jury instructions are a classic and crucial vehicle for shaping verdicts. Because jurors are the ultimate fact-finders in criminal trials, charged with the task of evaluating witness credibility and figuring out what "really" happened, their evaluation of informant testimony is central to the criminal process. For this reason, the Justice Project recommends that all states adopt jury instructions warning jurors of the special unreliability of jailhouse informants.[59]

While necessary, however, jury instructions are not enough to weed out lying informants. As described in chapter 3, research has cast doubt on the efficacy of jury instructions, demonstrating that jurors often find them confusing or counterintuitive and that jurors often do not apply instructions properly.[60] Psychological research also indicates that jury instructions alone are insufficient to overcome jurors' natural propensities to believe informant testimony.

Such research tells us that merely giving jurors information about informant rewards and instructing them to be wary of informant testimony are not effective safeguards against lying informants. Indeed, in the dozens of wrongful capital conviction cases studied in the Northwestern University Law School report, in each case jurors believed informant testimony, even though they were often aware that the informant was being rewarded.[61] Although jury instructions are important, they are not enough.

X. Improving Police-Community Trust

No discussion of informant reform would be complete without acknowledging the historic rift between police and communities of color that has fueled old controversies over snitching as well as outrage and protest over police violence. To state the obvious, improving trust between the police and low-income, heavily policed communities of color is a challenge that goes far beyond the problem of snitching. Indeed, it is a racial, economic, and social challenge that goes beyond law enforcement itself.[62] But informants are an important part of the trust conundrum. Procedural justice theories assert that community trust in police turns heavily on people's perceptions of the fairness of policing practices.[63] Community policing—through which many police departments endeavor to improve ties with the neighborhoods they patrol—is centrally about building trust.[64] Informant deals violate that trust. They represent a form of police surveillance that exploits and undermines personal, family, and community networks.[65] They tolerate ongoing informant crime in the very communities suffering from violence and personal insecurity. At the same time, informant deals devalue the moral weight of crime by commodifying it, trading away liability in exchange for information. This moral instrumentalism is a slap in the face to communities decimated by intrusive policing, long sentences, and decades of mass incarceration. Or as my young Baltimore student summed it up with so much disgust, "all they have to do is snitch and they can keep on dealing."

As the wide-ranging proposals in this chapter indicate, informant reform is an ambitious task potentially spanning the entire criminal process. When I published the first edition of this book, the drive for reform was relatively new. Today, the universe of possibilities is substantial and growing. Recent developments, and the ever-increasing attention to the problems of informant use and criminal justice writ large, indicate that this vital public debate will continue to flourish.

Conclusion

Russell[1] sat next to me at counsel table, polite and quiet, waiting for his arraignment to begin. We had just met in the courthouse lockup, and as his newly appointed public defender I was puzzled by his case. On the one hand, it looked relatively simple. Russell was charged with being a felon in possession of a gun, a common federal offense. On the other hand, it was an old state case that had been hastily transferred to federal court, and before I had even met my client, the prosecutor had rushed up to me in the courthouse hallway waving an already-drafted plea agreement, offering significant concessions if Russell would just hurry up and sign.

I only had a brief chance to ask Russell for his thoughts, but he just shrugged his shoulders. I guessed that his reticence might be due to his manic depression; he had been incarcerated and without his medication for a few days. As I sat musing over the situation, I felt Russell perk up in his seat. I turned, hoping for more insight, but he wasn't looking at me.

"Bobby!" he cried out, swiveling his body toward the police officer who had just entered the courtroom. As Bobby headed for our table, Russell rose to meet him, waving his hands. "How could you do this to me? You know I didn't have nothin' to do with that gun!"

I quickly reached for Russell's arm, reminding him in urgent tones that he shouldn't discuss his case with the government's agent. Russell ignored me.

The officer shook his head sadly. "I'm sorry, Russell, I know. I just needed you for this case."

Russell struck his thigh in frustration. "You know I would'a testified! You know I would'a done that for you. You didn't have to go and ARREST me!"

Bobby looked apologetic. "I'm sorry, man, I had to be sure." He jerked his head toward the prosecutor sitting across the room. "They made me do it this way." The two men stood in silence for a moment. "How's Monica and the kids?" Russell had five children; his wife was pregnant with their sixth.

Russell sighed. "They're alright. But they're scared now. Can you at least go check on 'em?"

Bobby grasped Russell's shoulder. "I will, man, I promise." Satisfied for the moment, Russell slumped back down in his seat as Bobby walked over to the prosecution table.[2]

From 2000 through 2003, I worked as an assistant federal public defender in Baltimore. Nothing in my law school education prepared me for the informant market. The omnipresent possibility of an informant deal reshaped my cases, it upended my role as defense counsel, and it sidelined all the legal rules and procedures that I had so painstakingly learned. At the same time, living and working in Baltimore, I could see for myself how informant practices shaped and distorted the community, changing residents' relationships to police and to each other. Many of these dynamics, moreover, were invisible from the outside. The kids in my neighborhood knew things about the informant market that I hadn't known, and my clients knew more about the realities of cooperation than many attorneys. Ever since then, as a professor and a scholar, I have been thinking about how much informant use impacts our criminal system and our democracy, even as it is largely hidden from view.[3] This book is the product of that thinking and those lessons from years ago.

I have come to understand the American snitching phenomenon as antithetical to basic principles of public, law-bound, evenhanded justice. The informant market is the wild child of plea bargaining, an extreme example of the deregulated wheeling and dealing that characterizes the bulk of the American criminal process. Plea bargaining itself has well-known risks and inequities, and informant deals ratchet them up. Facts and evidence are negotiable, which puts the innocent at risk and creates loopholes for the guilty. Crucial decisions about guilt and punishment are made in secret and off the record, which means that the public will never learn about the concrete ways in which the state wields its penal authority. The rich and powerful fare better than the poor and vulnerable, which, because the criminal system is full of poor, vulnerable people, is a recipe for inequality and injustice.

Nowhere are the governance implications of the informant market greater than in the disadvantaged communities of color in which the practice is most concentrated and least regulated. As we saw in chapter

6, the confluence of heavy drug enforcement and high rates of criminal-system involvement suggest that many people in these neighborhoods are cooperating or under pressure to cooperate with police. This means that some level of ongoing informant crime—and therefore victimization—is tolerated. It means that police rely on criminal suspects to make decisions about whose home to enter and which people to arrest. It means that residents, even the very young, know that some criminal actors get to act with impunity. And it means that the police are all too often perceived not as guardians of law and safety but as dealmakers who dispense justice on contingent, operational grounds. In neighborhoods with long histories of police-community tension, such disrespectful and inegalitarian tactics add fuel to long-simmering fires.[4] It is also bitterly ironic: snitching erodes the principled legitimacy of the criminal system in precisely those spaces where that system operates most harshly and destroys the lives of the most people.

For all these kinds of reasons, informant use should be understood not merely as a problematic criminal practice but broadly as a modern governance challenge. Short of the military, our criminal system is the most coercive, violent arm of the democratic state. It possesses extraordinary powers, including the authority to search our homes, our bodies, and our email; to stop us on the street and in our cars; to lock us up; and even to shoot at us.

In exchange for all this extraordinary authority, we ask the criminal system to make some basic promises. It must promise to go after people who have committed crimes, and only those people. As the philosopher Michael Walzer once explained, when we punish "it is critically important that we find the right people, that we put the mark of Cain *on Cain*."[5] The system must also promise to protect and vindicate the interests of victims.[6] And it must promise to do all this according to law, based on the legal rules and principles of criminal justice. Or as the Supreme Court wrote in *Marbury v. Madison* in 1803, ours should be "a government of laws, and not of men."[7]

The American criminal system is already infamous for breaking these basic promises. All too often it convicts the innocent. All too often it leaves victims unprotected. And all too often it makes coercive, punitive decisions based on money or politics or race.[8] But the informant market takes this promise-breaking to new heights. It affirmatively rewards criminals, sometimes the most culpable. It affirmatively creates new victims while intentionally choosing not to vindicate existing ones. And it openly throws legal rules, processes, and principles out the window. Such compromises, we are told, are necessary to convict other people for other crimes. But as the many stories in this book reveal, informant deals often punish the wrong people for the wrong things in ways that undermine public safety. This is the means-ends calculation, after all, that sacrificed Kathryn Johnston to the operational habits of local Atlanta drug enforcement. It is the means-ends calculation that permits serious offenders who have stolen millions of dollars or even killed multiple people to keep their freedom while people who have committed far less serious crimes remain in prison. And it is the means-ends calculation that permits drug dealers to remain on street corners where twelve-year-olds can watch them work.

The law enforcement gains from informant use thus come at a terrible normative cost to the integrity and legitimacy of the entire criminal ecosystem. While there may be individual cases where the trade-offs look acceptable, they should not be viewed in isolation: they do not account for the systemic social and institutional harms that flow from the practice. By letting the unregulated informant market run wild for this long, we have sacrificed too much. It is time to recalculate the normative math of informant use and to make better-informed, more rigorous decisions about the trade-offs that it inherently demands.

Such goals are especially realistic today because we live in such a fertile time of criminal justice change. To put it mildly, a lot has happened since this book was first published in 2009. Mass incarceration has been widely discredited as expensive, ineffective, and unfair. The police murder of George Floyd and the vitality of the Black Lives Matter movement have irrevocably elevated the issue of systemic racism in the public consciousness. But old habits die hard, and the informant market is a persistent holdover from mass incarceration culture. At its worst, it reflects an instrumental, dehumanizing mindset that prizes the short game of conviction over the long game of public safety and public faith in the criminal process. Regulating and restraining this market is thus not only an opportunity to improve the criminal apparatus. It is a chance to bring our criminal justice culture into better conformity with modern principles of equal justice and democratic accountability.

ACKNOWLEDGMENTS

When I wrote the first edition of this book in 2009, criminal informant use was a relatively obscure topic. Through the efforts of many, it now occupies an important place in the national conversation around criminal reform. I am deeply grateful to the legislators, attorneys, advocates, scholars, artists, journalists, and families with whom I have worked and who have taken up this issue. I learned an enormous amount from them; their insights are reflected throughout this second edition.

I have been honored to receive many letters from people in prison who told me that the book resonated with them and helped them to better understand their own experiences with the criminal system. I hope this second edition is equally helpful.

My thanks to all the educational institutions that have supported my work along the way, including Loyola Law School, Los Angeles, U.C. Irvine School of Law, and Harvard Law School. Special thanks to New York University Press for believing in this book for so many years and for having the chutzpah to put a rat on the cover. My partner Charles makes my work better in more ways than I can explain. As it was and always will be, this book is dedicated to my son Raphael.

NOTES

FOREWORD

1 "Informing Justice," Innocence Project, https://innocenceproject.org/informing-injustice.

2 Center on Wrongful Convictions, *The Snitch System* (Northwestern Univ. Law School, 2009), www.innocenceproject.org/wp-content/uploads/2016/02/Snitch-SystemBooklet.pdf.

3 *Report of the Independent Panel to Examine the Conviction and Sentence of Myon Burrell* (New York: Innocence Project, Dec. 2020), Appendix 2, https://innocenceproject.org/independent-panel-of-legal-experts-call-on-new-minnesota-cru-to-investigate-myon-burrells-2002-conviction.

INTRODUCTION

1 This narrative is drawn from events initially reported in the *Atlanta Journal-Constitution* and then in the *New York Times*. See Rhonda Cook, "Chain of Lies Led to Botched Raid: Feds detail woman's death, officers' plea," *Atlanta Journal-Constitution*, Apr. 27, 2007, at 1D; Bill Torpy, "Report Says Pot Bust Led to Raid: Suspected dealer told cops there was cocaine in slain woman's home," *Atlanta Journal-Constitution*, Dec. 8, 2006, at 1A; Ted Conover, "A Snitch's Dilemma," *N.Y. Times Magazine*, June 29, 2012.

2 Sarah Stillman, "The Throwaways," *New Yorker*, Aug. 27, 2012.

3 Nathan Levy, "Bringing Justice to Hearne," *Texas Observer*, Apr. 29, 2005; Wade Goodwyn, "Controversy over Federally Funded Regional Drug Task Forces in Texas," *All Things Considered*, National Public Radio, Nov. 4, 2002; Tim Carman & Steve McVicker, "Drug Crazed: Millions in federal tax dollars are being spent by narcotics task forces in Texas to nab low level users and dealers: Is this any way to wage a drug war?" *Dallas Observer*, Sept. 6, 2001. The film *American Violet* (Samuel Goldwyn Films, 2008) was based on Regina Kelly's story.

4 Travis Dorman, "Pills and lies in Grundy County: Was a Tennessee couple framed by police?" *Knoxville News Sentinel*, Mar. 12, 2020.

5 Matt Ferner, "A Mass Shooting Tore Their Lives Apart. A Corruption Scandal Crushed Their Hopes For Justice," *Huffington Post*, Mar. 9, 2018; see also Ted Rohrlich, "Miranda 'loophole': CA police use gang enforcers to win cellmate confessions," *Injustice Watch*, May 24, 2018.

6 Mathew R. Warren, "Whitewashing a Cartoon Rat's Message on Snitching," *N.Y. Times*, July 18, 2008, at B2.

7   See chapter 7.

8   Alexander v. DeAngelo, 329 F.3d 912, 914–15 (7th Cir. 2003).

9   Rebecca Spence, "Case of Informant Reverberates Through L.A.'s Orthodox Community," *The Forward*, Jan. 23, 2008.

10 Rahel Gebreyes, "Former FBI Informant Craig Monteilh: FBI Encouraged Me To Sleep With Muslim Women For Intel," *Huffington Post*, Mar. 4, 2015; Paul Harris, "The ex-FBI informant with a change of heart: 'There is no real hunt. It's fixed,'" *The Guardian*, Mar. 20, 2012. See also Fazaga v. Fed. Bureau of Investigation, 965 F.3d 1015, 1025, 1226 (9th Cir. 2020), rev'd, Fed. Bureau of Investigation v. Fazaga, No. 20-828, 595 U.S. __ (Mar. 4, 2022).

11 *A Tale of Two Countries: Racially Targeted Arrests in the Era of Marijuana Reform* (Washington, D.C.: ACLU, 2020), 5, 21; Ryan S. King, "Disparity by Geography: The War on Drugs in America's Cities" (Washington, D.C.: The Sentencing Project, 2008), 2, 10–11, www.sentencingproject.org. See chapter 6.

12 Laurence A. Benner, "Racial Disparity in Narcotics Search Warrants," 6 *J. Gender, Race & Just.* 183, 190–91, 196, 200–201 (2002).

13 See Benjamin Justice & Tracey L. Meares, "How the Criminal Justice System Educates Citizens," 651 *Annals Am. Acad. Pol. & Soc. Sci.* 159 (2014).

14 Elizabeth Hinton, *From the War on Poverty to the War on Crime: The Making of Mass Incarceration in America* (Cambridge: Harvard University Press, 2016); Loïc Wacquant, *Punishing the Poor: The Neoliberal Government of Social Insecurity* (Durham: Duke University Press, 2009); Jonathan Simon, *Governing Through Crime: How the War on Crime Transformed American Democracy and Created a Culture of Fear* (New York: Oxford University Press, 2007).

15 See Hinton, at 1; Wacquant, at 195–208; David Cole, *No Equal Justice: Race and Class in the American Criminal Justice System* (New York: New Press, 1999), 4–9. The disparate treatment of African Americans in particular is discussed in more depth in chapter 6.

16 See chapter 4.

17 Rob Warden, "The Snitch System: How Snitch Testimony Sent Randy Steidl and Other Innocent Americans to Death Row," Center on Wrongful Convictions, Northwestern University School of Law, 2004, www.law.northwestern.edu/wrongfulconvictions.

18 Samuel Gross & Kaitlin Jackson, "Snitch Watch," National Registry of Exonerations, May 13, 2015, www.law.umich.edu/special/exoneration/Pages/Features.Snitch. Watch.aspx.

19 Pamela Colloff, How This Con Man's Wild Testimony Sent Dozens to Jail, and 4 to Death Row, *N.Y. Times Magazine*, Dec. 4, 2019.

20 "Privilege," *In the Dark*, Episode 5, Season 2 (2019), www.apmreports.org/episode/2018/05/22/in-the-dark-s2e5; Flowers v. Mississippi, 139 S. Ct. 2228 (2019); Parker Yesko, "It's Over: Charges against Curtis Flowers are dropped," APM Reports, September 4, 2020.

21 Stillman, "The Throwaways"; "Young people are going undercover in the war on drugs," *60 Minutes*, Dec. 6, 2015.

22 Eric Bosco and Kayla Marchetti, "UMass police helped keep student's addiction secret," Boston Globe, Sept. 28, 2014.

23 State Court Caseload Digest 2018 Data, Court Statistics Project, Nat'l Ctr. for State Courts, 2018, at 14; *Sourcebook of Criminal Justice Statistics Online*, tbls. 5.44.2004 & 5.24.2006, Bureau of Justice Statistics, U.S. Dep't of Justice (2006), www.albany. edu/sourcebook (hereinafter "Sourcebook Online").

24 National Institute on Drug Abuse, "Words Matter—Terms to Use and Avoid When Talking About Addiction," Nat'l Institutes of Health, Washington D.C., www.drugabuse.gov/nidamed-medical-health-professionals/health-professions-education/words-matter-terms-to-use-avoid-when-talking-about-addiction. See also Akiba Solomon, "What Words We Use—and Avoid—When Covering People and Incarceration," *The Marshall Project*, Apr. 12, 2021.

1. THE REAL DEAL

1 Richard Rosenfeld, Bruce Jacobs & Richard Wright, "Snitching and the Code of the Street," 43 *Brit. J. Criminol.* 291, 303 (2003).

2 In practice, most crimes go unreported to police, and most reported crimes do not lead to arrest. Lynn Langston et al., "Victimizations Not Reported to the Police, 2006–2010," Bureau of Justice Statistics, U.S. Dep't of Justice, Aug. 2012 (finding that 52% of violent victimizations—over 3 million annually—were not reported to police and 67% of household theft crimes were not reported); Federal Bureau Investigation, tbl. 25, "Crime in the United States, 2019," https://ucr.fbi.gov/crime-in-the-u.s/2019/crime-in-the-u.s.-2019/topic-pages/tables/table-25 (reporting clearance rate for violent crimes reported to the police as 45.5% and clearance rate for property crimes as 17.2%).

3 See Stephanos Bibas, "Transparency and Participation in Criminal Procedure," 81 *N.Y.U. L. Rev.* 911, 923–24 (2006) (describing the secretive, off-the-record quality of plea bargaining).

4 Jaxon Van Derbeken, "Informant in Officer's Slaying, Gang Killings Was Repeatedly Freed to Pursue Life of Crime," *S.F. Chronicle*, Aug. 13, 2006.

5 Brian Day, "Four held in 2001 slaying of Whittier girl," *San Gabriel Valley Tribune*, June 28, 2012; "FBI tells of informant shooting," *Omaha World-Herald*, June 7, 2011.

6 United States v. Singleton, 144 F.3d 1343, 1347, rev'd en banc, 165 F.3d 1297 (10th Cir. 1999).

7 Graham Hughes, "Agreements for Cooperation in Criminal Cases," 45 *Vand. L. Rev.* 1, 3 (1992).

8 Dennis G. Fitzgerald, *Informants and Undercover Investigations: A Practical Guide to Law, Policy, and Procedure* (Boca Raton, FL: CRC Press, 2007), 45.

9 Stephen L. Mallory, *Informants: Development and Management* (Incline Village, NV: Copperhouse Publishing, 2000), 23.

10 Fitzgerald, *Informants and Undercover Investigations*, at 57.

11 Dan Herbeck and Michael Beebe, "Walking thin line in Village of Attica: Would-be informant says police coerced her into cooperation," *Buffalo News*, Nov. 8, 2009; Dan Herbeck and Michael Beebe, "Deal leaves informant fearing retribution Attica police accused of reneging on pledge," *Buffalo News*, Nov. 15, 2009; see also Erin McLaughlin, "Cops Use Traffic Tix to Force Woman Into Drug Buys, Lawyer Claims," ABC News, Sept. 26, 2012.

12 Mallory, *Informants*, at 18–19.

13 Id. at 52.

14 Id. at 42–43.

15 John Madinger, *Confidential Informant: Law Enforcement's Most Valuable Tool* (Boca Raton, FL: CRC Press, 2000), 122.

16 Id. at 168.

17 Ellen Yaroshefsky, "Cooperation with Federal Prosecutors: Experiences of Truth Telling and Embellishment," 68 *Fordham L. Rev.* 917, 952–56 (1999).

18 Kurt Eichenwald & Alexei Barrionuevo, "The Enron Verdict: The overview: Tough justice for executives in Enron era," *N.Y. Times*, May 27, 2006, at A1; Associated Press, "Lea Fastow Gets a Year in Enron Plea," *N.Y. Times*, May 7, 2004, at C1; Opinion, "A Family Pleads Guilty," *N.Y. Times*, Jan. 15, 2004.

19 Fitzgerald, *Informants and Undercover Investigations*, at 37.

20 See Stanley Z. Fisher, "'Just the Facts, Ma'am': Lying and the Omission of Exculpatory Evidence in Police Reports," 28 *New England L. Rev.* 1, 36 & n.179 (1993) (describing Chicago and New York "double file" systems in which police maintained two sets of reports and gave only the public versions to prosecutors).

21 Fitzgerald, *Informants and Undercover Investigations*, at 46.

22 Anna Clark, "He Was Wrongly Imprisoned for 25 Years. It Wasn't DNA Evidence That Got Him Out," *The New Republic*, Apr. 22, 2020; Aaron Miguel Cantú, "Ring of Snitches: How Detroit Police Slapped False Murder Convictions on Young Black Men," *TruthOut*, Mar. 31, 2015.

23 Daniel Richman, "Prosecutors and Their Agents, Agents and Their Prosecutors," 103 *Columbia L. Rev.* 749, 789 (2003).

24 See Massiah v. United States, 377 U.S. 201 (1964); Miranda v. Arizona, 384 U.S. 436 (1966); George C. Thomas & Richard A. Leo, "The Effect of *Miranda v. Arizona*: 'Embedded' in Our National Culture?" 29 *Crime & Justice* 203, 244 (2002) (at least 80 percent of suspects waive their Miranda rights and talk to police).

25 Fitzgerald, *Informants and Undercover Investigations*, at 46.

26 John G. Douglass, "Jimmy Hoffa's Revenge: White Collar Rights under the McDade Amendment," 11 *Wm. & Mary Bill of Rts. J.* 123, 124–25 (2002).

27 Michael S. Schmidt & Duff Wilson, "Prosecutors in Balco Case Turn to Wife of Trainer," *N.Y. Times*, June 20, 2008, at D1. See Sample Target Letter, United States Attorneys' Manual (U.S.A.M.) § 9, Criminal Resource Manual, at 160 (1997), www.usdoj.gov/usao/eousa/foia_reading_room/usam/title9/crm00160.htm.

28 Daniel Richman, "Cooperating Clients," 56 *Ohio St. L.J.* 69, 74 (1995).

29 See chapters 6 and 7.

30 See introduction.

31 Jay Atkinson, "Snitch: When cops trust a pair of criminals to help catch a major heroin dealer, it reveals the tangled relationship between police and confidential informants," *Boston Globe*, Aug. 20, 2006.

32 See chapter 2.

33 Michael D. Sorkin & Phyllis Brasch Librach, "Top U.S. Drug Snitch Is a Legend and a Liar," *St. Louis Post-Dispatch*, Jan. 16, 2006, at A1.

34 Mark Curriden, "The Informant Trap: Secret threat to justice," *Nat'l L. J.*, Feb. 20, 1995, at 2; see also Fitzgerald, *Informants and Undercover Investigations*, at 22, 63–74.

35 Rhonda Cook, "Chain of Lies Led to Botched Raid," *Atlanta Journal-Constitution*, Apr. 27, 2007, at D1; Beth Warren, "Kathryn Johnston Shooting: Informant hiding out, plans to sue city, police," *Atlanta Journal-Constitution*, Apr. 28, 2007, at 1B.

36 John Tucker, "Durham Police bonus payments to informants could violate defendants' rights," *IndyWeek*, Mar. 12, 2014.

37 Matthew Dolan, "Officers in Corruption Case Guilty of Gun, Drug Charges," *Baltimore Sun*, Apr. 8, 2006, at 1B.

38 Patrick McGreevy, "Case Not Closed Yet for LAPD: Despite progress since the Rampart scandal, the department still falls short of goals that would end U.S. oversight," *L.A. Times*, Apr. 20, 2006, at 1; Andrew Blankstein, "LAPD Eases Rules on Street Sources," *L.A. Times*, Aug. 13, 2005, at 4; Scott Glover, "Officers Allegedly Gave Drugs to Informant," *L.A. Times*, Feb. 13, 2000, at 1.

39 United States v. Burnside, 824 F. Supp. 1215, 1225, 1228, 1244, 1246 (N.D. Ill. 1993).

40 8 U.S.C.A. § 1101.

41 Todd Richmond, AP, "Witness Protection Programs Hurting: Programs don't have enough to keep witnesses safe," *Wisconsin State Journal*, May 1, 2008, at A1. See also Pete Earley and Gerald Shur, *WITSEC: Inside the Federal Witness Protection Program* (New York: Bantam, 2003).

42 United States v. Bernal-Obeso, 989 F.2d 331, 335 (9th Cir. 1993).

43 Simon & Schuster, Inc. v. New York State Crime Victims Bd., 502 U.S. 105, 112 (1991).

44 Jon Seidel and Frank Main, "Chicago twins who helped convict El Chapo face new probe after ending prison terms," *Chicago Sun-Times*, Mar. 9, 2021; Government's Sentencing Memorandum and Motion to Depart from the Applicable Guideline Range, United States v. Flores, Case No. 09-CR-00383 (N.D. Ill., Jan. 14, 2015) (describing the Flores twins' extensive cooperation).

45 United States v. Jack Abramoff, Plea Agreement (D.D.C. Jan. 3, 2006). See also chapter 7, discussing Abramoff cooperation in detail.

46 As described further in chapter 7.

47 Duff Wilson, "Witness in Track Doping Case Is Ready to Name Big Names," *N.Y. Times*, Apr. 13, 2008, at A1.

48 Nigel Smith, "Why Rick Singer, the Mastermind Behind the College Admissions Scandal, Is Still a Free Man," *People*, Mar. 17, 2021; Travis Andersen, "Lori Loughlin's attorneys receive documents taken from ringleader in college admissions

scandal," *Boston Globe*, Mar. 4, 2020. Singer, who took $25 million from parents and pled guilty to fraud, racketeering, and money laundering, remains free and unsentenced as of publication.

49 See chapter 2.

50 See chapter 5.

51 See, e.g., Alan Maimon, "A Plot That Failed," *Las Vegas Review-Journal*, Mar. 30, 2008, at 21A (documenting story of informant who falsified loan documents and tried to bribe a judge); United States v. Giffen, 473 F.3d 30 (2nd Cir. 2006) (businessman alleged that his bribery of foreign officials and money laundering were authorized by the U.S. government); United States v. Flemmi, 225 F.3d 78, 81–82 (1st Cir. 2000) (FBI handlers tolerated informants' extortion and murder); Michael D. Sorkin, "Top U.S. Drug Snitch Is a Legend and a Liar," *St. Louis Post Dispatch*, Jan. 16, 2000, at A1; David Rovella, "Some Superinformant: Lies, rap sheet of DEA's million dollar man starts a legal fire," *Nat'l L. J.*, Nov. 22, 1999 (DEA agents covered up their informant's tax fraud, prostitution, perjury).

52 Special Report: The Federal Bureau of Investigations's Compliance with the Attorney General's Investigative Guidelines, Office of the Inspector General, U.S. Dep't of Justice (Washington, D.C.: Sept. 2005), chapter 3, at 18, https://oig.justice.gov/sites/default/files/legacy/special/0509/final.pdf (hereinafter "OIG Report").

53 Al Baker, "Drugs-for-Information Scandal Shakes Up New York Police Narcotics Force," *N.Y. Times*, Jan. 23, 2008 (documenting police practice of keeping drugs from busts to give to informants as payment).

54 George Joseph, "The Mount Vernon Police Tapes: In Secretly Recorded Calls, Officer Says Some Drug Dealers Operate With 'Free Rein,'" *The Gothamist*, June 18, 2020.

55 United States v. Warren, 454 F.3d 752 (7th Cir. 2006).

56 United States v. Garcia, 193 Fed. Appx. 909 (11th Cir. 2006).

57 United States v. Smith, 481 F.3d 259 (5th Cir. 2007).

58 United States v. Abcasis, 45 F.3d 39 (2nd Cir. 1995).

59 David M. Zlotnick, "The Future of Federal Sentencing Policy: Learning Lessons from Republican Judicial Appointees in the Guidelines Era," 79 *U. Colo. L. Rev.* 1, 41–42 (2008).

60 Shelley Murphy, "Black Community Leaders Criticize Martorano Deal," *Boston Globe*, Sept. 29, 1999, at A21.

61 Crystal S. Yang, "Free at Last? Judicial Discretion and Racial Disparities in Federal Sentencing," 44 *J. Legal Stud.* 75, 105 (2015) ("[N]onwhite defendants are significantly less likely to receive substantial assistance motions in general."); Celesta A. Albonetti & Robert D. Baller, "Sentencing in Federal Drug Trafficking/manufacturing Cases: A Multilevel Analysis of Extra-Legal Defendant Characteristics, Guidelines Departures, and Continuity of Culture," 14 *J. Gender Race & Just.* 41, 67 (2010).

62 William J. Stuntz, "Plea Bargaining and Criminal Law's Disappearing Shadow," 117 *Harvard L. Rev.* 2548, 2564–65 (2004).

63 John Tierney, "For Lesser Crimes, Rethinking Life Behind Bars," *N.Y. Times*, Dec. 11, 2012.

64 West's Ann. Cal. Penal Code §§ 211, 213(a)(1)(A).

65 Welsh v. Wisconsin, 466 U.S. 740, 754 (1984) (legislative sentence set by law the "best indication of the State's interest" in establishing gravity of offense and authorizing law enforcement action against that conduct).

66 Criminal informant use is a strong version of the general phenomenon that, "[a] s criminal law expands, both lawmaking and adjudication pass into the hands of police and prosecutors; law enforcers, not the law, determine who goes to prison and for how long." William J. Stuntz, "The Pathological Politics of Criminal Law," 100 *Mich. L. Rev.* 505, 509 (2001).

67 Bruce A. Jacobs, "Contingent Ties: Undercover Drug Officers' Use of Informants," 48 *Brit. J. Sociol.* 36, 37 n.1 (1997) (study of U.S. city police describing "sentiment echoed by every officer").

68 Curriden, "The Informant Trap," at 4 (quoting Celerino Castillo, twelve-year veteran DEA agent).

69 Yaroshefsky, "Cooperation with Federal Prosecutors," at 937–38.

70 Curriden, "The Informant Trap," at 6 (quoting Michael Levine, twenty-five-year veteran of the DEA and Customs).

71 Yaroshefsky, "Cooperation with Federal Prosecutors," at 938.

72 See chapter 6. See also Laurence A. Benner, "Racial Disparity in Narcotics Search Warrants," 6 *J. Gender, Race & Just.* 183, 200–201 (2002) (attributing concentration of drug arrests in urban zip codes in part to heavy reliance on confidential informants).

73 Fitzgerald, *Informants and Undercover Investigations*, at 23–24, 36; Madinger, *Confidential Informant: Law Enforcement's Most Valuable Tool*, at 53–55; Mallory, *Informants*, at 48–50.

74 Morrison v. Olson, 487 U.S. 654, 727–28 (1988) (Scalia, J., dissenting) (quoting Justice Robert Jackson's view that the most dangerous and important power of the prosecutor is her ability to pick defendants). See also James Vorenberg, "Decent Restraint of Prosecutorial Power," 94 *Harvard L. Rev.* 1521, 1524–25 (1981) ("The core of prosecutors' power is charging, plea bargaining, and, when it is under the prosecutor's control, initiating investigations.").

75 See sources cited in note 2 above (showing that most crimes are not reported and most reported crimes are not prosecuted); Marc Mauer, *Race to Incarcerate* (New York: New Press, 2006), 114–19 (describing criminal system pyramid in which most reported crimes do not lead to arrest, and most arrests do not lead to cases or convictions); Berger v. United States, 295 U.S. 78, 88 (1935) ("The United States Attorney is the representative not of an ordinary party to a controversy, but of a sovereignty whose obligation to govern impartially is as compelling as its obligation to govern at all; and whose interest, therefore, in a criminal prosecution is not that it shall win a case, but that justice shall be done.").

76 Fitzgerald, *Informants and Undercover Investigations*, at 233 (quoting Integrity Assurance Notes, DEA, Planning and Inspection Division, vol. 1, no. 1 (Aug. 1991)).

77 Fitzgerald, *Informants and Undercover Investigations*, at 232.

78 Audit of the Drug Enforcement Administration's Management and Oversight of its Confidential Source Program, i–iv, Office of the Inspector General, U.S. Dep't of Justice (Sept. 2016).

79 "Everything Secret Degenerates: The FBI's Use of Murderers as Informants," H.R. Rep. no. 108-414, at 1 (2004), www.congress.gov/congressional-report/108th-congress/house-report/414/1.

80 United States v. Salemme, 91 F. Supp. 2d 141 (D. Mass. 1999), rev'd in part, United States v. Flemmi, 225 F.3d 78 (1st Cir. 2000); Amanda J. Schreiber, "Dealing with the Devil: An Examination of the FBI's Troubled Relationship with Its Confidential Informants," 34 *Colum. J.L. & Soc. Probs.* 301, 330–38 (2001); "Everything Secret Degenerates," at 2; Shelley Murphy & Brian Ballou, "U.S. Ordered to Pay $101.7 Million in False Murder Convictions: 'To the FBI, the plaintiffs' lives . . . just did not matter': FBI withheld evidence in '65 gangland slaying," *Boston Globe*, July 27, 2007, at 1A.

81 Bill Bush, "Arbitration Hearing: 2 officers keep jobs in identity dispute," *Columbus Dispatch*, Apr. 19, 2006, at 6E.

82 "Fake Drugs: Evolution of a scandal," *DallasNews.com*, www.dallasnews.com/s/dws/spe/2003/fakedrugs/fakedrug1103.html (no longer available online); see also Ross Milloy, "Fake Drugs Force an End to 24 Cases in Dallas," *N.Y. Times*, Jan. 16, 2002, at A1.

83 Hayes v. Brown, 399 F.3d 972 (9th Cir. 2005).

84 Silva v. Brown, 416 F.3d 980 (2005).

85 Shelley Murphy, "Detective, Dealer Convicted on Drug Charges: Pair sold cocaine worth $81,000," *Boston Globe*, Apr. 13, 2006, at B2.

86 Justin Fenton, "Former Baltimore Police detective sentenced to 14 months in prison for lying about '09 drug theft," *Baltimore Sun*, Jan. 26, 2021.

87 Van Derbeken, "Informant in Officer's Slaying."

88 Colloff, *This Con Man*, at 7.

89 Rob Warden & Patricia Haller, "Profile of a Snitch: A tragic choice," *Chicago Lawyer*, Oct. 1987.

90 "Privilege," *In the Dark*, Episode 5, Season 2 (2019), www.apmreports.org/episode/2018/05/22/in-the-dark-s2e5; Jeff Amy, "Man pleads guilty to killing 3, including ex-girlfriend," AP News, May 11, 2016.

91 Chuck Strouse, "Bosco Enriquez was beaten and raped after helping Miami cops bust Latin gangs," *Miami New Times*, Mar. 1, 2012; Chuck Strouse, "Bosco Enriquez snitched on Miami's Latin gangs; then cops abandoned him to rape and deportation," *Miami New Times*, Mar. 8, 2012; Chuck Strouse, "Save Bosco Enriquez, Part 3," *Miami New Times*, Mar. 15, 2012.

92 Hannah Dreier, "A Betrayal: The teenager told police all about his gang, MS-13. In return, he was slated for deportation and marked for death," ProPublica & *New*

York Magazine, Apr. 2, 2018; Hannah Dreier, "Former MS-13 Member Who Secretly Helped Police Is Deported," ProPublica & *New York Magazine*, Jan. 22, 2019. Henry is now seeking asylum in Europe.

93 Sharon Dolovich, "Exclusion and Control in the Carceral State," 16 Berkeley J. Crim. L. 259, 337–38 (2011).

94 Bryan Stevenson, *Just Mercy: A Story of Justice and Redemption* (New York: Spiegel and Grau, 2014), 15.

95 Alexander v. DeAngelo, 329 F.3d 912, 918 (7th Cir. 2003) (Posner, J.)

96 Rod Settle, *Police Informers: Negotiation and Power* (Sydney, Australia: Federation Press, 1995), 250; see also Martha A. Fineman, "The Vulnerable Subject: Anchoring Equality in the Human Condition," 20 *Yale J.L. & Feminism* 1, 8, 16, 18 (2008) (pointing out that political and institutional policies exacerbate personal vulnerabilities in derogation of social equality).

97 Fitzgerald, *Informants and Undercover Investigations*, at 57.

98 Mallory, *Informants*, at 21, 37–39.

99 Alexander v. DeAngelo, 329 F.3d at 917 (holding that informant stated a civil rights claim when police forced her to engage in oral sex with a suspect in exchange for avoiding prosecution). See also Susan S. Kuo, "Official Indiscretions: Considering Sex Bargains with Government Informants," 38 *U.C. Davis L. Rev.* 1643 (2005) (analyzing police practice at issue in Alexander—pressuring female informants to use sex to obtain incriminating information about others in order to avoid their own prosecution—as a form of gender subordination).

100 United States v. Simpson, 813 F.2d 1462 (9th Cir. 1987).

101 Erica Santiago, "Lake City Police Sergeant under investigation for reportedly having sex with informant," *First Coast News*, May 15, 2019; Nick Shepherd, "VSP officer charged with lying about sexual relationships with police informants," *SWVA. Today*, Aug. 28, 2018; Peter Farrell, "State Police Dismiss Detective Although He Escapes Indictment," *Portland Oregonian*, Sept. 23, 1998, at B07; Kathy Sanders, "Fort Worth Officer Put on Restricted Duty: A drug informant says he coerced her to have sex, the police say," *Fort Worth Star-Telegram*, Nov. 15, 1997, at 5.

102 Stillman, "The Throwaways"; "Young people going undercover in war on drugs," *60 Minutes*, Dec. 4, 2015; Simon McCormack, "College Student Andrew Sadek Busted For $80 Worth Of Pot, Then Found Dead," *Huffington Post*, Feb. 4, 2015; Albert Samaha and Alex Campbell, "Mississippi Cops Are Using College Kids as Drug Informants," *BuzzFeed*, Apr. 20, 2015; Sean Kirkby, "Undercover students used in drug busts at some University of Wisconsin campuses," *Wisconsin Watch*, Sept. 14, 2015; Dave Philipps, "Informant Debate Renewed as Air Force Revisits Cadet Misconduct," *N.Y. Times*, Aug. 9, 2014.

103 Ed White, "Family of slain police informant gets $1M settlement," *Detroit News*, Oct. 3, 2017. See Sharon Dolovich, "Two Models of the Prison: Accidental Humanity and Hypermasculinity in the L.A. County Jail," 102 *J. Crim. L. & Criminology* 965, 987 (2012) (describing special risks of violence faced by gay and transgender prisoners).

104 Ryan Katz, "Play to Stay: Undocumented Immigrant Faces a Choice: Become an Informant for ICE or Be Deported," *The Intercept*, Sept. 24, 2018; Talal Ansari and Siraj Datoo, "Welcome To America—Now Spy On Your Friends," *Buzzfeed*, Jan. 28, 2016. See also chapter 7.

105 Tristan Scott, "Family believes son's suicide partly caused by law enforcement's conscription as an informant," *The Missoulian*, Sept. 18, 2010.

106 Nathan Levy, "Bringing Justice to Hearne," *Texas Observer*, Apr. 29, 2005.

107 Henri E. Cauvin, "Witness Says Slain Girl Was Warned," *Wash. Post*, Feb. 11, 2004, at B01.

108 Craig R. McCoy, Nancy Phillips, and Dylan Purcell, "Justice: Delayed, Dismissed, Denied," *Philadelphia Inquirer*, Dec. 13, 2009; Report of the Advisor Committee of the Criminal Justice System, 21, 53–65 (Harrisburg, PA: Joint State Gov't Commission, January 2013), http://jsg.legis.state.pa.us.

109 Margaret S. Williams et al., "Survey of Harm to Cooperators," Fed. Jud. Ctr., 2016; Todd Richmond, AP, "Witness Protection Programs Hurting: Programs don't have enough to keep witnesses safe," *Wisconsin State Journal*, May 1, 2008, at A1.

110 Joel Rubin, "Slaying of Witness Spurs LAPD Changes," *L.A. Times*, July 18, 2008, at Cal. 1; Rauda v. City of Los Angeles, No. CV08–3128-CAS (PJW), 2010 WL 11549634, at *4 (C.D. Cal. Aug. 20, 2010).

111 Rosenfeld, Jacobs & Wright, "Snitching and the Code of the Street," at 306.

112 Tom R. Tyler & Jeffrey Fagan, "Legitimacy and Cooperation: Why Do People Help the Police Fight Crime in Their Communities?" 6 *Ohio St. J. Crim. L.* 231 (2008).

113 Northern Mariana Islands v. Bowie, 243 F.3d 1109, 1123 (9th Cir. 2001).

114 See chapter 5.

2. INFORMANT LAW

1 United States v. Dennis, 183 F.2d 201 (2nd Cir. 1950), aff'd, 341 U.S. 494 (1951).

2 Peter Reuter, "Licensing Criminals: Police and Informants," in Gerald M. Caplan, ed., *ABSCAM Ethics: Moral Issues and Deception in Law Enforcement* (Cambridge, MA: Ballinger, 1983), 100–17 (describing widespread licensing of criminal activities by informants); Jerome H. Skolnick, *Justice without Trial: Law Enforcement in Democratic Society* (New York: Wiley, 1966), 129; Amanda J. Schreiber, "Dealing with the Devil: An Examination of the FBI's Troubled Relationship with Its Confidential Informants," 34 *Colum. J.L. & Soc. Probs.* 301 (2000).

3 Miranda v. Arizona, 384 U.S. 436 (1966); Rhode Island v. Innis, 446 U.S. 291 (1980); Berkemer v. McCarty, 468 U.S. 420 (1984).

4 See Massiah v. United States, 377 U.S. 201 (1964); Rothgery v. Gillespie County, 554 U.S. 191 (2008).

5 United States v. White, 2004 WL 2182188, *4 (D. Kan. 2004).

6 Town of Castle Rock v. Gonzalez, 125 S. Ct. 2796 (2005) (finding no cause of action against police who failed to enforce domestic violence restraining order); see also DeShaney v. Winnebago County Dep't of Soc. Servs., 489 U.S. 189 (1989) (finding no constitutional guarantee for any minimal level of security); see also Joseph

Goldstein, "Police Discretion Not to Invoke the Criminal Process: Low-Visibility Decisions in the Administration of Justice," 69 *Yale L.J.* 543 (1960); Reuter, "Licensing Criminals," at 101 (describing police discretion to license crime).

7 See., e.g,. Section 607, Informants, Eureka Police Department Policy Manual, www.ci.eureka.ca.gov/depts/police/transparency_portal__sb_978/default.asp; Section 608.5, Informants, Lake County Sheriff's Office Policy Manual, www.lakesheriff.com/About/Policy.htm.

8 Las Vegas Metropolitan Police Department, Informants and Associated Funds Management, section 5/206.24.

9 Department of Justice, Guidelines Regarding the Use of Confidential Informants, at 3–4, 14 (Jan. 8, 2001), www.usdoj.gov/ag/readingroom/ciguidelines.htm ("DOJ Guidelines"); Attorney General Guidelines Regarding the Use of FBI Confidential Human Sources, at 5–7, 27, 30, 34–35 (Dec. 13, 2006), www.fas.org/irp/agency/doj/fbi/chs-guidelines.pdf (hereinafter "FBI Guidelines").

10 Daniel Richman, "Prosecutors and Their Agents, Agents and Their Prosecutors," 103 *Columbia L. Rev.* 749 (2003).

11 United States v. Abcasis, 45 F.3d 39, 43 (2nd Cir. 1995).

12 Fed. R. Crim. P. 12.3 (requiring defendants who "intend[] to assert a defense of actual or believed exercise of public authority on behalf of a law enforcement agency or federal intelligence agency at the time of the alleged offense" to notify the government in writing prior to trial).

13 United States v. Henry, 447 U.S. 264 (1980) (when jailhouse snitch deliberately elicited information from charged defendant it violated defendant's right to counsel). See also ABA Model Rule of Professional Conduct 4.2 (prohibiting lawyers from talking to represented defendants).

14 Imbler v. Pachtman, 424 U.S. 409 (1976).

15 See United States v. Williams, 47 F.3d 658 (4th Cir. 1995) (during plea negotiations prosecutor may threaten to charge defendant with more serious crimes, and carry out those threats, if the defendant refuses to cooperate with police).

16 See 18 U.S.C. § 6002 (federal immunity statute); Murphy v. Waterfront Commission, 378 U.S. 52, 77–79 (1964) (state grant of statutory immunity protects defendant in connection with federal prosecution as well); cf. State v. Edmondson, 714 So.2d 1233 (La. 1998) (cooperating defendant promised immunity in Mississippi was not entitled to immunity in Louisiana).

17 United States v. Pollard, 959 F.2d 1011, 1021 (D.C. Cir. 1992) ("Almost anything lawfully within the power of a prosecutor acting in good faith can be offered in exchange for a guilty plea.").

18 See description of proffer sessions in chapter 1.

19 Daniel Richman, "Cooperating Clients," 56 *Ohio St. L.J.* 69, 94–99 (1995); Graham Hughes, "Agreements for Cooperation in Criminal Cases," 45 *Vand. L. Rev.* 1 (1992).

20 Roberts v. United States, 445 U.S. 552 (1980) (upholding sentence that was enhanced in part on the basis of defendant's refusal to provide incriminating information about others); Bordenkirsher v. United States, 434 U.S. 357 (1978) (government

could charge defendant with more serious crimes in effort to get him to plead guilty); see also United States v. Williams, 47 F.3d at 661.

21 Meda Chesney-Lind, "Imprisoning Women: The Unintended Victims of Mass Imprisonment," in Marc Mauer & Meda Chesney-Lind, eds., *Invisible Punishment: The Collateral Consequences of Mass Imprisonment* (New York: New Press, 2002), 90.

22 United States v. Armstrong, 517 U.S. 456 (1996); Thigpen v. Roberts, 468 U.S. 27 (1984).

23 See, e.g., State v. Williams, 896 A.2d 973, 976, 392 Md. 194 (2006) (because of his cooperation in drug cases jailhouse snitch received time-served for theft charge and the dropping of numerous other charges).

24 Parrish v. State, 12 P.3d 953, 956 & n.5 (Nev. 2000) (noting statutory provisions for awarding cooperation credit in Nevada, Florida, and Georgia).

25 2007 Annual Report, Virginia Criminal Sentencing Commission (Richmond, VA: VCSC, 2007), 138, http://www.vcsc.virginia.gov/reports.html.

26 2019 Sourcebook of Federal Sentencing Statistics, tbls. 4, 37 & 43, U.S. Sentencing Comm'n, www.ussc.gov/research/sourcebook-2019.

27 Linda Drazga Maxfield & John H. Kramer, "Substantial Assistance: An Empirical Yardstick Gauging Equity in Current Federal Policy and Practice," United States Sentencing Commission (Jan. 1998), 9–10.

28 18 U.S.C. § 3553(e).

29 21 U.S.C. § 841(b)(1)(B)(iii).

30 The only exception is that first-time offenders may be eligible to receive a lower sentence under U.S.S.G. § 5C1.2.

31 U.S.S.G.§ 5K1.1.

32 See, e.g., United States v. Doe, 398 F.3d 1254, 1261 (10th Cir. 2005) ("[A] defendant's assistance should be fully considered by a district court at sentencing even if that assistance is not presented to the court in the form of a § 5K1.1 motion.").

33 2019 Sourcebook of Federal Sentencing Statistics, tbl. R, U.S. Sentencing Comm'n.; Fed. R. Crim. Pro. 35(b); see Kevin Blackwell and Jill Baisinger, *The Use of Federal Rule of Criminal Procedure 35(b)* (Washington, D.C.: U.S. Sentencing Comm'n, Jan. 2016).

34 Radley Balko, "Guilty before Proven Innocent: How police harassment, jailhouse snitches, and a runaway war on drugs imprisoned an innocent family," *Reason*, May 2008, at 51–52.

35 Mark Curriden, "The Informant Trap: Secret Threat to Justice," 17 *Nat'l Law J.* 1 (1995).

36 Hearing, House Committee on Oversight and Government Reform, U.S. Congress, Apr. 4, 2017; Audit of the Drug Enforcement Administration's Management and Oversight of its Confidential Source Program, Office of the Inspector General, U.S. Dep't of Justice (Sept. 2016); Audit of the Bureau of Alcohol, Tobacco, Firearms and Explosives' Management and Oversight of Confidential Informants, Office of the Inspector General, U.S. Dep't of Justice (Mar. 2017); Audit of the Federal Bureau of Investigation's Management of Its Confidential Human Source Validation Processes, Office of the Inspector General, U.S. Dep't of Justice (Nov. 2019).

37 28 U.S.C. § 524(c); Radley Balko, "The Forfeiture Racket," *Reason*, Feb. 2010.

38 Roy v. United States, 38 Fed. Cl. 184 (1997).

39 See Maya Harris et al., Letter from the ACLU of Northern California to the California Commission on the Fair Administration of Justice, Sept. 19, 2006 (describing sample vouchers used for paying informants); Beth Warren, "Kathryn Johnston Shooting: Informant hiding out, plans to sue city, police," *Atlanta Journal-Constitution*, Apr. 28, 2007, at 1B (describing payment arrangement for local snitch).

40 Richard Rosenfeld, Bruce Jacobs & Richard Wright, "Snitching and the Code of the Street," 43 *Brit. J. Criminol.* 291, 303 (2003); Jay Williams & L. Lynn Guess, "The Informant: A Narcotics Enforcement Dilemma," 13 *J. Psychoactive Drugs* 235 (1981) (noting that law enforcement provision of drugs to addict informants creates an ethical conflict); Stephen L. Mallory, *Informants: Development and Management* (Incline Village, NV: Copperhouse Publishing, 2000), 81 (noting that informants may skim money and/or drugs from controlled buys).

41 Rhode Island v. Innis, 446 U.S. 291 (1980); Massiah v. United States, 377 U.S. 201 (1964).

42 Title III, Omnibus Crime Control and Safe Streets Act, 18 U.S.C. §§ 2510 et seq. (governing electronic surveillance); State v. Mullens, 650 S.E.2d 169 (2007) (describing state statutory schemes); "Electronic Surveillance: Annual Review of Criminal Procedure," 36 *Geo. L.J.A.R.* 133, 157 (2007).

43 Hoffa v. United States, 385 U.S. 293, 303, 311 (1966).

44 Illinois v. Perkins, 496 U.S. 292 (1990).

45 United States v. White, 401 U.S. 745, 756, 764 (1971) (Douglas, J., dissenting); id. at 787 (Harlan, J., dissenting).

46 18 U.S.C. § 2518(3)(c).

47 18 U.S.C. § 2511(2)(c). See Mona R. Shokrai, "Double-Trouble: The Underregulation of Surreptitious Video Surveillance in Conjunction with the Use of Snitches in Domestic Government Investigations," 13 *Rich. J.L & Tech.* 3 (2006).

48 United States v. Nerber, 222 F.3d 597 (9th Cir. 2000).

49 State v. Mullens, 650 S.E.2d 169 (W.Va. 2007); see Recording Phone Calls and Conversations, Dig. Media L. Project, www.dmlp.org/legal-guide/recording-phone-calls-and-conversations.

50 State v. Goetz, 345 Mont. 421, 191 P.3d 489 (2008); State v. Blow, 157 Vt. 513 (1991); Commonwealth v. Blood, 400 Mass. 61 (1987); State v. Glass, 583 P.2d 872 (Alaska 1978); Commonwealth v. Brion, 539 Pa. 256 (1994).

51 Brady v. Maryland, 373 U.S. 83, 87 (1963).

52 United States v. Bagley, 473 U.S. 667 (1985).

53 Giglio v. United States, 405 U.S. 150, 154 (1972) ("When the 'reliability of a given witness may well be determinative of guilt or innocence,' nondisclosure of evidence affecting credibility falls within this general rule [of Brady v. Maryland]." (citation omitted)).

54 Giglio, 405 U.S. at 151.

55 United States v. Ruiz, 536 U.S. 622 (2002).

56 CSP STAT Criminal: Trial Court Caseload Overview, Court Statistics Project, Nat'l Ctr. for State Courts, 2019, www.courtstatistics.org/csp-stat-nav-cards-first-row/

csp-stat-criminal; Sourcebook Online, tbls. 5.46.2006 & 5.17.2006, Bureau of Justice Statistics, U.S. Dep't of Justice (2006), www.albany.edu/sourcebook.

57 See chapter 8.

58 D. Mass. Local Rule 116.2(B)(1)(c); Laural L. Hooper, Jennifer E. Marsh & Brian Yeh, "Treatment of *Brady v. Maryland* Material in United States District and State Courts' Rules, Orders, and Policies," Federal Judicial Center (U.S. Judicial Conference, Oct. 2004), 11.

59 In re: Amendments to Florida Rule of Criminal Procedure 3.220, Case No. SC13–1541 (Fla. May 29, 2014).

60 McCray v. Illinois, 386 U.S. 300, 311–13 (1967).

61 Roviaro v. United States, 353 U.S. 53, 59 (1957).

62 Roviaro, 353 U.S. at 60–61, 628–29.

63 Crawford v. Washington, 541 U.S. 36 (2004); United States v. Lombardozzi, 491 F.3d 61, 72–75 (2nd Cir. 2007) (admitting officer's expert testimony that was based on evidence obtained from out-of-court confidential informants).

64 18 U.S.C. § 3500; Ellen Podgor, "Criminal Discovery of Jencks Witness Statements: Timing Makes a Difference," 15 *Georgia St. U.L. Rev.* 651 (1999).

65 Ill. Comp. Stat., ch. 725, § 5/115–21.

66 Conn. Gen. Stat. § 51–286k; Conn. Gen. Stat. § 54–860-p.

67 Vernon's Ann. Tex. C.C.P. Art. 38–141; Cal. Penal Code § 1111.5.

68 See American Legislative Exchange Council, Model Jailhouse Informant Regulations, May 24, 2018, www.alec.org/model-policy/jailhouse-informant-regulations-2; American Bar Association, Resolution, Adopted by House of Delegates February 14, 2005 (urging nationwide adoption of corroboration requirements and documenting current state legislation), www.americanbar.org.

69 United States v. Singleton, 144 F.3d 1343, rev'd en banc, 165 F.3d 1297 (10th Cir. 1999).

70 Franks v. Delaware, 438 U.S. 154 (1978) (police reckless disregard for truth in warrant application will invalidate warrant); Napue v. Illinois, 360 U.S. 264 (1959) (prosecutor's knowing use of perjured informant testimony violated due process); Hayes v. Brown, 399 F.3d 972 (9th Cir. 2005) (prosecutor violated due process by knowingly using informant's false testimony).

71 Thomas Y. Davies, "Recovering the Original Fourth Amendment," 98 *Mich. L. Rev.* 547, 651 & n.288 (1999) ("The Burger Court made it virtually impossible for defendants to attack perjurious allegations in warrant affidavits."); Christopher Slobogin, "Testilying: Police Perjury and What to Do About It," 67 *U. Colo. L. Rev.* 1037, 1043 (1996) ("Most frequent, it seems, is the invention of 'confidential informants,' . . . a ploy that allows police to cover up irregularities in developing probable cause or to assert they have probable cause when in fact all they have is a hunch.").

72 Hampton v. United States, 425 U.S. 484 (1976) (holding that police overinvolvement would have to be "outrageous" before it would invalidate a conviction).

73 United States v. Twigg, 588 F.2d 373 (3rd Cir. 1978).

74 Sherman v. United States, 356 U.S. 369, 372 (1958).

75 Wadie E. Said, "The Terrorist Informant," 85 *Wash. L. Rev.* 687, 732 (2010); see also Center on Law & Security, NYU School of Law, Terrorist Trial Report Card: September 11, 2001–September 11, 2010, at 20 (2010), www.lawandsecurity.org/terrorist-trial-report-cards.

76 See, e.g., United States v. Dunlap, 593 F. App'x 619, 621 (9th Cir. 2014) (reversing lower court finding of outrageous government conduct).

77 United States v. Russell, 411 U.S. 423 (1973) (defining entrapment defense and also recognizing availability of outrageous government conduct claim); see United States v. Berkovich, 168 F.3d 64 (2nd Cir. 1999) (noting that courts rarely find government conduct to be outrageous).

78 See Slagle v. United States, 612 F.2d 1157 (9th Cir. 1980) (finding drug informant to be neither an employee of the United States nor an independent contractor and therefore finding the United States not liable under the Federal Torts Claims Act).

79 Pleasant v. Lovell, 876 F.2d 787, 798 (10th Cir. 1989); see also *Hoffa* at 311 ("This is not to say that a secret government informer is to the slightest degree more free from all relevant constitutional restrictions than is any other government agent.").

80 Town of Castle Rock v. Gonzalez, 545 U.S. 748 (2005) (finding no cause of action against police who failed to enforce domestic violence restraining order); DeShaney v. Winnebago County Dep't of Soc. Servs., 489 U.S. 189 (1989) (finding no constitutional guarantee for any minimal level of policing or security); see also Linda R. S. v. Richard D., 410 U.S. 614, 619 (1973) (mother lacked standing to complain of state's failure to prosecute father for failure to pay child support where prosecution would result in prison term but not necessarily payment, noting that "a private citizen lacks a judicially cognizable interest in the prosecution or non-prosecution of another").

81 JGE through Tasso v. United States, 772 F. App'x 608, 612 (10th Cir. 2019).

82 JGE, 772 F. App'x at 610.

83 Ostera v. United States, 769 F.2d 716 (11th Cir. 1985); Liuzzo v. United States, 508 F. Supp. 923 (E.D. Mich. 1981).

84 Buckley v. Fitzsimmons, 509 U.S. 259 (1993) (defining qualified immunity).

85 Alexander v. DeAngelo, 329 F.3d 912 (7th Cir. 2003) (holding that informant stated a civil rights claim under 42 U.S.C. § 1983 when police forced her to engage in oral sex with a suspect in exchange for avoiding prosecution).

86 Id. at 918. See also Susan S. Kuo, "Official Indiscretions: Considering Sex Bargains with Government Informants," 38 *U.C. Davis L. Rev.* 1643 (2005).

87 Shuler v. United States, 531 F.3d 930 (D.C. Cir. 2008).

88 SGS-92-X003 v. United States, Case No. 97–579C (Ct. Fed. Claims, Sept. 26, 2014).

89 Burns v. Martuscello, 890 F.3d 77 (2nd Cir. 2018).

90 Id. at 90 (quoting Justice Gorsuch, Transcript of Oral Argument at 82, Carpenter v. United States, 138 S.Ct. 2206, (2018)).

91 Id. at 93 ("We also wish to underscore that the rights at issue here do not implicate the widespread practice of conditioning pleas or other favorable prosecutorial treatment on the provision of information.").

92 Imbler v. Pachtman, 424 U.S. 409 (1976).

93 Burns v. Reed, 500 U.S. 478, 493–95 (1991). The Ninth Circuit briefly held that a wrongfully convicted defendant could sue the supervising district attorney for maintaining inadequate information-handling policies when those policies failed to disclose the use of unreliable informants in the prosecutors' office; the Supreme Court reversed. Goldstein v. City of Long Beach, 481 F.3d 1170 (9th Cir. 2007), rev'd, Van de Kamp v. Goldstein, 129 S. Ct. 855 (2009).

94 McGhee v. Pottawattamie Cty., Iowa, 547 F.3d 922, 933 (8th Cir. 2008). The Supreme Court granted certiorari and heard oral arguments in this case in 2009 but dismissed it when the case settled. Pottawattamie County, Iowa, et al., Petitioners, v. Curtis W. McGhee, Jr., et al., 2009 WL 3640088 (U.S.), 4 (U.S. Oral. Arg., 2009); Pottawattamie Cty., Iowa v. McGhee, 558 U.S. 1103 (2010).

95 See generally Cyrille Fijnaut & Gary T. Marx, eds., *Police Surveillance in Comparative Perspective* (The Hague: Kluwer Law International, 1995), 269–89.

96 Jacqueline E. Ross, "Impediments to Transnational Cooperation in Undercover Policing: A Comparative Study of the United States and Italy," 52 *Am. J. Comp. L.* 569, 571 (2004); see also Jacqueline E. Ross, "Undercover Policing and the Varieties of Regulatory Approaches in the United States," 62 *Am. J. Comp. L.* 673, 675 (2014) ("European legal systems authorize undercover operations primarily for the investigation of organized crime."); Jacqueline E. Ross, "Undercover Policing and the Shifting Terms of Scholarly Debate: The United States and Europe in Counterpoint," 4 *Ann. Rev. L. & Soc. Sci.* 239, 240 (2008).

97 Report of the Kaufman Commission on Proceedings Involving Guy Paul Morin (Ontario: 1997), 14, 599–636, www.attorneygeneral.jus.gov.on.ca.

98 Steven Skurka, "A Canadian Perspective on the Role of Cooperators and Informants," 23 *Cardozo L. Rev.* 759, 764 (2002).

99 See M. Maguire & T. John, "Covert and Deceptive Policing in England and Wales: Issues in Regulation and Practice," 4 *Euro. J. Crime, Crim. L. & Crim. Just.* 316, 329–31 (1996); John Steele, "Police Cut Army of Informers to Get 'Value for Money,'" *The Telegraph*, Dec. 25, 2001.

100 Ethan A. Nadelmann, "The DEA in Europe," in Fijnaut & Marx, *Police Surveillance in Comparative Perspective*, at 270–71, 280.

101 Maarten van Traa, "The Findings of the Parliamentary Inquiry Viewed from an International Perspective," in Monica den Boer, ed., *Undercover Policing and Accountability from an International Perspective* (Maastricht: European Institute of Public Administration, 1997), 15–24; Jacqueline E. Ross, "Tradeoffs in Undercover Investigations: A Comparative Perspective," 69 *U. Chi. L. Rev.* 1501, 1507–8, 1511 (2002).

102 Peter Klerks, "Covert Policing in the Netherlands," in Fijnaut & Marx, *Police Surveillance in Comparative Perspective*, at 119.

103 Ross, "Impediments to Transnational Cooperation," at 574, 587–88; see also Ross, "Shifting Terms."

104 Jacqueline E. Ross, "The Place of Covert Surveillance in Democratic Societies: A Comparative Study of the United States and Germany," 55 *Am. J. of Compara-*

tive Law 493, 494, 505, 508 (2007); see also Peter J. P. Tak, "Deals with Criminals: Supergrasses, Crown Witnesses, and Pentiti," 5 *Euro. J. Crim, Crim. L. & Crim. Justice* 2, 10, 12–18 (1997).

105 Louise Shelley, "Soviet Undercover Work," in Fijnaut & Marx, *Police Surveillance in Comparative Perspective*, at 155–56, 161.

106 Barbara Miller, *Narratives of Guilt and Compliance in Unified Germany: Stasi Informers and Their Impact on Society* (London: Routledge, 1999), 4, 133; James O. Jackson, "Fear and Betrayal in the Stasi State," *Time*, Feb. 3, 1992, at 32.

107 See Catherine Taylor, "How Israel Builds Its Fifth Column: Palestinian collaborators face mob justice and fuel a culture of suspicion," *Christian Sci. Monitor*, May 22, 2002, at P1 (describing a "culture of suspicion such that anyone who runs a successful business or has access to hard-to-get permits is often suspected"); Lee Hockstader, "Palestinians Battle the Enemy Within: Menace of Israeli collaborators spawns executions, vigilantism, revenge killings," *Wash. Post*, Feb. 2, 2001, at A1; Editorial, "Haunted by an Informer," *Boston Globe*, May 20, 2003 ("For generations, informers' whispers have sowed distrust, fear, and violence in Northern Ireland.").

108 Ethan A. Nadelmann, "The DEA in Europe," in Fijnaut & Marx, *Police Surveillance in Comparative Perspective*, at 269–89.

109 Ross, "Impediments to Transnational Cooperation," at 569, 602.

110 Gary T. Marx, *Undercover: Police Surveillance in America* (Berkeley: University of California Press, 1988), 50.

111 The original version of this chapter benefited immensely from the expertise and editorial assistance of Kathryn Frey-Balter.

3. JURIES AND EXPERTS

1 State v. Leniart, 333 Conn. 88, 215 A.3d 1104 (2019); State v. Leniart, 166 Conn. App. 142, 174 n.23 (2016).

2 State v. Leniart, 166 Conn. App. 142, 219, 140 A.3d 1026, 1075 (2016), aff'd in part, rev'd in part, 333 Conn. 88, 215 A.3d 1104 (2019).

3 Hoffa v. United States, 385 U.S. 293 (1966).

4 The Honorable Stephen S. Trott, "Words of Warning for Prosecutors Using Criminals as Witnesses," 47 *Hastings L.J.* 1381, 1383 (1996), 1385. See also K. N. Key et al., "Beliefs about secondary confession evidence: A survey of laypeople and defence attorneys," *Psychology, Crime and Law* 24, no. 1 (2018): 1–13. https://doi.org/10.1 080/1068316X.2017.1351968 (finding that laypeople perceive reported secondary confessions as less credible than forensics and DNA evidence and that they know that incentives may influence the veracity of those reported confessions).

5 Trott, "Words of Warning," at 1386.

6 Zach Lowe, "Drug Arrest Reveals Police Strategy: Possession Charges Lodged as Informants Don't Testify," *The Advocate* (Stamford, CT), Nov. 26, 2007, at A6.

7 Rob Warden, "The Snitch System: How Snitch Testimony Sent Randy Steidl and Other Innocent Americans to Death Row," Center on Wrongful Convictions, Northwestern University School of Law, 2004, www.law.northwestern.edu/wrongfulconvictions.

8 Id. at 4–5.

9 *In the Dark*, Season 2, Episoder 4: The Confessions, www.apmreports.org/epi-sode/2018/05/15/in-the-dark-s2e4; *In the Dark*, Season 2, Episode 5: Privilege, www.apmreports.org/episode/2018/05/22/in-the-dark-s2e5.

10 Brady v. Maryland, 373 U.S. 83, 87 (1963); Giglio v. United States, 405 U.S. 150, 154 (1972); United States v. Ruiz, 536 U.S. 622 (2002).

11 Russell D. Covey, "Suspect Evidence and Coalmine Canaries," 55 *Am. Crim. L. Rev.* 537, 574–76 (2018) (documenting dozens of exonerations where prosecutors with-held informant-related evidence). See also chapters 1 and 4 for additional examples.

12 Nat'l Registry of Exonerations, www.law.umich.edu/special/exoneration/Pages/ca-sedetail.aspx?caseid=5873.

13 Stanley Mozee and Dennis Allen, "Declared 'Actually Innocent' After 15 Years in Prison," Innocence Project, https://innocenceproject.org/stanley-mozee-and-dennis-allen-declared-actually-innocent-after-15-years-in-prison.

14 R. Michael Cassidy, "'Soft Words of Hope': Giglio, Accomplice Witnesses, and the Problem of Implied Inducements," 98 *Nw. U. L. Rev.* 1129, 1142 (2004).

15 Report of the 1989–90 Los Angeles County Grand Jury: Investigation of the In-volvement of Jail House Informants in the Criminal Justice System in Los Angeles County, July 1990, at 111–115.

16 "Everything Secret Degenerates: The FBI's Use of Murderers as Informants," H.R. Rep. no. 108-414, at 2 (2004).

17 Kelly Puente and Tony Saavedra, "O.C. deputies' logs reveal details of informant use, recordings in county jail," *O.C. Register*, Dec. 16, 2016, www.ocregister. com/2016/12/06/oc-deputies-logs-reveal-details-of-informant-use-recordings-in-county-jail.

18 *Hoffa*, 385 U.S. at 311.

19 John Henry Wigmore, Evidence in Trials at Common Law (2011), § 1367, at 32.

20 State v. Jones, No. 20261, 2020 WL 8257703, at *6 (Conn. Dec. 1, 2020).

21 George C. Harris, "Testimony for Sale: The Law and Ethics of Snitches and Ex-perts," 28 *Pepp. L. Rev.* 1, 54–55 (2000).

22 Cassidy, "'Soft Words of Hope,'" 1142 (2004) ("[D]efense counsel cannot effectively cross-examine an accomplice witness about his expectations of leniency unless the factual predicates for this expectation have been disclosed to the defense by the prosecutor.").

23 Cal. Pen. Code § 1127a.

24 Vernon's Okla. Forms 2d, OUJI-CR 9–43; State v. Charles, 2011 UT App. 291, 263 P.3d 469 (2011); State v. Patterson, 276 Conn. 452, 465, 886 A.2d 777, 787 (2005) (requiring an instruction telling the jury that informant testimony must "be reviewed with particular scrutiny and weighed . . . with greater care than the testimony of an ordinary witness"). See also chapter 8.

25 S. A., Wetmore et al., "Do Judicial Instructions Aid in Distinguishing Between Reli-able and Unreliable Jailhouse Informants?" *Criminal Justice and Behavior* 47, no. 5 (2020): 582–600.

26 United States v. Cohen, 145 F.2d 82, 93 (2nd Cir. 1944).

27 Walter W. Steele Jr., "Jury Instructions: A Persistent Failure to Communicate," 67 *N.C. L. Rev.* 77, 79 (1988) (finding that most instructions are incomprehensible to jurors but that rewriting them with an eye toward clarity improved comprehension).

28 See, e.g., State v. Knight, 161 N.H. 338, 343, 13 A.3d 244, 249 (2011) (upholding trial court refusal to give instruction); State v. DuBray, 2003 MT 255, ¶ 93, 317 Mont. 377, 399, 77 P.3d 247, 262 (same).

29 Melanie B. Fessinger et al.," Informants v. Innocents: Informant Testimony and Its Contribution to Wrongful Convictions," 48 *Cap. U. L. Rev.* 149, 162–173 (2020) (summarizing last decade of psychological and behavioral research).

30 Jeffrey S. Neuschatz et al., "The Effects of Accomplice Witnesses and Jailhouse Informants on Jury Decision Making," 32 *Law & Hum. Behav.* 137–49 (2008).

31 J. S. Neuschatz et al., "Secondary confessions, expert testimony, and unreliable testimony," *Journal of Police and Criminal Psychology* 27, no. 2 (2012): 17–192.

32 Evelyn M. Maeder and Emily Pica, "Secondary Confessions: The Influence (or Lack Thereof) of Incentive Size and Scientific Expert Testimony on Jurors' Perceptions of Informant Testimony," 38 *Law & Hum. Behav.* 560, 566 (2014) (observing "an overall effect of incentive on verdict decisions").

33 Jeffrey S. Neuschatz et al., "The truth about snitches: an archival analysis of informant testimony," *Psychiatry, Psychology and Law*, Nov. 10, 2020, 1–24, https://doi.org/10.1080/13218719.2020.1805810.

34 Ibid.

35 S. A. Wetmore, J. S. Neuschatz & S. D. Gronlund, "On the power of secondary confession evidence," *Psychology, Crime & Law* 20, no. 4 (2014): 339–57, 354, https://doi.org/10.1080/1068316X.2013.777963 ("[S]econdary confession was evaluated as the most incriminating.").

36 Jessica K. Swanner and Denise R. Beike, "Incentives Increase the Rate of False but Not True Secondary Confessions from Informants with an Allegiance to a Suspect," 34 *Law & Hum. Behav.* 418, 425 (2010) ("Offering incentive to implicate a close other increased the ease of obtaining a confession only when the other denied the misdeed (false secondary confessions)."). See also Jessica K. Swanner, Denise R. Beike & Alexander T. Cole, "Snitching, Lies and Computer Crashes: An Experimental Investigation of Secondary Confessions," 34 *Law & Hum. Behav.* 53, 63 (2010) (finding that "offers of incentive actually reduce the truth value of secondary confessions").

37 Los Angeles County Grand Jury Report, 72.

38 Fed. R. Evid. 702(a), Testimony by Expert Witnesses.

39 Fed. R. Evid. 702(b)–(c); Kumho Tire Co. v. Carmichael, 526 U.S. 137, 149 (1999).

40 Paul W. Grimm, "Challenges Facing Judges Regarding Expert Evidence in Criminal Cases," 86 *Fordham L. Rev.* 1601, 1604, 1607–08 (2018).

41 People v. Gardley, 14 Cal. 4th 605, 617 (1996), disapproved on other grounds.

42 State v. Torrez, 146 N.M. 331, 335, 210 P.3d 228, 232 (2009).

43 United States v. Avila, 557 F.3d 809, 820 (7th Cir. 2009).

44 Smith v. Commonwealth, 454 S.W.3d 283, 287 (Ky. 2015) (police expert permitted to testify regarding the meaning and significance of the term "snitching") (citing Hudson v. Com., 385 S.W.3d 411, 420 (Ky. 2012)); People v. Hill, 191 Cal. App. 4th 1104, 1120, 120 Cal. Rptr. 3d 251, 265 (2011) (permitting testimony on the stigma of snitching in gangs). See also Przybysz v. City of Toledo, 302 F. Supp. 3d 915, 922 (N.D. Ohio 2017), aff'd, 746 F. App'x 480 (6th Cir. 2018) (approving use of government informant expert who testified that a police officer's handling of her informant, who was eventually killed, was "perfectly reasonable").

45 Brandon L. Garrett & M. Chris Fabricant, "The Myth of the Reliability Test," 86 *Fordham L. Rev.* 1559, 1561–62 (2018). See also Christopher Slobogin, "The Structure of Expertise in Criminal Cases," 34 *Seton Hall L. Rev.* 105, 114 (2003) (explaining why the *Daubert* standard favors the prosecution).

46 Nat'l Research Council, *Strengthening Forensic Science in the United States: A Path Forward* (2009), 11, www.ncjrs.gov/pdffiles1/nij/grants/228091.pdf.

47 Jessica Savage, "Battered Woman Syndrome," 7 *Geo. J. Gender & L.* 761, 763 (2006).

48 Thomas Albright & Brandon L. Garrett, "The Law and Science of Eyewitness Evidence," 102 *B.U. L. Rev.* (forthcoming 2022), Appendix C: State Rulings on Admissibility of Eyewitness Experts. See also Brandon L. Garrett, "Contaminated Confessions Revisited," 101 *Va. L. Rev.* 395, 426 & n.143 (2015) (documenting how court records may create misleading impression of false confession expert inadmissibility).

49 United States v. Noze, 255 F. Supp. 3d 352, 354 (D. Conn. 2017), aff'd sub nom. United States v. Dugue, 763 F. App'x 93 (2nd Cir. 2019).

50 *The Wire* (HBO series) (created by David Simon); *Snitch* (Lionsgate, 2013) (starring Dwayne "The Rock" Johnson); *Black Mass* (Warner Bros., 2015) (starring Johnny Depp).

51 *See* Radley Balko, "Guilty Before Proven Innocent," *Reason*, May 2008, https://reason.com/2008/04/14/guilty-before-proven-innocent.

52 Los Angeles County Grand Jury Report, at 18, 26, 28.

53 Key et al., at 6 (summarizing survey results). See also Robert M. Bloom, "What Jurors Should Know About Informants: The Need for Expert Testimony," 2019 *Mich. St. L. Rev.* 345, 347 (2019).

54 United States v. Avila, 557 F.3d 809, 820 (7th Cir. 2009).

55 State v. Torrez, 146 N.M. 331, 335, 210 P.3d 228, 232 (2009).

56 Neuschatz et al., "Secondary Confessions" (2012) (finding that the "percentage of guilty verdicts did not vary with incentive, testimony history, or expert testimony"); see also Maeder et al., at 566 (expert testimony did not appear to affect juror credibility determinations).

57 State v. Leniart, 166 Conn. App. 142, 224–25, 140 A.3d 1026, 1078 (2016), aff'd in part, rev'd in part, 333 Conn. 88, 215 A.3d 1104 (2019).

58 State v. Jones, No. 20261, 2020 WL 8257703, at *1 (Conn. Dec. 1, 2020).

59 This chapter benefited greatly from comments provided by Brandon Garrett and Daniel Medwed.

4. BEYOND UNRELIABLE

1 John Madinger, *Confidential Informant: Law Enforcement's Most Valuable Tool* (Boca Raton, FL: CRC Press, 2000), 153.

2 Nat'l Registry of Exonerations (documenting over 2,800 exonerations in the U.S. since 1989), www.law.umich.edu/special/exoneration/Pages/graphs.aspx; Samuel R. Gross & Barbara O'Brien, "Frequency and Predictors of False Conviction: Why We Know So Little, and New Data on Capital Cases," *Journal of Empirical Legal Studies* 5, no. 4 (December 2008): 927–62.

3 Barry Scheck, Peter Neufeld & Jim Dwyer, *Actual Innocence: Five Days to Execution and Other Dispatches from the Wrongly Convicted* (New York: Doubleday, 2000), 156.

4 Rob Warden, "The Snitch System: How Snitch Testimony Sent Randy Steidl and Other Innocent Americans to Death Row," Center on Wrongful Convictions, Northwestern University School of Law, 2004, www.law.northwestern.edu/wrong-fulconvictions.

5 Nina Martin, "Innocence Lost," *San Francisco Magazine*, Nov. 2004, at 87–88 (estimating the number of California wrongful convictions as being in the hundreds or even thousands).

6 Innocence Project website, https://innocenceproject.org/informing-injustice.

7 Snitch Watch, National Registry of Exonerations, May 13, 2015, www.law.umich.edu/special/exoneration/Pages/Features.Snitch.Watch.aspx. The Registry does not sort cases by other types of informants.

8 Samuel R. Gross et al., "Exonerations in the United States, 1989 Through 2003," 95 *J. Crim. L. & Criminology* 523, 543–44 (2005).

9 The Honorable Stephen S. Trott, "Words of Warning for Prosecutors Using Criminals as Witnesses," 47 *Hastings L.J.* 1381, 1383 (1996).

10 United States v. Cervantes-Pacheco, 826 F.2d 310, 315 (5th Cir. 1987).

11 Radley Balko, "Guilty before Proven Innocent," *Reason*, May 2008, at 42–55.

12 Report of the 1989–90 Los Angeles County Grand Jury: Investigation of the Involvement of Jail House Informants in the Criminal Justice System in Los Angeles County, July 1990, at 119–22, http://grandjury.co.la.ca.us/pdf/1989-90_Final.pdf (hereinafter "Los Angeles County Grand Jury Investigation Report"). See also Robert M. Bloom, *Ratting: The Use and Abuse of Informants in the American Justice System* (Westport, CT: Praeger, 2002), 64–66.

13 Los Angeles County Grand Jury Investigation Report, at 55, 58.

14 Matt Ferner, "A Mass Shooting Tore Their Lives Apart. A Corruption Scandal Crushed Their Hopes For Justice," *Huffington Post*, Mar. 9, 2018.

15 Robert P. Mosteller, "The Special Threat of Informants to the Innocent Who Are Not Innocents: Producing 'First Drafts,' Recording Incentives, and Taking a Fresh Look at the Evidence," 6 *Ohio St. J. Crim. L.* 101, 104, 164 (2009).

16 George C. Harris, "Testimony for Sale: The Law and Ethics of Snitches and Experts," 28 *Pepperdine L. Rev.* 1, 54 (2000).

17 See Joint Oversight Hearing on Law Enforcement Confidential Informant Practices before the House Comm. on the Judiciary Subcomm. on Crime, Terrorism, and Homeland Security and the Subcomm. on the Constitution, Civil Rights, and Civil Liberties, 110th Congr. (2007) (statement of J. Patrick O'Burke, Deputy Commander, Narcotics Service, Texas Dep't of Safety) (describing the need to measure police performance in terms other than numbers of arrests).

18 Ellen Yaroshefsky, "Cooperation with Federal Prosecutors: Experiences of Truth Telling and Embellishment," 68 *Fordham L. Rev.* 917, 944 (1999).

19 Steven M. Cohen, "What Is True? Perspectives of a Former Prosecutor," 23 *Cardozo L. Rev.* 817, 825 (2002).

20 Daniel S. Medwed, *Prosecution Complex: America's Race to Convict and It's Impact on the Innocent* (New York: New York Universty Press, 2012), 22–24.

21 Harris, "Testimony for Sale," at 54; Darryl Brown, "The Decline of Defense Counsel and the Rise of Accuracy in Criminal Adjudication," 93 *Cal. L. Rev.* 1585, 1600 (2005) (describing path-dependence of law enforcement decision-making).

22 See chapter 2.

23 Trott, "Words of Warning," at 1383–84.

24 Alisa Bralove, "Murder-Prosecutor's Ignorance Was No Excuse for Brady Flaw," *Daily Record* (Baltimore), Sept. 5, 2003.

25 Heather Ratcliffe, "City cops told to ID informers to bosses," *St. Louis Post Dispatch*, Sept. 12, 2009; "St. Louis Police Bristle at Bosses' Inquiry on Their Confidential Informers," *Police*, Aug. 20, 2009.

26 Goldstein v. City of Long Beach, 481 F.3d 1170 (9th Cir. 2007), rev'd, Van de Kamp v. Goldstein, 129 S. Ct. 855 (2009).

27 Los Angeles County Grand Jury Investigation Report, at 111–15.

28 Banks v. Dretke, 540 U.S. 668 (2004).

29 Walker v. City of New York, 974 F.2d 293 (2nd Cir. 2002).

30 Sivak v. Hardison, 658 F.3d 898, 911 (9th Cir. 2011).

31 Anna Clark, "He Was Wrongly Imprisoned for 25 Years. It Wasn't DNA Evidence That Got Him Out," *The New Republic*, Apr. 22, 2020; Aaron Miguel Cantú, "Ring of Snitches: How Detroit Police Slapped False Murder Convictions on Young Black Men," *TruthOut*, Mar. 31, 2015.

32 Clark, "Wrongly Imprisoned"; Cantú, "Ring of Snitches."

33 Maurice Possley, "The Prosecutor and the Snitch," The Marshall Project, Aug. 3, 2014; David Grann, "Trial By Fire," *New Yorker*, Aug. 31, 2009.

34 John A. Torres, "Citing sham of trial, prominent law firm to take on case of Gary Bennett," *FloridaToday*, May 29, 2020.

35 Raymond Bonner and Sara Rimer, "A Closer Look at Five Cases That Resulted in Executions of Texas Inmates," *N.Y. Times*, May 14, 2000; Daniele Selby, "Why Bite Mark Evidence Should Never Be Used in Criminal Trials," Innocence Project, Apr. 26, 2020, https://innocenceproject.org/what-is-bite-mark-evidence-forensic-science.

36 Commonwealth of N. Mariana Islands v. Bowie, 243 F.3d 1109, 1124 (9th Cir. 2001).

37 Brad Heath, "Federal prisoners use snitching for personal gain," *USA Today*, Dec. 14, 2012, www.usatoday.com/story/news/nation/2012/12/14/jailhouse-informants-for-sale/1762013.

38 Los Angeles County Grand Jury Report, at 18, 26, 28.

39 Cash v. Maxwell, 565 U.S. 1138 (2012) (denying cert.). The emphatic italicization is Justice Sotomayor's.

40 Cal. Penal Code § 1111.5.

41 For deeper analyses of the wrongful conviction dynamics in plea bargaining, see Alexandra Natapoff, "Negotiating Accuracy: DNA in the Age of Plea Bargaining," in Daniel S. Medwed, *Wrongful Convictions and the DNA Revolution: Twenty-Five Years of Freeing the Innocent* 85–98 (Cambridge: Cambridge University Press, 2017); Alexandra Natapoff, *Punishment without Crime: How Our Massive Misdemeanor System Traps the Innocent and Makes America More Unequal* (New York: Basic Books, 2018), 87–112.

42 John Caniglia, "Judge to Free 15 Convicted on Drug Informant's Tainted Testimony," *Cleveland Plain Dealer*, Jan. 23, 2008.

43 See introduction.

44 U.S.S.G. § 3E1.1 (rewarding defendants who plead guilty with a reduction in offense level).

45 Gross & O'Brien, "Frequency and Predictors of False Conviction," at 931.

46 Id. at 931–32.

47 Mosteller, "The Special Threat of Informants," at 104.

5. SECRET JUSTICE

1 John Emerich Edward Dalberg Acton, *Lord Acton and His Circle* (Abbot Gasquet, ed., 1968), 166, quoted in United States v. Salemme, 91 F. Supp.2d 141, 148 (D. Mass. 1999).

2 Michael J. Sniffen & John Solomon, "Thousands of Federal Cases Kept Secret," Associated Press, Mar. 5, 2006.

3 Survey of Harm to Cooperators: Final Report, Fed. Jud. Ctr., 2016; Andrew Cohen, "Is the Internet Endangering Criminal Informants?" The Marshall Project, Aug. 1, 2016.

4 Shannon Duffy, "Pa. Courts Move to Protect Informants from 'Who's a Rat' Web Site," *Legal Intelligencer*, July 17, 2007.

5 See Darryl Brown, "The Decline of Defense Counsel and the Rise of Accuracy in Criminal Adjudication," 93 *Cal. L. Rev.* 1585, 1589 (2005).

6 Town of Castle Rock v. Gonzalez, 545 U.S. 748, 761 (2005) (reaffirming "deep-rooted nature of law-enforcement discretion"); see also Linda R. S. v. Richard D., 410 U.S. 614, 619 (1973) (mother lacked standing to complain of state's failure to prosecute father for failure to pay child support, noting that "a private citizen lacks a judicially cognizable interest in the prosecution or non-prosecution of another").

7 This reflects the general fact that regulated processes tend to produce more public information, whereas discretionary, unregulated processes tend not to. See, e.g., United States v. Armstrong, 517 U.S. 456, 464–66 (1996) (holding that defendants were not entitled to discovery regarding discretionary prosecutorial functions that "courts are properly hesitant to examine").

8 See Stanley Z. Fisher, "'Just the Facts, Ma'am': Lying and the Omission of Exculpatory Evidence in Police Reports," 28 *New England L. Rev.* 1 (1993).
9 Id. at 36 & n.179.
10 David Alan Sklansky, "Police and Democracy," 103 *Mich. L. Rev.* 1699 (2005).
11 Brandon Garrett, "Remedying Racial Profiling," 33 *Colum. Hum. Rts. L. Rev.* 41, 43–44 & n.128 (2001).
12 See Mary D. Fan, "Justice Visualized: Courts and the Body Camera Revolution," 50 *U.C. Davis L. Rev.* 897 (2017).
13 See Hoffa v. United States, 385 U.S. 293, 302–03 (1966); United States v. White, 401 U.S. 745, 752–53 (1971); Illinois v. Perkins, 496 U.S. 292 (1990). See chapter 2 for a detailed explanation.
14 John Hopkins, "Man Claims He Broke into Garage, Was Police Informant," *Virginian-Pilot*, Sept. 19, 2008.
15 Illinois v. Gates, 462 U.S. 213 (1983); U.S. Const. Amend. IV.
16 Rich Lord, "Confidential informants are an integral but problematic part of federal law enforcement," *Pittsburgh Post Gazette*, Oct. 19, 2014; Rich Lord, "How data on confidential informants was gathered and analyzed," *Pittsburgh Post Gazette*, Oct. 19, 2014, www.post-gazette.com/local/region/2014/10/19/How-data-on-confidential-informants-was-gathered-and-analyzed/stories/201410190077.
17 Lawrence A. Benner & Charles T. Samarkos, "Searching for Narcotics in San Diego: Preliminary Findings from the San Diego Search Warrant Project," 36 *Cal. West. L. Rev.* 221, 239 (2000).
18 Benner & Samarkos, "Searching for Narcotics in San Diego," at 239–40.
19 Id. at 241.
20 Chapters 1 and 4 contain more detailed descriptions of these examples.
21 Court Statistics Project, 2019 Criminal Trial Court Caseload Overview: Data Table: Bench and Jury Trial Rates, www.courtstatistics.org/court-statistics/interactive-caseload-data-displays); see also Lafler v. Cooper, 566 U.S. 156, 170 (2012) ("Ninety-seven percent of federal convictions and ninety-four percent of state convictions are the result of guilty pleas.").
22 Stephanos Bibas, "Transparency and Participation in Criminal Procedure," 81 *N.Y.U. L. Rev.* 911, 942 (2006).
23 United States v. White, 2004 WL 2182188, *1 (D. Kan. 2004).
24 See chapter 7.
25 Plea Agreement, United States v. William "Rick" Singer, Case 1:19-cr-10078-RWZ (Mar. 5, 2019), www.documentcloud.org/documents/5985479-Rick-Singer-Plea-Agreement.html.
26 Freedom of Information Act ["FOIA"], 5 U.S.C. § 552; see Bennett v. Drug Enforcement Administration, 55 F. Supp.2d 36 (D.D.C. 1999) (FOIA request to DEA for records pertaining to informant Andrew Chambers).
27 Giglio v. United States, 405 U.S. 150, 154 (1972) ("When the reliability of a given witness may well be determinative of guilt or innocence, nondisclosure of evidence affecting credibility falls within this general rule [of *Brady v. Maryland*].").

28 See, e.g., United States v. Villarman-Oviedo, 325 F.3d 1 (1st Cir. 2003) (describing impeachment material); see also Roviaro v. United States, 353 U.S. 53 (1957) (in deciding whether government can withhold identity of confidential informant, court must "balance the public interest in protecting the flow of information against the right of the defendant to prepare his defense").

29 Roviaro, 353 U.S. at 60–61, 628–29.

30 United States v. Ruiz, 536 U.S. 622, 625 (2002).

31 United States v. Ruiz, 241 F.3d 1157, 1164 (9th Cir. 2001). The Court further reasoned that "a defendant's decision whether or not to plead guilty is often heavily influenced by his appraisal of the prosecution's case. . . . [Moreover,] if a defendant may not raise a *Brady* claim after a guilty plea, prosecutors may be tempted to deliberately withhold exculpatory information as part of an attempt to elicit guilty pleas." Ruiz, 214 F.3d at 1164 (internal citations and quotation marks omitted) (citing Sanchez v. United States, 50 F.3d 1448 (9th Cir. 1995) (holding that Brady rights are not automatically waived by entry of guilty plea)).

32 Ruiz, 536 U.S. at 633.

33 Id. at 631–32.

34 Jerome H. Skolnick, *Justice Without Trial: Law Enforcement in Democratic Society* (New York: Wiley, 1966), at 133.

35 Benner & Samarkos, "Searching for Narcotics in San Diego," at 239; Fisher, "'Just the Facts, Ma'am,'" at 36. See also Maya Harris et al., Letter from the ACLU of Northern California to the California Commission on the Fair Administration of Justice, Sept. 19, 2006 (documenting police and prosecutorial practices in California designed to conceal informants).

36 See R. Michael Cassidy, "'Soft Words of Hope': Giglio, Accomplice Witnesses, and the Problem of Implied Inducements," 98 *Northwestern U.L. Rev.* 1129 (2004); Ellen Yaroshefsky, "Cooperation with Federal Prosecutors: Experiences of Truth Telling and Embellishment," 68 *Fordham L. Rev.* 917, 962 (1999) (describing how prosecutors avoid taking notes when debriefing informants to avoid creating discoverable material).

37 Gary T. Marx, *Undercover: Police Surveillance in America* (Berkeley: University of California Press, 1988), xix.

38 Richmond Newspapers, Inc. v. Virginia, 448 U.S. 555, 576 (1980).

39 Id. at 572–73 (establishing right of public access to trial proceeding). See also Press-Enterprise Co. v. Superior Court of California, 464 U.S. 501 (1984) (establishing right of public access to voir dire proceeding); Press-Enterprise Co. v. Superior Court of California II, 478 U.S. 1 (1986) (establishing public access right to preliminary hearings).

40 First National Bank of Boston v. Bellotti, 435 U.S. 765, 783 (1978) (quoted in Richmond Newspapers Inc. v. Virginia, 448 U.S. 555 (1980) (establishing public right of access to criminal trials)).

41 Press-Enterprise Co. v. Superior Court, 464 U.S. 501 (1984).

42 CBS, Inc. v. U.S. Dist. Ct. for Central Dist. California, 765 F.2d 823 (9th Cir. 1985).

43 Id. at 825.

44 Id. at 826.

45 Gannett Co. Inc. v. DePasquale, 443 U.S. 368, 383 (1979); see also New York v. Hill, 528 U.S. 110 (2000) (public interest in speedy trial did not preclude defendant's waiver of time limits).

46 Id. at 383.

47 "Everything Secret Degenerates: The FBI's Use of Murderers as Informants," H.R. Rep. no. 108-414, at 126 (2004).

48 Caren Myers Morrison, "Privacy, Accountability, and the Cooperating Defendant: Towards a New Role for Internet Access to Court Records," 62 *Vanderbilt L. Rev.* 921 (2009).

49 Katherine J. Strandburg, "Home, Home on the Web and Other Fourth Amendment Implications of Technosocial Change," 70 *Maryland L. Rev.* 614, 674 (2011) ("The extent of undercover surveillance possible in the online world is drastically greater than the possibilities for similar surveillance in the physical world."); John Browning, "#Snitches Get Stitches: Witness Intimidation in the Age of Facebook and Twitter," 35 *Pace L. Rev.* 192 (2014).

50 "Witness Protection," *N.Y. Times*, June 1, 2007 (editorial).

51 Edward Burch, "Fake informant list posted on social media," ABC3340 News, Mar. 5, 2016; Shelly Bradbury, "No snitching: Facebook page 'outed' identities of cooperating witnesses in Pittsburgh," *Pittsburgh Post-Gazette*, Aug. 10, 2018.

52 Kevin Poulsen, "The Ukrainian Hacker Who Became the FBI's Best Weapon—And Worst Nightmare," Wired.com, May 2016.

53 Memorandum from John R. Tunheim and Paul Cassell, Website Posting Information on Criminal Case Cooperation (Nov. 9, 2006).

54 Report of the Judicial Conference Committee on Court Administration and Case Management on Privacy and Public Access to Electronic Case Files (December 2006), www.privacy.uscourts.gov/Policy.htm.

55 Andrew Cohen, "Is the Internet Endangering Criminal Informants?" The Marshall Project, Aug. 1, 2016.

6. THE COMMUNITY COST

1 Charles Lane and Keith Humphreys, "Opinion: Black imprisonment rates are down. It's important to know why." *Wash. Post*, Apr. 30, 2019; John Gramlich, "Black imprisonment rate in the U.S. has fallen by a third since 2006," Pew Research Ctr., May 6, 2020; E. Ann Carson, *Prisoners in 2019* (Washington, D.C.: U.S. Dep't of Justice, Bureau of Justice Statistics, Oct. 2020), at 10; *Report to the United Nations Special Rapporteur on Contemporary Forms of Racism, Racial Discrimination, Xenophobia, and Related Intolerance Regarding Racial Disparities in the United States* (Washington D.C.: The Sentencing Project, Mar. 2018): 3–4; Bruce Western & Becky Pettit, "Incarceration and social inequality," *Daedelus* (Summer 2010): 8–11.

2 William J. Sabol et al., *Trends in Correctional Control by Race and Sex* (Washington D.C.: Council on Criminal Justice, Dec. 2019), 8.

3 Ricky Camplain et al., "Racial/Ethnic Differences in Drug- and Alcohol-Related Arrest Outcomes in a Southwest County From 2009 to 2018", *Am. J. Public Health* 110, no. S1 (Jan. 2020): 85–87; Barbara Ferrer and John M. Connolly, "Racial Inequities in Drug Arrests: Treatment in Lieu of and After Incarceration," *Am. J. Public Health* 108, no. 8 (August 2018): 968–69.

4 Alexandra Natapoff, *Punishment without Crime: How Our Massive Misdemeanor System Traps the Innocent and Makes America More Unequal* (New York: Basic Books, 2018), 151–57.

5 Floyd v. City of New York, 959 F. Supp. 2d 540 (S.D.N.Y. 2013); *Investigation of the Baltimore City Police Department* (U.S. Department of Justice, Civil Rights Division, August 10, 2016).

6 Gabriel L. Schwartz and Jaquelyn L. Jahn, "Mapping fatal police violence across U.S. metropolitan areas: Overall rates and racial/ethnic inequities, 2013–2017," *PLoS ONE* 15, no. 6 (2020): e0229686. https://doi.org/10.1371/journal.pone.0229686; Fatal Force: Policing Shootings Database, *Wash. Post*, Mar. 17, 2021, www.washingtonpost.com.

7 *Black Homicide Victimization in the United States: An Analysis of 2016 Homicide Data*, Violence Policy Center, May 2019, 1; Jill Leovy, *Ghettoside: A True Story of Murder in America* (New York: Spiegel & Grau, 2015).

8 See, e.g., Jonathan Kozol, *The Shame of the Nation: The Restoration of Apartheid Schooling in America* (New York: Crown Publishers, 2005), 19. Kozol documents the continuing poor quality and pervasive segregation in U.S. public schools, with 75 percent of nonwhite children in predominantly nonwhite schools and 2 million children of color in "apartheid schools" in which 99 percent of the students are nonwhite. See also Gary B. v. Whitmer, 957 F.3d 616, 624 (6th Cir.), reh'g en banc granted, opinion vacated, 958 F.3d 1216 (6th Cir. 2020) (describing low-performing Detroit schools that "fail to provide access to literacy").

9 Jeffrey Fagan & Tracey L. Meares, "Punishment, Deterrence and Social Control: The Paradox of Punishment in Minority Communities," 6 *Ohio St. J. Crim. L.* 173, 193–196 (2008) (describing community impact of illegal economic work); Sudhir Alladi Venkatesh, *Off the Books: The Underground Economy of the Urban Poor* (Cambridge, MA: Harvard University Press, 2006), xviii–xix; see also Naomi F. Sugie, "Work as Foraging: A Smartphone Study of Job Search and Employment after Prison," *Am. J. Sociol.* 123, no. 5 (2108):1453–91.

10 Robert J. Sampson & William Julius Wilson, "Toward a Theory of Race, Crime, and Urban Inequality," in J. Hagan & R. Peterson, eds., *Crime and Inequality*, 37, 38 (reprinted in R. Crutchfeld et al., eds., *Crime Readings* (Thousand Oaks, CA: Pine Forge Press, 2000), at 127) ("[T]he macrosocial or community-level of explanation [for crime] asks what it is about community structures and cultures that produces differential rates of crime.").

11 See, e.g., Benjamin Justice & Tracey L. Meares, "How the Criminal Justice System Educates Citizens," 651 *Annals Am. Acad. Pol. & Soc. Sci.* 159 (2014); Amy Lerman and Vesla Weaver, *Arresting Citizenship: The Democratic Consequences of American Crime Control* (Chicago: University of Chicago Press, 2014).

12 Monica C. Bell, "Police Reform and the Dismantling of Legal Estrangement," 126 *Yale L.J.* 2054, 2067 (2017).

13 *A Tale of Two Countries: Racially Targeted Arrests in the Era of Marijuana Reform* (Washington, D.C.: ACLU, 2020), 5, 21; Ryan S. King, "Disparity by Geography: The War on Drugs in America's Cities," at 2 (Washington, D.C.: The Sentencing Project, May 2008).

14 2019 Sourcebook of Federal Sentencing Statistics, tbl. 37 (2019) ("Of the 76,538 cases, in 7,272 the offender received a §5K1.1 substantial assistance departure below the guideline range."); id. at tbl. D-14 (4,409 of 5K1.1 departures were drug trafficking cases, out of a total of 19,830 drug trafficking cases, or 22.6%), www.ussc.gov/research/sourcebook-2019. In addition, another 1,070 people received a postconviction departure pursuant to Rule 35, Fed. R. Crim. P. Id. at tbl. R.

15 Linda Drazga Maxfield & John H. Kramer, "Substantial Assistance: An Empirical Yardstick Gauging Equity in Current Federal Policy and Practice," 11 *Fed. Sent. Rep.* 6, 9, 1998 WL 911926 (1998).

16 FBI FY 2008 Authorization and Budget Request to Congress, 4–24 (2007) (stating that the FBI maintains 15,000 confidential human sources); Audit of the Drug Enforcement Administration's Management and Oversight of Its Confidential Source Program, i–iv, Office of the Inspector General, U.S. Dep't of Justice (Sept. 2016) (reporting that the DEA maintains 18,000 informants).

17 "Prisoners in 2019," at tbls. 13 & 14 (Black people comprised 29.5% of drug defendants sentenced in state courts); cf. Brian A. Reaves, *Felony Defendants in Large Urban Counties, 2009—Statistics Tables* (Washington D.C.: Bureau of Justice Statistics, U.S. Dep't of Justice, December 2013), 7 (Black people comprised 45% of convicted drug defendants in large urban counties); "2019 Crime in the United States," tbl. 43, Arrests by Race and Ethnicity (Washington, D.C., FBI, 2019).

18 ACLU, *A Tale of Two Countries*, at 5, 21.

19 Id. at 33–34, tbl. 8; King, "Disparity by Geography," at 11–12.

20 Eric Lotke and Jason Ziedenberg, "Tipping Point: Maryland's Overuse of Incarceration and the Impact on Public Safety," *Policy Brief, Washington, DC: Justice Policy Institute* (2005), 8–9.

21 Marc V. Levine, "Milwaukee 53206: The Anatomy of Concentrated Disadvantage In an Inner City Neighborhood 2000–2017," University of Wisconsin–Milwaukee Center for Economic Development (Mar. 2019), 7–8, 51 & n.53.

22 Nancy G. La Vigne & Vera Kachnowski, "A Portrait of Prisoner Reentry in Maryland," 2, 50–53, 57–60 (Washington, D.C.: Urban Institute Justice Policy Center, Mar. 2003).

23 Nancy G. La Vigne & Cynthia A. Mamalian, "A Portrait of Prisoner Reentry in Illinois," 2, 50–51 (Washington, D.C.: Urban Institute Justice Policy Center, Apr. 2003).

24 "State Court Caseload Digest: 2018 Data," Court Statistics Project, National Center for State Courts (2020), 14; "Prisoners in 2019," at 20.

25 "Prisoners in 2019," at 20; "Estimated number of arrests by offense and race, 2019," *Statistical Briefing Book* (Washington, D.C.: Office of Justice Programs, U.S. Dep't

of Justice); "Arrests by Race and Ethnicity," *Crime in the United States, 2019*, tbl. 43 (FBI, 2019).

26 "Prisoners in 2019," at 20; Jerome H. Skolnick, *Justice without Trial: Law Enforcement in Democratic Society* (New York: Wiley, 1966), 126–30.

27 Jennifer Bronson et al., "Drug Use, Dependence, and Abuse Among State Prisoners and Jail" (Washington, D.C.: Bureau of Justice Statistics, U.S. Dep't of Justice, June 2017), 6.

28 Id. at 1.

29 See, e.g., N.J.S.A. § 2C:35–12 (permitting adjustment of mandatory minimum sentences where defendants have entered into a cooperation agreement); N.J.S.A. § 2C:44–1(b)12 (instructing courts to consider defendant cooperation in sentencing).

30 George Joseph, "The Mount Vernon Police Tapes: In Secretly Recorded Calls, Officer Says Some Drug Dealers Operate With 'Free Rein,'" *The Gothamist*, June 18, 2020.

31 Opinion and Order, United States v. Ail, CR 05-323-01-RE (Aug. 14, 2007) (Redden, J.); see also Ashbel S. Green, "Shop Owner Demands FBI Records," *Portland Oregonian*, Aug. 15, 2006, B10.

32 Ken Armstrong, "The Problem With Hiring Liars to Catch Crooks: Can you really trust an informant who's been arrested in 43 states?" The Marshall Project, Sept. 14, 2015.

33 David Conti & Richard Byrne Reilly, "Decision to Release Jailhouse Snitch Backfires," *Pittsburgh Tribune Review*, Apr. 17, 2005.

34 Editorial, "Police Debacle Earns Courageous Rebuke," *St. Petersburg Times*, Apr. 10, 2008, at 8A.

35 Joseph, "The Mount Vernon Police Tapes," at 10.

36 Skolnick, *Justice without Trial*, at 129.

37 Richard Rosenfeld, Bruce A. Jacobs & Richard Wright, "Snitching and the Code of the Street," 43 *British J. Criminol.* 291, 303, n.7 (2003).

38 John Madinger, *Confidential Informant: Law Enforcement's Most Valuable Tool* (Boca Raton, FL: CRC Press, 2000), 187.

39 Jerome G. Miller, *Search and Destroy: African-American Males in the Criminal Justice System* (New York: Cambridge University Press, 1996), 102.

40 Rosenfeld, "Snitching and the Code of the Street," at 304–06.

41 See Omri Yadlin, "The Conspirator Dilemma: Introducing the 'Trojan Horse' Enforcement Strategy" 2 *Rev. L. & Econ.* 25 (2006).

42 Peter Finn & Kerry Murphy Healey, "Preventing Gang- and Drug-Related Witness Intimidation," National Institute of Justice, U.S. Dep't of Justice, Nov. 1996, at 4–5, 6, www.ncjrs.gov/pdffiles/163067.pdf; Kerry Murphy Healey, "Victim and Witness Intimidation: New Developments and Emerging Responses," National Institute of Justice, U.S. Dep't of Justice, Oct. 1995, at 2, www.ncjrs.gov/pdffiles/witintim.pdf.

43 Scott Jacques & Richard Wright, "The Relevance of Peace to Studies of Drug Market Violence," 46 *Criminology* 221, 222 (2008).

44 Joel Rubin, "Slaying of Witness Spurs LAPD Changes," *L.A. Times*, July 18, 2008, California section, 1.

45 "Slain Teen's Mother Wins Suit: Court: Award of at least $1 million to go to woman whose son, killed in Norwalk Drug house, was police informant," *Long Beach Press-Telegram*, Aug. 27, 2002, at A2.

46 Laurence A. Benner, "Racial Disparity in Narcotics Search Warrants," 6 *J. Gender, Race & Just.* 183, 190–91, 194, 196, 200–201 & n.60 (2002). See also Laurence A. Benner & Charles T. Samarkos, "Searching for Narcotics in San Diego: Preliminary Findings from the San Diego Search Warrant Project," 36 *Cal. West. L. Rev.* 221 (2000).

47 See Andrew E. Taslitz, "Wrongly Accused Redux: How Race Contributes to Convicting the Innocent: The Informants Example," 37 *Southwest U. L. Rev.* 101 (2008).

48 I have written more extensively about the phenomenon of urban underenforcement in Alexandra Natapoff, "Underenforcement," 75 *Fordham L. Rev.* 1715 (2006). See also Randall Kennedy, *Race, Crime, and the Law* (New York: Pantheon Books, 1997), 4, 11, 113–25.

49 Charles R. Epp, Steven Maynard-Moody & Donald Haider-Markel, *Pulled Over: How Police Stops Define Race and Citizenship* (Chicago: University of Chicago Press, 2014).

50 Elizabeth Hinton, *America on Fire: The Untold History of Police Violence and Black Rebellion Since the 1960s* (New York: Liveright, 2021); Amna A. Akbar, "Toward A Radical Imagination of Law," 93 *N.Y.U. L. Rev.* 405, 416 (2018); Kennedy, *Race, Crime, and the Law*, at 115–18.

51 Robert J. Sampson & Dawn Jeglum Bartusch, "Legal Cynicism and (Subcultural?) Tolerance of Deviance: The Neighborhood Context of Racial Differences," 32 *Law & Soc. Rev.* 777, 783–84 (1998).

52 Monica C. Bell, "Anti-Segregation Policing," 95 N.Y.U. L. Rev. 650, 733–34 (2020).

53 Associated Press, "Reno Urges Officers to Try to Regain Trust: Department to gather data on police brutality," *Baltimore Sun*, Apr. 16, 1999, at 7A.

54 "Excerpts of Attorney General Eric Holder's Remarks at a Community College," St. Louis, MO, August 20, 2014, www.justice.gov/opa/speech/excerpts-attorney-general-eric-holder-s-remarks-community-college.

55 Matthew Desmond and Andrew V. Papachristos, Opinion: "Why Don't You Just Call the Cops?," *N.Y. Times*, Sept. 30, 2016.

56 Tom Farrey, "'Melo Looks Past Hoops to Street," *ESPN The Magazine*, Jan. 18, 2006.

57 Jeremy Kahn, "The Story of a Snitch," *Atlantic Monthly*, Apr. 2007, at 3.

58 See, e.g., Tommie Shelby, *Dark Ghettos: Injustice, Dissent and Reform* (Cambridge: Harvard University Press, 2016), 238–45 (arguing that the state loses its moral authority to condemn crime—although not its institutional authority to enforce it—when it engages in systemic injustice); Kathryne M. Young & Joan Petersilia, "Keeping Track: Surveillance, Control, and the Expansion of the Carceral State," 129 *Harv. L. Rev.* 1318 (2016) (book review of *Pulled Over*, *On the Run*, and *The Eternal Criminal Record*); Michelle Alexander, *The New Jim Crow: Mass Incarcera-*

tion in the Age of Colorblindness (New York: New Press, 2012); Loïc Wacquant, *Punishing the Poor: The Neoliberal Government of Social Insecurity* (Durham: Duke University Press, 2009), 195–208.

59 Tracey L. Meares and Tom R. Tyler, "Justice Sotomayor and the Jurisprudence of Procedural Justice," 123 *Yale L.J. Forum* 525, 526–27 (2014); Tom R. Tyler and Jeffrey Fagan, "Legitimacy and Cooperation: Why Do People Help the Police Fight Crime in Their Communities?," 6 *Ohio St. J. Crim. L.* 231 (2008); Tom R. Tyler & Yuen J. Huo, *Trust in the Law: Encouraging Public Cooperation with the Police and Courts* (New York: Russell Sage Foundation, 2002); Tom R. Tyler, *Why People Obey the Law* (New Haven, CT: Yale University Press, 1990).

60 Tyler & Fagan, "Legitimacy and Cooperation," at 266–67.

61 Id. at 239; see Tracey L. Meares, "The Path Forward: Improving the Dynamics of Community-Police Relationships to Achieve Effective Law Enforcement Policies," 117 *Colum. L. Rev.* 1355, 1362 (2017) (describing theory of procedural justice).

62 Tyler & Fagan, "Legitimacy and Cooperation," at 235; see also Jocelyn Simonson, "Police Reform Through a Power Lens," 130 *Yale L.J.* 778, 788 (2021) (arguing for a view of police reform that is broader than evaluating trust in police).

63 Cheryl W. Thompson, "Dozens in D.C., Maryland paid the ultimate price for cooperating with police," *Wash. Post*, Jan. 10, 2015.

64 Jeffrey Fagan & Daniel Richman, "Understanding Recent Spikes and Longer Trends in American Murders," 117 *Colum. L. Rev.* 1235, 1282 (2017) (connnecting low crime clearance rates to reluctance to cooperate with police in Los Angeles, New York and Chicago).

65 Jill Leovy & Doug Smith, "Mortal Wounds: Getting away with murder in South L.A.'s killing zone," *L.A. Times*, Jan. 1, 2004, at A1.

66 Id.

67 Fagan & Richman, "Understanding Recent Spikes," at 1284.

68 See Alexandra Natapoff, "Underenforcement," 75 *Fordham L. Rev.* 1715, 1719 (2006) ("Over- and underenforcement are twin symptoms of a deeper democratic weakness of the criminal system: its non-responsiveness to the needs of the poor, racial minorities, and the otherwise politically vulnerable.").

69 See James Q. Wilson & George L. Kelling, "Broken Windows: The Police and Neighborhood Safety," *Atlantic Monthly*, Mar. 1982, at 29–83 ("Some Chicago officers tell of times when they were afraid to enter [high-crime housing projects].").

70 Leovy & Smith, "Mortal Wounds," at A1; see also Jeremy M. Wilson & K. Jack Riley, "Violence in East and West Oakland," WR-129-OJP, at 14 (RAND, Feb. 2004, prepared for Office of Justice Programs) (describing high-crime community's "general contempt for the police").

71 See chapter 5.

72 Ofra Bickel, "Frontline: Snitch," Transcript (PBS, Jan. 12, 1999), 32.

73 Art Barnum, "Mom Called 'Snitch' on Son in Murder Case," *Chicago Tribune*, Nov. 29, 2006.

74 Bickel, "Frontline: Snitch," at 7–10.

75 See Venkatesh, *Off the Books*, at 6–13.

76 Sampson & Wilson, "Toward a Theory of Race, Crime, and Urban Inequality" (describing social disorganization theory); Robert J. Sampson, Stephen W. Raudenbush & Felton Earls, "Neighborhoods and Violent Crime: A Multilevel Study of Collective Efficacy," 277 *Science* 918 (1997) (arguing that social dislocation and disadvantage undermine collective efficacy of communities, which in turn disables those communities from internally regulating violence and crime).

77 Jeffrey Fagan & Tracey L. Meares, "Punishment, Deterrence and Social Control: The Paradox of Punishment in Minority Communities," 6 *Ohio St. J. Crim. L.* 173, 189 (2008).

78 Michael Tonry, *Malign Neglect: Race, Crime, and Punishment in America* (New York: Oxford University Press, 1995), 105–06.

79 This is true with respect to carceral policies in general. Fagan & Meares, "Punishment, Deterrence and Social Control," at 204 (arguing that "the increasing likelihood and severity of punishment . . . has approached normative levels, compromising the moral component of punishment and in turn the logic of deterrence").

80 See *Key Substance Use and Mental Health Indicators in the United States: Results from the 2019 National Survey on Drug Use and Health* (Washington D.C.: Substance Abuse and Mental Health Services Administration (SAMHSA), Sept. 2020), 14–15; "Federal Drug Sentencing Laws Bring High Cost, Low Return: Penalty Increases Enacted in 1980s and 1990s Have Not Reduced Drug Use or Recidivism," 28 *Fed. Sent. Rep.* 4, 6, 2015 WL 7906229 (Vera Institute of Justice).

81 William K. Rashbaum, "'Last Don' Reported to Be the First One to Betray the Mob," *N.Y. Times*, Jan. 28, 2005, at A1 (describing numerous high-level mafia operatives turned informant). Of course, this policy had its costs as well. See "*Everything Secret Degenerates: The FBI's Use of Murderers as Informants*," H.R. Rep. no. 108-414, at 126 (2004), 1–9.

82 Michael Tonry, "Making American Sentencing Just, Humane, and Effective," 46 *Crime & Just.* 441, 457 (2017) (describing replacement effects in illegal drug markets).

7. HOW THE OTHER HALF LIVES

1 David Glovin and David Voreacos, "From entangled trader to FBI secret weapon," *Wash. Post*, Dec. 9, 2012; Bob Van Voris and Ian Thomas, "Ex-Galleon Trader Who Led U.S. to Probe Rajaratnam Avoids Prison," *Bloomberg News*, Jan. 21, 2012; Reynolds Holding et al., "Insider trading snitch got off too lightly," *Reuters Breakingviews*, Jan. 23, 2012; United States v. Goffer, No. 10-CR-56–1 (RJS), 2017 WL 203229, at *2 (S.D.N.Y. Jan. 17, 2017).

2 Darryl K. Brown, "Street Crime, Corporate Crime, and the Contingency of Criminal Liability," 149 *U. Pa. L. Rev.* 1295, 1306–08 (2001).

3 Gary T. Marx, *Undercover: Police Surveillance in America* (Berkeley: University of California Press, 1988), 8.

4 2020 Sourcebook of Federal Sentencing Statistics, Race of Federal Offenders by Type of Crime, tbl. 5 (Washington D.C.: U.S. Sentencing Commission, 2020);

Kristin M. Finklea, Organized Crime in the United States: Trends and Issues for Congress (Congressional Research Service, Apr. 16, 2009), 12–14; Center on Law & Security, NYU School of Law, Terrorist Trial Report Card: September 11, 2001-September 11, 2010, at 20 (2010), www.lawandsecurity.org/terrorist-trial-report-cards.

5 Dick Lehr, "The Information Underworld: Police Reliance on Criminal Informants Is a Dangerous Game for Both," *Boston Globe*, Oct. 16, 1988, at A27.

6 FBI FY 2008 Authorization and Budget Request to Congress, 4–24 (2007). The more recent 2019 DOJ OIG audit redacts the number of informants currently maintained by the FBI. Audit of the Federal Bureau of Investigation's Management of Its Confidential Human Source Validation Processes, Office of the Inspector General, U.S. Dep't of Justice (Nov. 2019) (hereinafter "OIG Audit of FBI"), at 1.

7 See OIG Audit of FBI, at i; FBI Guidelines, at 18.

8 Ben A. Franklin, "Informer Is a Witness at Sentence Hearing for Teamster's Chief," *N.Y. Times*, Feb. 8, 1983, at A1; Joseph P. Fried, "Ex-Mob Underboss Given Lenient Term for Help as Witness," *N.Y. Times*, Sept. 27, 1994, at A1.

9 Jess Bidgood and Katharine Q. Seelye, "At Boston Trial of 'Cadillac Frank,' a Who's Who of Mobsters in Sensible Shoes," *N.Y. Times*, May 11, 2018.

10 OIG Report, chapter 3, at 3.

11 Alan Feuer, "Gravano and Son Are to Enter Guilty Pleas in Ecstasy Case," *N.Y. Times*, May 25, 2001, at B2; Tom Troncone, "Pals Say Gravano Ordered Hit on Cop," *N.J. Record*, Nov. 7, 2006, at A1.

12 "Everything Secret Degenerates: The FBI's Use of Murderers as Informants," H.R. Rep. no. 108-414 (2004), www.gpoaccess.gov/serialset/creports/everything-secret.html).

13 The Attorney General's Guidelines Regarding the Use of Confidential Informants (2002), 1–2 (hereinafter "DOJ Guidelines"), www.justice.gov/archives.

14 FBI Guidelines. Other federal agencies such as the DEA, ATF, and the United States Marshals Service remain governed by the general 2002 guidelines.

15 OIG Report, chapter 3, at 18.

16 OIG Audit of FBI, at 5, 31.

17 Letter from Representative Stephen Lynch to Attorney General Eric Holder, Aug. 22, 2013, https://lynch.house.gov/2013/8/congressman-lynch-urges-attorney-general-holder-strengthen-guidelines-fbi-confidential; Letter from Representative Stephen Lynch to Congressman Darrell Issa, Oct. 1, 2013, https://oversight.house.gov/sites/democrats.oversight.house.gov/files/migrated/uploads/2013-10-01.Lynch%20to%20Issa%20re%20FBI%20Hearing.pdf.

18 FBI Guidelines, at 8, 13, 15, 17–18, 27.

19 United States v. Friedrick, 842 F.2d 382, 384 (D.C. Cir. 1988); Schreiber, "Dealing with the Devil," at 323–24.

20 Letter from Representative Darrell Issa and Senator Charles Grassley to Attorney General Eric Holder, September 27, 2011; Report of the Committee on Oversight

and Gov't Reform, House Rep. 112–546, 112th Congr., June 22, 2012, at 43; Richard Serrano, "Drug lords targeted by Fast and Furious were FBI informants," *L.A. Times*, Mar. 21, 2012.

21 Joint Oversight Hearing on Law Enforcement Confidential Informant Practices before the House Comm. on the Judiciary Subcomm. on Crime, Terrorism, and Homeland Security and the Subcomm. on the Constitution, Civil Rights, and Civil Liberties, 110th Congr. (2007), Hearing Transcript, Thursday, July 19, 2007, at 59–61 (hereinafter "Oversight Hearing Transcript").

22 See Law Enforcement Cooperation Act of 2006, H.R. 4132, 109th Cong. (2006).

23 Dina Temple-Raston, "Legislator Aims to Regulate FBI Behavior," *Morning Edition*, National Public Radio, Oct. 15, 2008.

24 Lynch Letter to Holder, at 2.

25 H.R. 1857 (115th Cong.); H.R. 2985 (114th Cong.); H.R. 265 (113th Cong.); H.R. 3228 (112th Cong.)

26 Daniel C. Richman & William J. Stuntz, "Al Capone's Revenge: An Essay on the Political Economy of Pretextual Prosecutions," 105 *Colum. L. Rev.* 583, 601 (2005); cf. Carlos Berdejó, "Small Investments, Big Losses: The States' Role in Protecting Local Investors from Securities Fraud," 92 *Wash. L. Rev.* 567, 572 (2017) (describing the underregulation of small-scale state and local securities transactions). See also Sourcebook *Online*, tbls. 5.44.2004 & 5.10.2006, Bureau of Justice Statistics, U.S. Dep't of Justice (2006), www.albany.edu/sourcebook/pdf/t5442004.pdf and www.albany.edu/sourcebook/pdf/t5102006.pdf.

27 Darryl Brown, "Street Crime, Corporate Crime, and the Contingency of Criminal Liability," 149 *U. Pa. L. Rev.* 1295, 1327–28 (2001).

28 Clifton Leaf, "White Collar Criminals: They lie, they cheat, they steal, and they've been getting away with it for too long: Enough is enough," *Fortune*, Mar. 18, 2002, at 60–76.

29 Brooke Masters, "Are Executives' Sentences Too Harsh? Debate is rising about deterrence of corporate crime," *Houston Chronicle*, July 15, 2005, at 2; Ronald Sullivan, "Milken's Sentence Reduced by Judge; 7 Months Are Left," *N.Y. Times*, Aug. 6, 1992.

30 Robert D. McFadden, "Charles Keating, 90, Key Figure in '80s Savings and Loan Crisis, Dies," *N.Y. Times*, Apr. 2, 2014; see 21 U.S.C. § 841(b)(1)(B)(iii).

31 Christine Hurt, "The Undercivilization of Corporate Law," 33 *J. Corp. L.* 361, 373–75 (2008).

32 Masters, "Are Executives' Sentences Too Harsh?" at 2.

33 Jed S. Rakoff, "The Financial Crisis: Why Have No High-Level Executives Been Prosecuted?," *N.Y. Rev. Books* (Jan. 9, 2014). See also Brandon L. Garrett, "Declining Corporate Prosecutions," 57 *Am. Crim. L. Rev.* 109 (2020); William D. Cohan, "A Clue to the Scarcity of Financial Crisis Prosecutions," *N.Y. Times*, July 21, 2016; William D. Cohan, "How Wall Street's Bankers Stayed Out of Jail," *Atlantic Monthly*, Sept. 2015.

34 See Sara Sun Beale, "Is Corporate Criminal Liability Unique?" 44 *Am. Crim. L. Rev.* 1503, 1529–31 (2007); see also Leaf, "White Collar Criminals," at 62.

35 See, e.g., Ewing v. California, 538 U.S. 11, 18 (2003) (upholding Ewing's sentence of twenty-five years to life for stealing three golf clubs); Robin Kaiser-Schatzlein, "How White-Collar Criminals Get Away With It," *The New Republic*, Sept. 15, 2020 (quoting Professor Jennifer Taub's finding that white-collar crime costs victims between $300 and $800 billion per year while street-level crimes like burglary, larceny, and theft cost victims approximately $16 billion).

36 Honorable Stephen J. Fortunato, Jr., "Judges, Racism, and the Problem of Actual Innocence," 57 *Maine L. Rev.* 481, 489–90 (2005).

37 Max Schanzenbach & Michael L. Yaeger, "Prison Time, Fines, and Federal White Collar Criminals: The Anatomy of a Racial Disparity," 96 *J. Crim. L. & Criminology* 757, 758 (2006).

38 Brown, "Street Crime," at 1312–15.

39 Grant McCool, "FBI sees more hedge fund trading probe informants," Reuters, Feb. 27, 2012.

40 Alexei Barrionuevo & Kurt Eichenwald, "What Remains Unanswered at the Enron Trial," *N.Y. Times*, May 9, 2006, at C1.

41 See Sample Target Letter, United States Attorney's Manual (U.S.A.M.) § 9, Criminal Resource Manual, at 160 (1997), www.usdoj.gov/usao/eousa/foia_reading_room/usam/title9/crm00160.htm.

42 Kenneth Mann, *Defending White Collar Crime: A Portrait of Attorneys at Work* (New Haven, CT: Yale University Press, 1985), 5.

43 Daniel C. Richman, "Cooperating Clients," 56 *Ohio St. L.J.* 69, 89, 109 (1995).

44 Id. at 109–10 (quoting Michael H. Metzger, Advertisement, *Nat'l L.J.*, May 24, 1993, at 26 (letter dated Apr. 20, 1993) from Michael H. Metzger to Roberto Martinez, United States Attorney for the Southern District of Florida).

45 Kurt Eichenwald & Alex Barrionuevo, "The Enron Verdict: The overview: Tough justice for executives in Enron era," *N.Y. Times*, May 27, 2006, at A1.

46 See 18 U.S.C. §§ 6001–6005 (governing formal grants of immunity); Ian Weinstein, "Regulating the Market for Snitches," 47 *Buff. L. Rev.* 563 (1999); Richman, "Cooperating Clients," at 94–109.

47 Graham Hughes, "Agreements for Cooperation in Criminal Cases," 45 *Vand. L. Rev.* 1, 3 (1992).

48 Steven M. Cohen, "What Is True? Perspectives of a Former Prosecutor," 23 *Cardozo L. Rev.* 817, 825 (2002); see also Claudia M. Landeo & Kathryn E. Spier, "Optimal Law Enforcement with Ordered Leniency," 63 *J.L. & Econ.* 71 (2020).

49 Ellen Yaroshefsky, "Cooperation with Federal Prosecutors: Experiences of Truth Telling and Embellishment," 68 *Fordham L. Rev.* 917, 929 (1999).

50 Arthur Andersen v. United States, 544 U.S. 696 (2005).

51 Memorandum from Mark R. Filip, Deputy Attorney General, to Heads of Department Components and U.S. Attorneys, Principles of Federal Prosecution of Business Organizations, Aug. 28, 2008, www.usdoj.gov/opa/documents/corp-charging-guidelines.pdf (hereinafter "Filip Memo").

52 Filip Memo, at 7.

53 Memorandum from Sally Quillian Yates, Deputy Att'y Gen., U.S. Dep't of Justice, To Heads of Dep't Components & All U.S. Attorneys, Individual Accountability for Corporate Wrongdoing (Sept. 9, 2015), www.justice.gov/dag/file/769036/download, (hereinafter "Yates Memo"). See Elizabeth E. Joh and Thomas W. Joo, "Essay, The Corporation as Snitch: The New DOJ Guidelines on Prosecuting White Collar Crime," 101 *Va. L. Rev. Online* 51 (2015–2016).

54 Filip Memo, at 5.

55 United States Sentencing Guidelines [U.S.S.G.] § 8C2.5 & note 13.

56 U.S.S.G. § 8C4.1.

57 Garrett, "Declining Corporate Prosecutions," at 110 (documenting declining numbers of federal prosecutions); David M. Uhlmann, "Deferred Prosecution and Non-Prosecution Agreements and the Erosion of Corporate Criminal Liability," 72 *Md. L. Rev.* 1295 (2013). See also Gibson Dunn & Crutcher LLP, *2020 Year-End Update on Corporate Non-Prosecution Agreements and Deferred Prosecution Agreements* (Jan. 19, 2021), www.gibsondunn.com/2020-year-end-update-on-corporate-non-prosecution-agreements-and-deferred-prosecution-agreements/?utm_source=Mondaq&utm_medium=syndication&utm_campaign=LinkedIn-integration; Brandon L. Garrett & Jon Ashley, "Corporate Prosecution Registry," Duke University and University of Virginia School of Law, http://lib.law.virginia.edu/Garrett/corporate-prosecution-registry/index.html.

58 See 18 U.S.C. § 3154(10) (authorizing pretrial diversion program); United States Attorneys' Manual § 9–22.010 (Apr. 2011) (establishing criteria for pretrial diversion eligibility), www.usdoj.gov/usao/eousa/foia_reading_room/usam/title9/22mcrm.htm#9-22.100.

59 See Eric Lichtblau, "In Justice Shift, Corporate Deals Replace Trials," *N.Y. Times*, Apr. 9, 2008, at A1; Lisa Kern Griffin, "Compelled Cooperation and the New Corporate Criminal Procedure," 82 *N.Y.U. L. Rev.* 311 (2007).

60 Daniel Fisher & Peter Lattman, "Ratted Out: That reassuring corporate attorney who asked you a few questions may turn out to be the long arm of the law," *Forbes*, July 4, 2005, at 49.

61 United States v. Stein, 435 F. Supp. 2d 330, 350 (S.D. N.Y. 2006).

62 Griffin, "Compelled Cooperation," at 323–24.

63 Garrett, Declining Corporate Prosecutions, at 112.

64 Griffin, "Compelled Cooperation," at 330–32.

65 Julia Rose O'Sullivan, "The DOJ Risks Killing the Golden Goose Through Computer Associates/Singleton Theories of Obstruction," 44 *Am. Crim. L. Rev.* 1447, 1450, 1452 (2007).

66 Filip Memo, at 8.

67 Philip Shenon, "New Guidelines Ahead of Ashcroft Testimony," *N.Y. Times*, Mar. 11, 2008.

68 Rick Claypool, "Corporate Criminals Above the Law," Public Citizen, May 3, 2021, www.citizen.org/article/corporate-criminals-above-the-law-prosecutions-plunged.

69 Lichtblau, "Justice Shift," at A1.

70 Northern Mariana Islands v. Bowie, 243 F.3d 1109, 1123 (9th Cir. 2001).

71 Yates Memo, at 2.

72 Uhlmann, at 1298; Joh & Joo, at 58.

73 Ellen S. Podgor, "White-Collar Cooperators: The Government in Employer-Employee Relationships," 23 *Cardozo L. Rev.* 795 (2002).

74 United States v. Stein, 440 F.Supp.2d 315, 318 (S.D.N.Y. 2006) ("Stein II").

75 Id. at 337–38; United States v. Stein, 435 F.Supp.2d 330, 365–66, 382 (S.D.N.Y. 2006) ("Stein I"), aff'd, United States v. Stein, 541 F.3d 130 (2nd Cir. 2008).

76 Filip Memo, at 13.

77 Uhlmann, at 1298; Joh & Joo, at 58; Podgor, "White-Collar Cooperators," at 804.

78 Filip Memo, at 4.

79 Darryl Brown, "Street Crime, Corporate Crime," at 1330–31; Beale, "Is Corporate Criminal Liability Unique?" at 1505–06.

80 David Cole, *No Equal Justice: Race and Class in the American Criminal Justice System* (New York: New Press, 1999), 7–8. See Alexandra Natapoff, "The Penal Pyramid," in *The New Criminal Justice Thinking,* 72–73, Sharon Dolovich and Alexandra Natapoff, eds. (New York: New York University Press, 2017) (arguing that rule of law wanes at the bottom of the penal pyramid where defendants are most vulnerable); see also conclusion.

81 Margaret M. Blair & Lynn A. Stout, "Trust, Trustworthiness, and the Behavioral Foundations of Corporate Law," 149 *U. Penn. L. Rev.* 1735, 1737 (2001).

82 Id. at 1740; see also Orly Lobel, "Citizenship, Organizational Citizenship, and the Laws of Overlapping Obligations," 97 *California L. Rev.* 433 (2009) (describing the powerful role of loyalty in maintaining organizational health).

83 Wadie E. Said, *Crimes of Terror: The Legal and Political Implications of Federal Terrorism Prosecutions* (Oxford: Oxford University Press, 2015), 47–50 (describing informant-based prosecutions of Occupy activists); Gary T. Marx, "Thoughts on a Neglected Category of Social Movement Participant: The Agent Provocateur and the Informant," 80 *Am. J. Sociol.* 402, 404–9 (1974); see also Joe Sexton, "He Spent Years Infiltrating White Supremacist Groups. Here's What He Has to Say About What's Going on Now," ProPublica, Aug. 30, 2019.

84 Hampton v. Hanrahan, 600 F.2d 600, 609, 613–15 (7th Cir. 1979); see also Elizabeth Hinton, "The Unsettling Message of Judas and the Black Messiah," *Atlantic Monthly,* Feb. 13. 2021.

85 David J. Garrow, "The FBI and Martin Luther King," *Atlantic Monthly,* July/Aug. 2002.

86 Gary May, *The Informant: The FBI, The Ku Klux Klan, and the Murder of Viola Liuzzo* (New Haven, CT: Yale University Press, 2005), 164–83, 367–69; Liuzzo v. United States, 508 F. Supp. 923 (E.D. Mich. 1981).

87 Henry Pierson Curtis, "Neo-Nazi Rally Was Organized by FBI Informant," *Orlando Sentinel,* Feb. 15, 2007; Henry Pierson Curtis, "FBI: No Role in Staging March," *Orlando Sentinel,* Feb. 17, 2007, at B1.

88 Complaint, Ctr. for Media Justice v. FBI, Case 3:19-cv-01465 (N.D. Cal. Mar. 21, 2019), at 6, www.aclu.org/sites/default/files/field_document/1-_complaint_0.pdf.

89 Robert D. McFadden, "City Is Rebuffed on the Release of '04 Records," *N.Y. Times*, Aug. 7, 2007, at A1.

90 Paul Vitello and Kirk Semple, "Muslims Say F.B.I. Tactics Sow Anger and Fear," *N.Y. Times*, Dec. 17, 2009.

91 Fazaga v. Fed. Bureau of Investigation, 965 F.3d 1015, 1025, 1226 (9th Cir. 2020), rev'd, Fed. Bureau of Investigation v. Fazaga, No. 20-828, 595 U.S. __ (Mar. 4, 2022).

92 Ghandi v. Police Dep't of Detroit, 747 F.2d 338, 350 (6th Cir. 1984) (citing NAACP v. Alabama, 360 U.S. 240 (1958)).

93 Laird v. Tatum, 408 U.S. 1 (1972).

94 *Ghandi*, 747 F.2d at 347 (quoting Handschu v. Special Services Division, 349 F. Supp. 766, 769–70 (S.D.N.Y. 1972)).

95 *Handschu*, 349 F. Supp. at 769–71.

96 *Ghandi*, 747 F.2d at 349–50.

97 Presbyterian Church v. United States, 870 F.2d 518, 521–22 (9th Cir. 1989).

98 Fazaga v. Fed. Bureau of Investigation, 965 F.3d 1015, 1025, 1226 (9th Cir. 2020), rev'd, Fed. Bureau of Investigation v. Fazaga, No. 20-828, 595 U.S. __ (Mar. 4, 2022) (holding that the Foreign Intelligence Surveillance Act does not displace the state secrets privilege).

99 Marx, "The Agent Provocateur and the Informant," at 404, 409, 434.

100 "Press Release: CBC Task Force on Foreign Affairs and National Security Hosts Briefing Examining FBI Black Identity Extremism Report," Congressional Black Caucus, Mar. 20, 2018, https://cbc.house.gov/news/documentsingle.aspx?DocumentID=866.

101 Shirin Sinnar, "Separate and Unequal: The Law of 'Domestic' and 'International' Terrorism," 117 *Mich. L. Rev.* 1333, 1336 & n.12 (2019).

102 Bennett L. Gershman, "Abscam, the Judiciary, and the Ethics of Entrapment," 91 *Yale L.J.* 1565 (1982); see United States v. Jannotti, 673 F.2d 578 (3rd Cir. 1982) (en banc); United States v. Williams, 529 F.Supp. 1085 (E.D.N.Y.1981), aff'd, 705 F.2d 603 (2nd Cir. 1983); United States v. Myers, 527 F. Supp. 1206 (E.D.N.Y. 1981), aff'd, 692 F.2d 823 (2nd Cir. 1982); United States v. Kelly, 539 F.Supp. 363 (D.D.C. 1982), rev'd, 707 F.2d 1460 (D.C. Cir. 1983).

103 United States v. Kelly, 707 F.2d 1460, 1471–72 (D.C. Cir. 1983).

104 Paul Chevigny, "A Rejoinder," *The Nation*, Feb. 23, 1980, at 205, quoted in United States v. Jannotti, 673 F.2d 578, 613 n. 5 (3rd Cir. 1982) (Aldisert, J., dissenting).

105 United States v. Jack Abramoff, Plea Agreement (D.D.C. Jan. 3, 2006).

106 Anne E. Kornblutt, "The Abramoff Case: The overview: Lobbyist accepts plea deal and becomes star witness in a wider corruption case," *N.Y. Times*, Jan. 4, 2006, at A1; Philip Shenon, "Federal Lawmakers from Coast to Coast Are under Investigation," *N.Y. Times*, July 27, 2007, at A16.

107 Neil Lewis, "Abramoff Gets 4 Years in Prison for Corruption," *N.Y. Times*, Sept. 5, 2008, at A13.

108 Del Quentin Wilber and Carrie Johnson, "Abramoff Gets Reduced Sentence of Four Years in Prison," *Wash. Post*, Sept. 5, 2008; Editorial, "From Backslapper to Back Stabber," *N.Y. Times*, Jan. 5, 2006; Editorial, "Guilty-Plea Aftershocks: When D.C. lobbyist Abramoff starts to name elected officials he bought and sold, Washington will quake," *Atlanta Journal-Constitution*, Jan. 4, 2006, at A10.

109 Editorial, "Kicking and Screaming towards Reform," *N.Y. Times*, Mar. 13, 2008, at A24.

110 2 U.S.C. § 1603(b)(7); Pub. L. 115–5440 (115th Cong. Jan. 3, 2019) (the Justice Against Corruption on K Street Act of 2018, or the JACK Act).

111 Nathaniel Popper, "Disgraced Lobbyist Jack Abramoff Headed Back to Jail," *N.Y. Times*, June 25, 2020; Kate Ackley, "K Street Files: Abramoff Returns as Government Reformer," *Roll Call*, Feb. 6, 2012; Order, Pretrial Services Modification, U.S. v. Abramoff, Case No. 3:20-cr-00260-RS-1 (July 22, 2020) (removing Abramoff from pretrial services supervision); Plea Agreement, U.S. v. Abramoff, Case No. 3:20-cr-00260-RS-1 (May 14, 2020); Danielle I. Pingue et al., "Blog Post: The First Criminal Conviction Under the Lobbying Disclosure Act," *Enforcement Edge*, July 15, 2020, www.arnoldporter.com/en/perspectives/blogs/enforcement-edge/2020/07/the-first-criminal-conviction-under-lda.

112 18 U.S.C. § 2331(1), (5) (defining international and domestic terrorism).

113 Joseph Fried, "The Terror Conspiracy: The overview: Sheik and nine followers guilty of a conspiracy of terrorism," *N.Y. Times*, Oct. 2, 1995, at A1.

114 Wadie E. Said, "The Terrorist Informant," 85 *Wash. L. Rev.* 687 (2010); see also Center on Law & Security, New York University School of Law, *Terrorist Trial Report Card: September 11, 2001–September 11, 2010*, at 20 (2010), www.lawandsecurity.org/terrorist-trial-report-cards.

115 See, e.g., Wadie E. Said, *Crimes of Terror: The Legal and Political Implications of Federal Terrorism Prosecutions* 23–50 (Oxford: Oxford University Press, 2015); Trevor Aaronson, *The Terror Factory: Inside the FBI's Manufactured War on Terrorism* (New York: Ig Publishing, 2013); Diala Shamas, "A Nation of Informants: Reining in Post-9/11 Coercion of Intelligence Informants," 83 *Brook. L. Rev.* 1175 (2018); Amna Akbar, "National Security's Broken Windows," 62 *UCLA L. Rev.* 834, 853 (2015).

116 Adam Goldman, "Domestic Terrorism Threat Is 'Metastasizing' in U.S., F.B.I. Director Says," *N.Y. Times*, Mar. 2, 2021; *National Strategy for Countering Domestic Terrorism*, Nat'l Security Council, The White House, June 2021. See Shirin Sinnar, "Separate and Unequal: The Law of 'Domestic' and 'International' Terrorism," 117 *Mich. L. Rev.* 1333, 1337 (2019) (challenging the law's formal distinction between international and domestic terrorism). Compare 18 U.S.C. § 2331(1) (defining interational terrorism) with 18 U.S.C. § 2331(5) (defining domestic terrorism).

117 22 U.S.C. § 2708; Rewards for Justice, U.S. Dep't of State, https://rewardsforjustice.net/english.

118 8 U.S.C. § 1101(S)(i)(I) (requiring that the immigrant provide "critical reliable information"); 8 U.S.C. § 1184 (limiting number of S-visas to 200); Talal Ansari

and Siraj Datoo, "Welcome To America—Now Spy On Your Friends," *Buzzfeed*, Jan. 28, 2016; Neil A. Lewis, "A Nation Challenged: The informants: Immigrants offered incentives to give evidence on terrorists," *N.Y. Times*, Nov. 30, 2001, at B7; Karma Ester, "Immigration: S Visas for Criminal and Terrorist Informants," Congressional Research Service, Library of Congress, January 19, 2005; Douglas Kash, "Rewarding Confidential Informants: Cashing In on Terrorism and Narcotics Trafficking," 34 *Case West. Res. J. Int'l L.* 231, 235 (2002).

119 United States v. Nixon, 418 U.S. 683, 710 (1974).

120 E.g., Hamdi v. Rumsfeld, 542 U.S. 507, 509 (2004) (holding that due process still protects American citizen held not as a criminal defendant but as an enemy combatant).

121 United States v. U.S. District Court (Keith), 407 U.S. 297, 308–9 (1972) (distinguishing between Fourth Amendment regulation of domestic security and foreign security matters); United States v. Truong Dinh Hung, 629 F.2d 908, 914–16 (4th Cir. 1980).

122 Fed. Bureau of Investigation v. Fazaga, No. 20-828, 595 U.S. __ (Mar. 4, 2022) (holding that the Foreign Intelligence Surveillance Act does not displace the state secrets privilege and that Muslim plaintiffs' FISA claims could thus be dismissed); United States v. Mejia, 448 F.3d 436, 453–58 (D.C. Cir. 2006) (describing procedures for the discovery of classified information); United States v. Yunis, 867 F.2d 617, 623 (D.C. Cir. 1989) (same).

123 18 U.S.C. §§ 2511, 2518, 2519, 50 U.S.C. § 1801 et. seq.

124 Peter P. Swire, "The System of Foreign Intelligence Surveillance Law," 72 *Geo. Wash. L. Rev.* 1306, 1332–33 (2004).

125 Foreign Intelligence Surveillance Act Court Orders 1979–2017, Electronic Privacy Information Center, https://epic.org/privacy/surveillance/fisa/stats/default. html#background; *Wiretap Report 2016*, U.S. Courts, Dec. 31, 2016, www.uscourts. gov/statistics-reports/wiretap-report-2016.

126 Kash, "Rewarding Confidential Informants," at 232. But see Joby Warrick, "'The Triple Agent': The final days of the suicide bomber who attacked the CIA," *Wash. Post*, June 28, 2011 (documenting the path of a CIA informant).

127 The Attorney General's Guidelines for FBI National Security Investigations and Foreign Intelligence Collection (Oct. 31, 2003), at 23, www.justice.gov/archive/olp/ ag-guidelines-10312003.pdf.

128 Attorney General Guidelines on General Crimes, Racketeering Enterprise, and Terrorism Enterprise Investigations (May 2002), at 1, 18–19 , www.justice.gov/archives/ag/ attorney-generals-guidelines-general-crimes-racketeering-enterprise-and-domestic.

129 Kim Lane Scheppele, "Law in a Time of Emergency: States of Exception and the Temptations of 9/11," 6 *U. Pa. J. Const. L.* 1001, 1040 (2004).

130 FBI Guidelines, at 2, 18, 20, 21, 31.

131 "FBI: Informants Key to Breaking Up Terror Plots," Associated Press, June 4, 2007 (quoting Tom Corrigan, former member of the FBI–NYPD Joint Terrorism Task Force).

132 Center on Law & Security, *Terrorist Trial Report Card*, at 4, 26 (2010), www.lawa-ndsecurity.org/terrorist-trial-report-cards.

133 Michael Powell & William Rashbaum, "Plot Suspects Described as Short on Cash and a Long Way from Realizing Goals," *N.Y. Times*, June 4, 2007, at B1. See also Said, *Crimes of Terror*, at 31 (noting that "the NYPD has admitted that its systemic spying on New York's Muslim community did not lead to one successful prosecution, in contrast to the FBI's longer and more fruitful history in garnering federal criminal convictions").

134 Rozina Ali, "The 'Herald Square Bomber' Who Wasn't," *N.Y. Times Magazine*, Apr. 23, 2021; William K. Rashbaum and Carla Baranauckas, "30-Year Sentence in Subway Bomb Plot Case," *N.Y. Times*, Jan. 8, 2007.

135 Christopher Drew & Eric Lichtblau, "Two Views of Terror Suspects: Die-hards or dupes," *N.Y. Times*, July 1, 2006, at A1.

136 Said, *Crimes of Terror*, at 44 (quoting Aaronson, *The Terror Factory*, at 234).

137 Lance Williams & Erin McCormick, "Al Qaeda Terrorist Worked with FBI: Ex–Silicon Valley resident plotted embassy attacks," *San Francisco Chronicle*, Nov. 4, 2001.

138 Warrick, "'The Triple Agent.'"

139 Danny Hakim & Eric Lichtblau, "Trial and Errors: The Detroit terror case: After convictions, the undoing of a U.S. terror prosecution," *N.Y. Times*, Oct. 7, 2004, at A1.

140 Douglas Pasternak, "Squeezing Them, Leaving Them," *U.S. News & World Report*, July 8, 2002, at A12.

141 Caryle Murphy & Del Quentin Wilbur, "Terror Informant Ignites Himself Near White House: Yemeni was upset at treatment by FBI," *Wash. Post*, Nov. 16, 2004, at A1; William Glaberson, "Behind Scenes, Informer's Path Led U.S. to 20 Terror Cases," *N.Y. Times*, Nov. 18, 2004, at B1.

142 See, e.g., Jennie Pasquarella, "Muslims Need Not Apply: How USCIS Secretly Mandates the Discriminatory Delay and Denial of Citizenship and Immigration Benefits to Aspiring Americans," ACLU of Southern California, Aug. 2013, at 1–2.

143 Said, "The Terrorist Informant," at 690. See also Paul Vitello and Kirk Semple, "Muslims Say F.B.I. Tactics Sow Anger and Fear," *N.Y. Times*, Dec. 17, 2009 (FBI using informants and "agent[s] provocateurs to trap unsuspective Muslim youth").

144 Sinnar, "Separate and Unequal," at 1335.

145 Shamas, "A Nation of Informants," at 1202.

146 Tanzin v. Tanvir, 141 S. Ct. 486, 489 (2020).

147 See, e.g., James Risen, "Propping Up a Drug Lord, Then Arresting Him," *N.Y. Times*, Dec. 11, 2010 (describing U.S. arrest of Afghan drug lord who was also a longtime CIA informant).

148 Oversight Hearing Transcript, at 8.

8. REGULATION AND REFORM

1 Olmstead v. United States, 277 U.S. 438, 468 (1928) (Brandeis, J., dissenting).

2 American Law Institute, *Principles of the Law: Policing*, Council Draft No. 5, Ch. 12 (Dec. 3, 2020) (on file with author).

3 William J. Stuntz, "The Uneasy Relationship between Criminal Procedure and Criminal Justice," 107 *Yale L.J.* 1, 5, 26 (1997).

4 Cyrille Finjaut & Gary T. Marx, "The Normalization of Undercover Policing in the West: Historical and Contemporary Perspectives," in Cyrille Finjaut & Gary T. Marx, eds., *Undercover: Police Surveillance in Comparative Perspective* (The Hague: Klewer Law International, 1995) (noting that the increase in covert means in the United States is related to the growth of civil liberties and public protections against police, whereas in Europe, where police are less regulated, covert means have been less developed).

5 Wash. Stat. § 10.56.040 (2020).

6 L.B. 465, 100th Leg., 1st Sess. (Neb. 2008); Neb. Rev. Stat. § 29–1929 (2004).

7 See chapter 6. See also Andrew E. Taslitz, "Racial Auditors and the Fourth Amendment: Data with the Power to Inspire Political Action," 66 *L. & Contemp. Probs.* 221 (2003).

8 The Federal Bureau of Investigation's Compliance with the Attorney General's Investigative Guidelines, Office of the Inspector General, U.S. Dep't of Justice (Sept. 2005), at 3.

9 Attorney General's Guidelines Regarding the Use of FBI Confidential Human Sources, § V(B)(10)(b), U.S. Dep't of Justice (Dec. 2006), at 40.

10 An act to amend the criminal procedure law, in relation to the regulation of the use of informants, A. 01124, 2008 Gen. Assem. (NY 2008), www.assembly.state.ny.us/leg/?bn=A01124&term=2007.

11 Dan Herbeck and Michael Beebe, "Walking thin line in Village of Attica: Would-be informant says police coerced her into cooperation," *Buffalo News*, Nov. 8, 2009; Dan Herbeck and Michael Beebe, "Deal leaves informant fearing retribution Attica police accused of reneging on pledge," *Buffalo News*, Nov. 15, 2009; Erin McLaughlin, "Cops Use Traffic Tix to Force Woman Into Drug Buys, Lawyer Claims," ABC News, Sept. 26, 2012.

12 H.B. 564, Tex. Leg. (2015).

13 D.C. Code Ann. § 5–333.08 (2005).

14 Cal. Penal Code § 701.5 (2008).

15 Editorial, "Chad MacDonald's Legacy," *L.A. Times*, Sept. 1, 2002, at C18; "Slain Teen's Mother Wins Suit: Court: Award of at least $1 million to go to woman whose son, killed in Norwalk Drug house, was police informant," *Long Beach Press-Telegram*, Aug. 27, 2002, at A2.

16 N. Dak. Stat. § 29-29-5.

17 Roper v. Simmons, 543 U.S. 55, 569 (2005) (eliminating the death penalty for children).

18 Elizabeth S. Scott, "'Children Are Different': Constitutional Values and Justice Policy," 11 *Ohio St. J. Crim. L.* 71, 72 (2013); Andrea L. Dennis, "Collateral Damage? Juvenile Snitches in America's 'Wars' on Drugs, Crime, and Gangs," 46 *Am. Crim. L. Rev.* 1145 (2009).

19 Cf. "Matthew's Law" (discussed below), House Bill 63, 211-H0063-2, sec. 29, Minn. House of Rep. (enacted June 30, 2021) (requiring "consideration of an informant's diagnosis of mental illness, substance abuse, or disability").

20 See "Rachel's Law"; "Matthew's Law."

21 Joint Oversight Hearing on Law Enforcement Confidential Informant Practices Before the House Comm. on the Judiciary Subcomm. on Crime, Terrorism, and Homeland Security and the Subcomm. on the Constitution, Civil Rights, and Civil Liberties, 110th Cong. (2007) (statement of J. Patrick O'Burke, Deputy Commander, Narcotics Service, Texas Dep't of Safety).

22 Fla. Stat. § 914.28.

23 Dennis G. Fitzgerald, *Informants and Undercover Operations: A Practical Guide to Law, Policy, and Procedure* (Boca Raton, FL: CRC Press, 2007), 262–63. See also Pete Earley and Gerald Shur, *WITSEC: Inside the Federal Witness Protection Program* (New York: Bantam, 2003).

24 Todd Richmond, AP, "Witness Protection Programs Hurting: Programs don't have enough to keep witnesses safe," *Wisconsin State Journal*, May 1, 2008, at A1. See also chapter 1.

25 Julie Bykowicz & Chris Yakaitis, "Lawyers Use Sister's Prior Testimony without Her: Brother's murder trial marks first use of law," *Baltimore Sun*, July 20, 2006, at 1B.

26 Hoffa v. United States, 385 U.S. 293, 321 (1966).

27 George C. Harris, "Testimony for Sale: The Law and Ethics of Snitches and Experts," 28 *Pepp. L. Rev.* 1, 64–68 (2000).

28 Confidential Informants: Model Policy, Law Enforcement Policy Center, International Association of Chiefs of Police (December 2020), at 8.

29 The FBI's guidelines are discussed in chapters 2 and 7.

30 Regulations of the Las Vegas Metropolitan Police Department, § 5/206.24, at 454.

31 Confidential Informants, Policy Number 7.12, Deschutes County Sheriff's Office, June 29, 2016.

32 Compare Maya Harris et al., Letter from the ACLU of Northern California to the California Commission on the Fair Administration of Justice, Sept. 19, 2006 (documenting lacks of Stanislaus and Lake County informant policies), with Stanislaus County Sheriff Department Southern California Policy Manual § 608.1 and Lake County Sheriff's Office Southern California Policy Manual § 608.

33 United States Attorney's Manual (U.S.A.M.) § 9–27.620, Entering into Non-prosecution Agreements in Return for Cooperation—Considerations to be Weighed, updated July 2020, www.justice.gov/jm/jm-9-27000-principles-federal-prosecution#9-27.600.

34 American Bar Association, ABA Standards on Prosecutorial Investigation § 2.5, Feb. 2008, www.americanbar.org/groups/criminal_justice/publications/criminal_justice_section_archive/crimjust_standards_pinvestigate.

35 Conn. Gen. Stat. §§ 51–286k et seq.; Neb. Code § 29–4702 et seq.; 22 Okl. St. Ann. § 2002(A)(4); Tex. Code Crim. Pro. § 2.024. See also "Jailhouse Informants," ch. 19, Legal Policies Manual, Los Angeles County District Attorney's Office, Apr. 2005, at 187–90.

36 Letter from Maya Harris et al., ACLU of Northern California, to the California Commission on the Fair Administration of Justice, Sept. 19, 2006.

37 See Myrna S. Raeder, "See No Evil: Wrongful Convictions and the Prosecutorial Ethics of Offering Testimony by Jailhouse Informants and Dishonest Experts," 76 *Fordham L. Rev.* 1413 (2007).

38 Rule 104(a), Fed. R. Evid.

39 Rule 403, Fed. R. Evid.

40 Rule 104(c), Fed. R. Evid.

41 See Crystal S. Yang, "Free at Last? Judicial Discretion and Racial Disparities in Federal Sentencing," 44 *J. Legal Stud.* 75, 105 (2015) ("[N]onwhite defendants are significantly less likely to receive substantial assistance motions in general."); Celesta A. Albonetti & Robert D. Baller, "Sentencing in Federal Drug Trafficking/manufacturing Cases: A Multilevel Analysis of Extra-Legal Defendant Characteristics, Guidelines Departures, and Continuity of Culture," 14 *J. Gender Race & Just.* 41, 67 (2010) (finding that § 5K1.1 substantial assistance departures result in significantly less sentence reduction for African American and Hispanic defendants compared to white defendants); Brian D. Johnson et al., "The Social Context of Guidelines Circumvention: The Case of Federal District Courts," 46 *Criminology* 737, 769 (2008) (finding that racial minority defendants were especially disadvantaged relative to whites in receiving substantial assistance departures).

42 Stephanos Bibas, "Plea Bargaining in the Shadow of Trial," 117 *Harv. L. Rev.* 2463 (2004).

43 Conn. Gen. Stat. § 51–286k; Neb. Code § 29–4703; see also American Legislative Exchange Council, *Model Jailhouse Informant Regulations*, May 24, 2018, www.alec.org/model-policy/jailhouse-informant-regulations-2 (requiring data collection and disclosure).

44 Fla. R. Crim. Pro. 3.220(b)(1)(M); Ill. Comp. Stat. ch. 725, § 5/115–21; Md. Code Ann., Cts. & Jud. Proc. § 10–924; "Matthew's Law," House Bill 63, 211-H0063-2, Minn. House of Rep. (enacted June 30, 2021); Neb. Code § 29–4702 et seq.; 22 Okl. St. Ann. § 2002(A)(4); Tx. Code Crim. Pro. § 39.14(h-1); Wash. Stat. §§ 10.56.030 & 10.56.040.

45 Conn. Gen. Stat. § 54–860.

46 Ill. Comp. Stat., ch. 725, § 5/115–21(d).

47 Dodd v. State, 993 P.2d 778, 785 (Okla. Crim. App. 2000) (Strubhar, J., specially concurring); D'Agostino v. State, 107 Nev. 1001, 823 P.2d 283 (Nev. 1992) (holding that before "jailhouse incrimination" testimony is admissible, the "trial judge

[must] first determine . . . that the details of the admissions supply a sufficient indicia of reliability").

48 Daubert v. Merrell Dow Pharmaceuticals, Inc., 509 U.S. 579, 595 (1993).

49 See chapter 3.

50 Harris, "Testimony for Sale."

51 Sandra Guerra Thompson, "Beyond a Reasonable Doubt? Reconsidering Uncorroborated Eyewitness Identification Testimony," 41 *U.C. Davis L. Rev.* 1487, 1528–29 (2008).

52 Steve Barnes, "Rogue Narcotics Agent in Texas Found Guilty in Perjury Case," *N.Y. Times*, Jan. 15, 2005, at A1.

53 Vernon's Ann. Tex. Crim. Code Art. 38–141.

54 No More Tulias: Drug Law Enforcement Evidentiary Standards Improvement Act of 2005, H.R. 2620, 109th Cong. §3(a)(2)(A) (2005).

55 Resolution 108B, American Bar Association, Adopted by House of Delegates, Feb. 14, 2005.

56 Cal. Penal Code § 1111.5.

57 Cal. Jury Instruction, Crim. 3.20—Cautionary Instruction-In-Custody Informant (6th ed. 2008).

58 State v. Jones, No. 20261, 2020 WL 8257703, at *1 (Conn. Dec. 1, 2020); see also "Jailhouse Snitch Testimony: A Policy Review," The Justice Project (2007), 7.

59 "Jailhouse Snitch Testimony: A Policy Review."

60 Nancy S. Marder, "Bringing Jury Instructions into the 21st Century," 81 *Notre Dame L. Rev.* 449, 454–55 (2006).

61 See chapter 3.

62 See, e.g., Monica C. Bell, *Anti-Segregation Policing*, 95 N.Y.U. L. Rev. 650 (2020) (describing the broad socioeconomic and racial contours of policing).

63 Tracey L. Meares and Tom R. Tyler, "Justice Sotomayor and the Jurisprudence of Procedural Justice," 123 *Yale L.J. Forum* 525, 526–27 (2014) ("The primary factor that people consider when they are deciding whether they feel a decision is legitimate and ought to be accepted is whether or not they believe that the authorities involved made their decision through a fair procedure, irrespective of whether members of the public are evaluating decisions made by the Supreme Court or by local courts."). See also chapter 6 (discussing procedural justice theories).

64 See David Alan Sklansky, *Democracy and the Police* (Stanford: Stanford University Press, 2008), 116–19 (discussing the promises and pitfalls of community policing).

65 Compare I. Bennett Capers, "Crime, Surveillance, and Communities," 40 Fordham Urb. L.J. 959 (2013) (arguing that mass surveillance can benefit and protect communities of color), with Kimberly D. Bailey, "Watching Me: The War on Crime, Privacy, and the State," 47 *U.C. Davis L. Rev.* 1539 (2014) (describing the subordinating effects of pervasive surveillance on poor urban communities of color). See also *An End of the Mass Surveillance of Black Communities, Policy Brief No. 10*, Movement for Black Lives, https://m4bl.org/resources/?issue=end-the-war-on-black-people&category=policy-demands.

CONCLUSION

1 The names in this actual case have been changed to protect attorney-client privilege. The incident was reconstructed from my memory and notes taken during the case. The story originally appeared in Alexandra Natapoff, "Deregulating Guilt: The Information Culture of the Criminal System," 30 *Cardozo L. Rev.* 965, 1004–05 (2008).

2 Russell eventually pled guilty to the gun charge and testified at the trial that Bobby wanted him to. A correctional officer reported that another prisoner shouted at Russell: "There goes that rat! We're going to kill you when you get into the system." Russell was subsequently placed in protective custody.

3 Alexandra Natapoff, "Snitching: The Institutional and Communal Consequences," 73 *U. Cincinnati L. Rev.* 645 (2004); Alexandra Natapoff, "Beyond Unreliable: How Snitches Contribute to Wrongful Convictions," 37 *Golden Gate U. L. Rev.* 107 (2006); Alexandra Natapoff, "Deregulating Guilt: The Information Culture of the Criminal System," 30 *Cardozo L. Rev.* 965 (2009); Alexandra Natapoff, "Snitching and the Use of Criminal Informants," *Oxford Bibliographies* in Criminology, Richard Wright, ed. (New York: Oxford University Press, 2012); Alexandra Natapoff, "Negotiating Accuracy: DNA in the Age of Plea Bargaining," in *Wrongful Convictions and the DNA Revolution: Twenty-Five Years of Freeing the Innocent*, Daniel Medwed, ed. (Cambridge: Cambridge University Press, 2017).

4 Elizabeth Hinton, *America on Fire: The Untold History of Police Violence and Black Rebellion Since the 1960s* (New York: Liveright, 2021).

5 Michael Walzer, *Spheres of Justice: A Defense of Pluralism and Equality* (New York: Basic Books, 1983), 269 (emphasis in original).

6 Principles of Construction, Model Penal Code § 1.02 (describing the purpose of the Code is "to forbid and prevent conduct that unjustifiably and inexcusably inflicts or threatens substantial harm to individual or public interests").

7 Marbury v. Madison, 5 U.S. 137 (1803).

8 Alexandra Natapoff, "The Penal Pyramid," in *The New Criminal Justice Thinking*, 72–73, Sharon Dolovich and Alexandra Natapoff, eds. (New York: New York University Press, 2017) (arguing that rule of law wanes at the bottom of the penal pyramid where defendants are most vulnerable).

INDEX

ABOUT THE AUTHOR

ALEXANDRA NATAPOFF is the Lee S. Kreindler Professor of Law at Harvard Law School.

Lightning Source UK Ltd.
Milton Keynes UK
UKHW010702061022
410025UK00006B/234